WALK OFF WEIGHT™

Quick & Easy
COOKBOOK

150 Delicious Recipes to Fill You Up and Slim You Down!

Heidi McIndoo, MS, RD, with the Editors of **Prevention.**

Foreword by **Michele Stanten**, Fitness Director

RODALE

Direct edition first published in 2010. Trade edition published in 2011.
© 2010 by Rodale Inc.

Rodale books may be purchased for business or promotional use or for special sales. For information, please write to: Special Markets Department, Rodale Inc., 733 Third Avenue, New York, NY 10017.

Walk Off Weight™ and *Prevention*® are registered trademarks of Rodale Inc.

Printed in the United States of America
Rodale Inc. makes every effort to use acid-free ♾, recycled paper ♻.

Book design by Jessica Sokol

Photographs © 2010 by Marcus Nilsson; food styling by Stephana Bottom; prop styling by Deborah Williams

Library of Congress Cataloging-in-Publication Data

McIndoo, Heidi.
    Walk off weight quick & easy cookbook : 150 Delicious Recipes to Fill You Up and Slim You Down! /
Heidi McIndoo and the Editors of Prevention.
        p.   cm.
    Includes index.
    ISBN-13 978–1–60529–305–9   direct hardcover
    ISBN-10 1–60529–305–9   direct hardcover
    ISBN-13 978–1–60529–304–2   trade hardcover
    ISBN-10 1–60529–304–0   trade hardcover
    1. Reducing diets—Recipes.   I. Title.
RM222.2.M35 2010
613.2′5′—dc22   2010013021

2   4   6   8   10 9 7 5 3   direct hardcover
2   4   6   8   10 9 7 5 3 1   trade hardcover

We inspire and enable people to improve their lives and the world around them.

For more of our products, visit prevention.com.

CONTENTS

Introduction

I HAVE A CONFESSION TO MAKE. Even I am surprised by the power of Walk Off Weight (WOW).

Let me explain. As the fitness director of *Prevention* magazine, with nearly 2 decades of experience as a certified fitness instructor, I've tried just about every training routine out there. I know with certainty that walking ranks right up near the top of health-enhancing exercises.

Moderate daily walking can lower women's risk of heart disease, stroke, and type 2 diabetes by up to 40 percent and the risk of breast cancer by up to 30 percent. It also boosts energy, your immune system, and your odds for living longer and better. It keeps your brain humming and your disposition positive.

So naturally when I implemented the trials for the WOW program with the initial test group of 24 women, I anticipated a positive outcome. The results exceeded my expectations. All the participants lost weight, but the ones who followed both the exercise and diet portions, as opposed to exercise only, shed more than double the number of pounds, on average, and 65 percent more inches than the exercise-only group.

For a summary of the WOW exercise program, turn to page 224. For now, I want to focus on the WOW eating plan. When I envisioned the food component of the original WOW plan, I knew I wanted the expertise of someone who understands the real-life challenges that dieters face. Heidi McIndoo, MS, RD, fit the bill perfectly. Not only is she a respected dietitian, she's a wife, mother, and walker.

Over and over again, our WOW participants told us that Heidi's meal plans, guidelines, and tips gave them the strategies they needed to understand calories and conquer cravings. And the recipes! "Family friendly," "delicious," "quick," and "yummy" are typical of the comments. Our original WOW walkers continue to walk for additional weight loss and better health. They've asked for even more wonderful recipes to keep them well fed on the journey. In this book, we're sharing more than 150 recipes that meet the WOW standards.

For those just catching on to WOW, the first three chapters are your guide to what the program is all about. We'll acquaint you with nutrients that go the distance: fiber, calcium and vitamin D, good fats, and protein, accompanied by plenty of pure water and antioxidant-rich green tea.

You'll find information on how you can personalize the eating plan for your specific caloric needs and food preferences. Like the good support and increased endurance you get from a well-fitting pair of walking shoes, this eating program gives you a nourishing foundation with lots of options. You'll also find savvy tips for dining out and choosing carry-out, an explanation of how excess weight affects your health, and a primer on sodium.

If you're already walking and working out the WOW way, feel free to turn right to the recipe pages (we know that's where you want to go anyway). It's all here for you: breakfasts, lunches, dinners, snacks, and desserts. Each recipe includes a nutritional analysis so you can see how the dish works with your healthy eating program. Each recipe also includes the total time required for preparing and cooking so you can see how it fits into your lifestyle and schedule.

You'll find daily menus for 28 days, combining WOW recipes with easy-to-prep foods for complete meals that are quick and simple to make *and* give you all the nutrients you need. Ingredient lists are short and made up of products found in any supermarket, so shopping is a breeze. Canned beans, bagged spinach, loose-pack frozen produce, and other healthful packaged foods save time and energy in many meals. If you don't like a particular meal, feel free to mix and match—we've also given you additional breakfasts, lunches, dinners, and snacks you can substitute in Build Your Own WOW Menus.

Eating smarter the WOW way means savoring delicious meals and snacks that will keep you satisfied and energized while you slim down and shape up from your walks and workouts. The result? A stronger, leaner, firmer body that will wow you.

—*Michele Stanten, Fitness Director,*
Prevention

REV UP YOUR WEIGHT LOSS

PART
one

THE PRINCIPLES OF THE WOW DIET

IF YOU'RE FOLLOWING THE WOW exercise and eating program and reading this cookbook to get healthier, tastier weight-loss recipes, you probably know one important tenet of the program: "Walk smarter—not longer." The concept of interval training—interspersing short, vigorous workouts with slower endurance training—enables you to shed unwanted fat while energizing and toning your body.

This same enlightened concept applies to the WOW Diet. Success comes not only from eating less but also from eating smarter. By now, most of us understand that the body loses weight when it takes in fewer calories than it burns (see "Do the Math" on page 4). But calories are only part of the story when you're walking off weight. The quality, not just the quantity, of the calories is vital. Because you'll be moving your body more and working it in different ways than you've been used to, it's important to eat foods that give you the right nutrients to fuel your workouts. This chapter explains why.

FOODS THAT GO THE DISTANCE

WHEN WE FEED OUR BODIES consistently with refined or simple carbohydrates such as white bread and pasta, white rice, doughnuts, sodas, and sugary drinks, we feel energized for a short time but quickly crash. That's because those simple carbohydrates have been processed to remove the fiber found in plant foods such as whole grains and produce. With no fiber, these foods metabolize very fast. They don't provide the body with the staying power needed to benefit from the WOW program.

The fitness benefits of walking begin with the first step. The step you take to get up from the couch. The step you take to lace up your walking shoes and head out the door. The step you take to accelerate the pace.

The fitness benefits of healthy eating also begin with the first step. Breaking a lifetime of negative habits must be a series of gradual steps if it's to have lasting impact. It's no secret that our society thrives on instant gratification. We want everything now, now, now! Combine that with the ease with which we can obtain calorie-dense, sugar-filled, and sodium-laden foods and we've got a recipe for weight gain.

Per person, Americans eat far more calories than we did a half century ago. Not surprisingly, our waistlines have kept pace with our intake. We currently eat almost eight times as many pounds of processed sugar per year as we did in the 1950s.[2] And it doesn't come from the granulated stuff in the sugar bowl. It's hidden in a myriad of food products. Processed sweeteners such as corn syrup and high-fructose corn syrup are found not only in items you would expect, such as cookies, soda, and fruit drinks, but are also ingredients in breads, pizza, hot dogs, flavored rices, noodle side-dish mixes, and much, much more.

We also eat at least 60 percent more added fats and oils than we did 50 years ago. Is it any wonder the percentage of obese Americans has skyrocketed from 13 percent in the early 1960s to 35 percent in 2006?[3]

DO THE MATH

Losing weight is a numbers game. To lose 1 pound a week, you need to create a deficit of 3,500 calories. Over the course of 7 days, that's 500 fewer calories per day. There are three ways to accomplish this goal.

1. Eat 500 fewer calories than usual per day—a simple or difficult task, depending on how much you typically eat each day.
2. Burn off 500 calories by increasing your activity each day. For a 160-pound person, that equals about 45 minutes on the stairclimber, 1 hour of high-impact aerobics, or 2½ hours of walking at 2 MPH.[1] If you weigh less, the times are longer—and that's every day.
3. Eat 250 fewer calories and burn 250 more calories each day. Because exercise helps you maintain your fat-burning muscle, you burn calories more efficiently. That makes this option the winning combination.

Make Better Choices

Perhaps you've fallen into the bad habit of eating mostly processed foods because of perceived convenience. But at what price to your health? Don't worry. If you take it one step at a time, you can wean yourself from the junk. Don't attempt to ban these items from your diet cold turkey. It's more realistic to transition to including them in your diet in moderation. You can either eat the processed food less frequently, eat it in smaller portions, or do both.

For example, if you now drink five 12-ounce cans of soda a day (to the tune of a whopping 680 calories), set a goal to limit yourself to one can per day, one can per week, or another number that works for you. Then take small steps to reach that goal—first cut down to three cans a day for a week, then two, and so on. Eventually, you may find that your craving for sweet soda disappears as your body responds to the real thirst-quenching provided by water.

Perhaps you can't resist grabbing that 3-ounce bag of chips every day to crunch with your sandwich at lunch. It's become a habit—a habit that's costing you 462 calories every day! Start by carrying a 1-ounce bag (154 calories) from home. Immediately, without denying yourself a "treat," you've

Custom Calories

How do you assess an accurate calorie level for safe and steady weight loss? Several factors affect this calculation: height, age, activity level, and gender. Many Web sites have calculators in which you can input all of these numbers to determine how many calories you need to meet your weight loss goals. Try www.prevention.com/healthtrackers for one such tool. Then adjust your calorie intake according to the tips in "Do the Math" on the opposite page.

cut 308 calories from your daily intake. That's progress. Next, try replacing the chips every couple of days with pretzels or even veggie sticks, for a crunch that packs some nutrient power.

No matter what your junk-food habit, start by setting goals just for portion size and how often you'll eat the item. Then set equally important goals for incorporating more whole foods into your eating plan. High-caliber, nutritious foods will fuel your body during exercise. You'll feel more energetic, fitter, and less likely to overeat on those junk foods you once craved. Let's face it, why would you continue to choose foods that make you feel bad?

And, as the WOW program proves, incorporating more activity and fewer but better calories is ideal for a number of reasons. Foremost is that even though you're cutting calories, exercise allows you to eat a truly satisfying amount of food and

Kathy Ashenfelter, 63

LOST 22½ POUNDS AND 12¾ INCHES

Kathy Ashenfelter lost 60 pounds a decade ago, but over the years the weight came back. Though she always loved walking, her weekend strolls weren't enough to keep the pounds at bay. The WOW program gave her the tools she needed to turn her walks into fat-fighting workouts and the diet into a doable way of eating for life. "I found a lot of freedom on this eating plan; I could eat out, on vacation, and at parties and still find good choices." Kathy lost nearly 23 pounds over the course of the 8-week program—more than 10 percent of her body weight—and reported that she no longer craves sweets. "Now it's no big deal to give away my dessert. I just head for the skinniest person in the room; I figure that they can afford the extra calories." Three months after the official end of the program, Kathy recorded an additional 5½-pound weight loss and shaved another 6¾ inches off her figure, for a grand total of 28 pounds and 20½ inches lost in 5 months.

still lose weight. The WOW Diet is a slightly less-restrictive eating plan than many trendy crash diets, but it is ultimately easier to follow and more sustainable for the long term than some ridiculously low-calorie diet that bans all of your favorite foods and leaves you hungry all the time.

STRIVE FOR BALANCE

WHILE YOU STRIDE to burn more calories through the WOW program, you'll also want to strive for greater equilibrium in your intake of nutritious foods.

A balanced eating plan is basically composed of three macronutrients—protein, fat, and carbohydrates—plus essential micronutrients—fiber, vitamins, and minerals. Each one is important and unique in its own right.

The easiest way to ensure you're getting the necessary amounts of each nutrient is to choose a variety of foods from every food group every day. In upcoming chapters, we share plenty of recommendations and tips on how to accomplish this. In addition to basic nutrients, the WOW plan identifies other dietary guidelines that help improve results. To feel your best, walk and work out at your peak, and accelerate weight loss, strive for the following daily goals:

At least 20 grams of fiber

3 servings of calcium-rich and vitamin D–rich foods

3 to 4 servings of healthy fats

3 servings of lean protein

At least 4 cups of water

3 cups of green tea

In the next chapter, you'll find plenty of examples of the WOW Diet foods you'll be enjoying from each category. We include recommended daily servings and serving sizes—everything you need to start satisfying your hunger while you achieve your calorie-reduction goals. You'll learn just how each category of foods in the plan contributes to real satiety. No more hunger. No more deprivation. Just slimming results. Now that's an eating plan that's truly appetizing.

WEIGHING IN FOR HEALTH

We live in a society that's seemingly obsessed with thinness. Celebrity weight gain—or loss—is scrutinized by the media. Impossibly rail-thin supermodels flaunt the latest fashions. The visual and verbal messages bombard us, and so we struggle to lose those postholiday pounds or slim down for swimsuit season. Focusing on short-term goals may indeed motivate us for a while, but to succeed for a lifetime of healthy body weight, we need to focus on the forest, not just the trees.

It's easy to see when excess pounds prevent us from zipping our jeans, but it's the factors that aren't visible to the naked eye that should grab our attention. Carrying too much excess weight is a major health risk factor, a fact we frequently choose to ignore.

For instance, overweight is often associated with high blood-cholesterol levels, which can lead to fat buildup within your arteries. This fatty buildup makes the arteries narrow, which in turn makes it harder and harder for blood to get where it needs to go. The narrowing can get so severe that it becomes a total blockage, which, if it happens in the heart, is a heart attack. In the brain, it's a stroke.

Developing high blood pressure is another associated risk that can damage arteries and lead to peripheral artery disease and coronary artery disease.[4] That's because excess body weight causes the heart to pump much harder to circulate blood throughout the body. All of this extra work can lead to weakened artery walls and increased risk of blood clots and plaque buildup,[5] which can lead to a stroke or heart attack.

Yet another risk is that the body can't produce enough insulin to control the levels of sugar in the blood. Diabetes can result. Long-term, excessively high blood-sugar levels damage many parts of the body. That's why diabetes is the silent killer. It can lead to blindness, kidney disease, heart disease, stroke, loss of limbs, and more.[6]

But there is a way to prevent these outcomes. Losing weight can lower your risk of developing all of these conditions and the associated problems. A recent Spanish study involved participants with elevated blood pressure, LDL-cholesterol levels, and blood sugar levels. The participants who lost even minor amounts of body weight achieved healthy goals for cholesterol, blood pressure, and blood sugar. You can do it, too.[7]

THE FOODS OF THE WOW DIET

FOR THE PARTICIPANTS in *Prevention* fitness director Michele Stanten's original WOW Diet program, there's no turning back. In only 2 months, these women lost as much as 22½ pounds of body weight and almost 14 inches all over. Perhaps you're ready to join their slimmer ranks—or already have begun the WOW program.

Whether you're maintaining your ideal body or walking your way toward it, the wonderful recipes and meals in this book will nourish and satisfy you every step of the way. The more you know about eating smarter, the better off you'll be.

First we'll take a look at the major nutrients of the WOW Diet and the role they play in keeping your eating plan on track. Then we'll give you simple guidelines for what foods to eat to ensure that you get the right balance of nutrients without having to track and calculate every gram of fiber or ounce of water—and don't worry, you won't be limited to cabbage and rice cakes! Finally, we'll give you some shopping and cooking tips.

FILL UP TO TRIM DOWN

THE FIRST THING YOU NEED to lose on the WOW eating plan is the idea that starving and weight loss go hand in hand. These two foes are more likely to be locked in hand-to-hand combat. If you've tried losing weight before, you know hunger pangs can often be the biggest barrier to controlling your eating. Let's take a look at the key elements you need in your diet.

Fiber for Fullness

When you invite fiber into your eating plan in a regular way, you'll never be hungry again. Fiber is found in all plant foods—whole grains, fruits, vegetables, dry beans, and legumes. Among other health benefits, fiber fills you up! In fact, in 2009, researchers found that women who eat diets higher in fiber typically weigh less than women who don't eat comparable amounts of fiber. Every additional gram of fiber a woman eats is associated with ½ pound less of body weight.[1]

GOAL: At least 20 grams a day

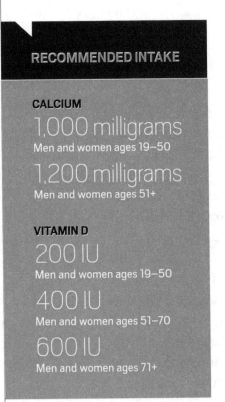

RECOMMENDED INTAKE

CALCIUM

1,000 milligrams
Men and women ages 19–50

1,200 milligrams
Men and women ages 51+

VITAMIN D

200 IU
Men and women ages 19–50

400 IU
Men and women ages 51–70

600 IU
Men and women ages 71+

Dairy Do

We all know calcium and vitamin D—nutritional partners that are often found together, particularly in dairy foods—build strong bones, but did you know these nutrients may play a role in weight loss as well?

At Johns Hopkins University, scientists tracked college students who followed a healthy diet. Those who consumed three servings of dairy foods a day weighed less, gained less, and in fact lost belly fat in contrast to those whose diets included little or no dairy foods.[2] There's more—vitamin D serves a bonus purpose. Vitamin D can be "kidnapped" within our bodies by extra fat, which holds it hostage and doesn't let the body use it.[3] The body is tricked into thinking it is deficient in vitamin D, and that perception hinders the work of the hormone leptin, which signals the brain when the stomach is full. If your brain isn't receiving the signal, you may not recognize that you're satiated and may eat more than you actually need.

GOAL: 3 servings of calcium-rich and vitamin D-rich foods a day

Fats You Can Love

Fat has a reputation as a dietary bad boy. But, as with calories, it's not just the quantity of fat that impacts the body—quality counts, too. While there certainly are fats, such as saturated fat and trans fat, that can be harmful in high amounts, some particular fats are beneficial, even essential, to your well-being.

Monounsaturated fatty acids, found in vegetable oils such as olive, canola, sunflower, sesame, and peanut, as well as avocados, nuts, seeds, and nut butters, are one group of healthy fats.[4] Another is omega-3 fatty acids, found primarily in walnuts, ground flaxseed, flaxseed oil, and fatty fish such as salmon and mackerel.[5] One of the many benefits of these types of fats is that they help you feel fuller longer after you eat—a big plus when you're trying to lose weight by reducing calorie intake. A recent study from Spain revealed that participants who consumed the greatest amount of omega-3 fatty acids—more than 1,300 milligrams a day—were less hungry immediately after their meals, as well as 2 hours later, than those who ate less than 260 milligrams per day of the omega-3s.[6]

GOAL: 3 to 4 servings of an omega-3–rich food a day

Staying Power from Protein

Protein is another nutrient that quells hunger pangs. It is digested more slowly than simple carbohydrates, so getting enough protein steadily through the day can help combat hunger and help prevent unnecessary munching. In a small 2009 study, those who ate a high-protein breakfast reported feeling more satiated after their meal than those who ate a low-protein breakfast.[7]

Don't fall into the trap of believing that only red meat can satisfy your protein needs. Legumes such as dried beans and lentils, as well as some grains such as quinoa, contain good amounts of protein and practically no fat. And because these foods are incredibly filling, they make a welcome ally in staving off hunger pangs. Other top-notch sources of lean protein include fish, skinless chicken and turkey, tofu, eggs, and low-fat and fat-free cottage cheese, yogurt, and ricotta cheese.

GOAL: 3 servings of lean protein a day

High on Hydration

Be sure to drink enough water! We've probably all heard this diet advice a hundred times. But did you ever really know why? Two reasons are standouts. Researchers at the Stanford School of Medicine Prevention Research Center tell us that the way water helps promote weight loss is twofold. As little as 4 cups of water each day could help you lose up to 5 pounds a year! Not too shabby for plain old H_2O. Water increases the amount of calories the body burns, explain the scientists. If this water is replacing sweetened drinks such as sodas, sports beverages, fruit drinks, or sweetened coffee and tea, you could lose even more weight. How much exactly depends on how many of these drinks you're replacing with water. Changing from sweetened drinks to diet ones will also result in weight loss, just not as much.[8]

GOAL: At least 4 (8-ounce) cups a day

SODIUM SIMPLIFIED

Salt is a natural compound that has been used as a food seasoning and preservative since ancient times. Yet these days, the role of salt in a healthy diet can be downright confusing—and scary. The risks associated with eating too much sodium over a long period of time include hypertension, congestive heart failure, and kidney disease. But is sodium the same thing as salt? Is eating any salt bad for us? How much is enough? How much is too much?

First let's clear up the difference between salt and sodium. As mentioned already, salt is found in nature, underground and in the oceans, and is a compound of 40 percent sodium and 60 percent chloride (NaCl). The sodium in salt is a mineral that is required by the body. It assists in nutrient transport, fluid regulation, muscle contraction, and other bodily functions. In addition to being part of salt, sodium is present in foods—from beef to celery, from milk to salmon. Although not technically accurate, the terms *salt* and *sodium* have become interchangeable.

We get sodium from three sources: first, the small amounts that occur naturally in foods; second, from salt used in cooking or as seasoning at the table; and third, from food products that are commercially processed. In fact, more than three-quarters of the sodium we eat comes from processed foods.[9] This includes canned soups, tomato products, and vegetables juices, as well as breads, frozen pizzas, rice and noodles mixes, and much more. Also ramping up the intake are meals from fast-food places and restaurants where we have little control over sodium intake.

The average American adult needs only about 1,500 milligrams per day.[10] The average American actually eats more than 3,400 milligrams of sodium a day,[11] according to the Centers for Disease Control and Prevention. (Just one Big Mac contains more than 1,000 milligrams.) The most recent Dietary Guidelines for Americans fall between those extremes, recommending that most healthy adults take in no more than 2,300 milligrams a day. This is the guideline that we've followed in creating the WOW meal plans.

As your taste buds adjust to less heavily salted foods, you'll begin to appreciate vibrant, natural flavors. Here are some tips to get started.

- Eat whole foods—fresh produce, unseasoned frozen produce, legumes, unprocessed meats, whole grains—as often as possible.

- In the supermarket, check out the sodium content on the nutrition facts label so you can monitor and control your intake. When purchasing nutritious canned foods, such as tomatoes and beans, seek out no-salt-added brands.

- In the kitchen, flavor dishes with lemon, garlic, fresh herbs, spices, and other sodium-free seasonings (see page 18).

- Replace the salt on your table with a salt-free seasoning or freshly ground black pepper.

Make Time for Tea

Tea is the most-consumed beverage in the world. Just wait until word gets out that tea—specifically, green tea—may help get rid of belly fat and promote weight loss! A 2009 Tufts University study reveals that drinking the equivalent of 3 cups of green tea a day assisted participants in losing twice as much weight, as well as more belly fat, as the ones who did not drink tea.[12] Catechins, a type of antioxidant in the tea, are thought to be responsible. To get even more bang for the buck, brew the tea with citrus juice such as lemon, lime, grapefruit, or orange. The citrus allows your body to use more of the catechins.[13] (For every 8 ounces, replace 2 to 4 ounces of water with citrus juice.) Be warned, some of these drinks may be a tad on the sour side. If you like, mix in 1 teaspoon of honey for only 21 calories.

GOAL: 3 (8-ounce) cups a day

THE WOW FACTOR FOODS

YOU'RE ALL SET to start getting enough fiber, calcium, vitamin D, good fats, and protein. Your tea is brewing and water is chilling. But you're wondering what actual foods you should eat and hoping that it will be enough to keep you from feeling hungry all the time. Fear not. The simple rules that follow will help you easily meet the WOW nutritional guidelines (we've done all the math for you!). And you'll find that this combination of foods will keep you feeling satisfied and energized all day long—some test panelists even felt that this was a bit too much food. Remember, these lists are examples and are by no means all-inclusive. If certain fruits, veggies, or other foods don't appear here, it doesn't mean that you can't eat them. As long as it's an unprocessed whole food, enjoy it. In fact, making a game of sampling new foods can add vitality and variety to your daily dining. Boredom be gone!

Basic Brewed Green Tea

Place 1 tea bag or 1 teaspoon of loose tea leaves in your cup. Bring a little more than 1 cup of cold water to a boil. Remove from the heat and add an ice cube, if you'd like; this will help bring the water to the ideal temperature for brewing tea, which is 180°F. Pour the water over the tea and let it steep for 3 to 5 minutes.

For convenience, you may brew 24 ounces at one time by combining 3 tea bags and 3 cups of hot water in a heatproof jar. After steeping, remove and discard the tea bags. To reheat a single-cup serving, pour the desired amount into a microwaveable cup and heat on high power for 60 to 90 seconds.

WHOLE GRAINS, STARCHY VEGGIES, AND BEANS:
Eat 5 or 6 servings a day

Bread *(1 serving = 1 slice)*
- Bagel *(1/2 mini)*
- English muffin *(1/2)*
- Pita *(1/2 small)*
- Tortilla *(1 small)*

Cereal, dry *(1 serving = 1 cup)*

Crackers *(1 serving = 1 ounce)*

Pancake/waffle *(1 serving = 1 medium)*

Popcorn, light microwave *(1 serving = 3 cups popped)*

Cooked whole grains *(1 serving = 1/2 cup)*
- Coucous
- Hot cereal
- Oatmeal
- Pasta
- Rice

Canned and cooked beans, all kinds *(1 serving = 1/2 cup)*

Cooked starchy veggies *(1 serving = 1/2 cup)*
- Corn
- Peas
- Potatoes, all kinds

> **Tip**
>
> When buying foods, check the ingredient list found on the label—the first ingredient should be something such as whole wheat flour, oats, or brown rice—to make sure you are getting whole grains.

FRUIT: Eat 3 servings a day

Whole fresh fruit *(1 serving = 1 medium piece)*
- Apple
- Banana *(1/2)*
- Grapefruit *(1/2)*
- Kiwifruit
- Nectarine
- Orange
- Peach
- Pear
- Plum
- Tangerine

Canned or cut-up fresh fruit *(1 serving = 1/2 cup)*
- Blueberries
- Cherries
- Grapes
- Mango
- Melon
- Papaya
- Pineapple
- Pomegranate
- Raspberries
- Strawberries

Dried fruit *(1 serving = 1/4 cup)*
- Apricots
- Craisins
- Prunes (dried plums)
- Raisins

100% fruit juice, all kinds *(1 serving = 1/2 cup)*

> **Tip**
>
> When buying canned or frozen fruit, be sure to avoid sugar- or syrup-packed products.

VEGETABLES: Eat 4 or 5 servings a day

Cooked *(fresh, frozen, or canned; 1 serving = ½ cup)*

- Asparagus (3 spears)
- Bell pepper
- Broccoli
- Brussels sprouts
- Cabbage
- Carrots
- Cauliflower
- Eggplant
- Green beans
- Mushrooms
- Onion
- Spinach
- Zucchini

Cut-up raw vegetables *(1 serving = 1 cup)*

- Baby carrots
- Bell pepper
- Broccoli
- Cauliflower
- Cucumber
- Greens, all kinds
- Lettuce, all kinds
- Tomato

100% vegetable juice, all kinds *(1 serving = ½ cup)*

Tip

When buying frozen vegetables, avoid butter, cheese, or other creamy sauces. When buying vegetable juices, look for reduced-sodium products.

DAIRY: Eat 3 servings a day

Milk, fat-free or soy *(1 serving = 1 cup)*

Yogurt *(1 serving = 1 cup)*

Shredded or crumbled cheese *(1 serving = ⅓ cup)*

- Blue cheese
- Cheddar
- Feta cheese
- Mozzarella
- Parmesan
- Romano

Sliced or cubed cheese *(1 serving = 1 ounce or 1 slice or 2 domino-sized cubes)*

- American
- Cheddar
- Colby
- Monterey Jack
- Swiss

Soft cheese *(1 serving = ½ cup)*

- Cottage cheese
- Ricotta

Tip

When buying dairy products, choose fat-free or reduced-fat versions whenever possible. If you're lactose intolerant, you can try dividing your dairy into smaller servings throughout the day, making sure to pair them with other foods. Also, look for lactose-reduced foods and beverages, or consider Lactaid or other lactase supplements. You can get some calcium and vitamin D from nondairy foods, such as dark leafy greens and fortified orange juice, or, of course, from supplements.

HEALTHY FATS: Eat 3 or 4 servings a day

Monounsaturated fatty acids and omega-3 fatty acids

Avocado *(1 serving = ⅓ medium)*

Chocolate, dark *(1 serving = ¼ cup chips or a 2-ounce piece)*

Fatty fish *(1 serving = 3 ounces)*
- Herring
- Mackerel
- Salmon
- Sardines
- Trout

Nut butter *(1 serving = 1 tablespoon)*
- Almond
- Cashew
- Peanut
- Soy

Nuts *(1 serving = 1 ounce)*
- Almonds *(24)*
- Cashews *(18)*
- Peanuts *(28)*
- Pecan halves *(20)*
- Pistachios *(46)*
- Macadamias *(12)*
- Walnut halves *(7)*

Oil *(1 serving = 2½ teaspoons)*
- Canola
- Flaxseed
- Olive

Olives *(1 serving = 10 medium)*

Pesto *(1 serving = 1 tablespoon)*

Polyunsaturated and trans fats:

The following are unhealthy fats and should be eaten sparingly.

Reduced-fat mayonnaise *(1 serving = 2 tablespoons)*

Reduced-fat salad dressing *(1 serving = 2½ tablespoons)*

Regular salad dressing *(1 serving = 1½ tablespoons)*

Soft/tub/stick margarine, butter, or regular mayonnaise *(1 serving = 1 tablespoon)*

Tip

You should limit your total fat consumption to no more than 5 servings per day, so limit unhealthy fats to 1 or 2 servings. Even better, make all 5 servings healthy fats.

LEAN PROTEIN: Eat 3 servings a day

Meat *(1 serving = 3 ounces)*
- Beef
- Deli meat (roast beef or ham)
- Ground beef
- Pork, boneless loin

Poultry, white meat preferred *(1 serving = 3 ounces)*
- Chicken, boneless, skinless

- Chicken or turkey, ground
- Deli meat (chicken or turkey)
- Turkey, boneless, skinless

Seafood, low fat content *(1 serving = 3 ounces)*
- Shrimp, without shells
- Tuna, canned, water-packed

- Whitefish (such as cod and haddock)

Nonmeat protein *(1 serving = 3 ounces)*
- Egg, large *(1)*
- Egg substitute *(¼ cup)*
- Tofu or soy foods

Tip

Choose 2 servings from the meat, poultry, or seafood groups and 1 serving from the nonmeat group per day. If you're a vegetarian, simply choose all 3 servings from the nonmeat group.

PUTTING IT ALL TOGETHER

NOW THAT YOU HAVE all the basic information you need to start eating smarter, how do you find time to actually do it in today's busy world? We have the strategies you can use to select, store, and prepare the wonderful, nutritious foods that are going to transform your life and health.

Super Marketing

When it comes to changing to healthier eating habits, the place to start is the supermarket. Making a conscious choice to buy whole grains, lean meats, low-fat dairy, and fresh produce will put you on the fast track to meeting your weight-loss goals.

Many of us go grocery shopping on autopilot. We coast through the aisles, putting the same bags, boxes, and cans in our cart. At home, we perhaps prepare a couple of the same old meals and then find ourselves with "nothing to eat." So it's takeout or another quick grocery-store run to grab something convenient.

Applying a new mind-set to grocery shopping can dramatically reframe the experience. Instead of looking at it as a chore, consider it one of the most empowering activities you can do to change your life for the better. Do you want to hand your health and well-being over to food marketers who are motivated by profit? Or do you want to make the decisions about what's best for you?

This creative new mind-set starts with menus. Start by selecting a week's worth of meals. We've made it easy for you to with 28 Days of WOW Menus (page 182) and Build Your Own WOW Menus (page 212) from which to choose. And remember, just because you're selecting 7 days' worth of meals doesn't mean you have to cook every day. See page 19 for ways to prepare for no-cook meals.

Now it's time for the grocery list. Jot down the ingredients you'll need for each meal, then scan your fridge, freezer, and cupboards for what you already have and write down what you don't. Now it's off to the supermarket. You'll discover that it's suddenly become easier to resist impulse buying. In fact, since you're focusing on whole foods, you won't be spending nearly as

LEAN MEAT CUTS

Keep this checklist in hand when you shop so you know you're choosing the cuts of beef and pork with the least amount of fat. Ask the meat cutter to trim off all visible fat, or do it yourself at home.[14]

BEEF

- Top round roast and steak
- Bottom round roast and steak
- Eye round roast and steak
- Sirloin tip side steak
- Top sirloin steak
- 95% lean or greater ground beef

PORK

- Top loin chop
- Tenderloin

much time in the center aisles, where the highly processed foods are shelved.

Shopping this way assures you'll have the ingredients on hand to make healthy meals that fit your new eating plan. You'll also save money and time by cutting last-minute trips to the market or fast-food joints a few times a week.

FLAVOR FOR FREE

Focus on "freebies"—condiments and seasonings to stock in the pantry that add big flavor to meats, vegetables, and grains with virtually no added calories, fat, or salt.

There's a world of flavors out there! What are you waiting for?

- Dried herbs, such as oregano, rosemary, sage, and thyme
- Dried mushroom powder
- Dried mustard powder
- Dried pepper flakes
- Flavoring extracts such as vanilla, almond, coconut, maple, peppermint, and more
- Fresh ginger
- Fresh herbs, such as basil, cilantro, dill, parsley, and tarragon
- Fresh or dried chiles
- Garlic
- Grated fresh horseradish or prepared horseradish
- Juices—lemon, lime, and orange—and grated zest
- Reduced-sodium soy sauce
- Salt-free seasoning mixes
- Spices, such as cayenne, cinnamon, coriander, cumin, ginger, nutmeg, paprika, pepper, and turmeric
- Vinegars, such as balsamic, sherry, red or white wine, and rice
- Wasabi

Prepped in the Pantry

The right convenience foods can be your allies in healthier eating. There are loads of healthful food products that you should stock in your pantry that will cut preparation time dramatically. Also listed below are some basics you'll want to always have on hand.

IN THE CUPBOARD

Canola and olive oils

Old-fashioned oats

Whole grain pasta in various shapes

Instant or heat-and-eat whole grain brown rice

Whole wheat tortillas

Chicken, beef, and/or vegetable broth or stock in an aseptic pack

Reduced-sodium, canned, broth-based, or bean soups

Low-sodium canned beans

Low-sodium canned tomatoes

Low-sodium spaghetti sauce

Canned, water-packed fish, such as tuna and salmon

Juice-packed canned fruit

Canned pumpkin puree (not pumpkin pie mix)

Nuts

Mini chocolate chips

IN THE REFRIGERATOR

Bagged, washed spinach and kale

Precut veggies from the salad bar

Shredded reduced-fat cheese

Reduced-fat sour cream

Fat-free plain or vanilla yogurt

Loose-pack boneless, skinless chicken breasts
Loose-pack fish fillets such as cod, salmon, or tilapia
Loose-pack peeled and cooked shrimp
Loose-pack fruits and vegetables

Strategies for No-Cook Meals

Eating healthy meals does not mean you'll be tied to the stove each and every day. We know the demands on your time and energy from work, family, and community. By cooking smarter, not longer, you can create multiple meals with no extra work.

Start by doubling recipes to have extra portions for the refrigerator or freezer. You'll have instant brown-bag lunches and microwaveable dinners. Utilize the slow cooker for dishes that require long cooking, such as soups and stews. Dinner is ready when you come home from work or walking.

Cook whole grains such as wheat berries, barley, quinoa, and brown rice in big batches to keep on hand for quick-to-eat cereals or side dishes or as soup or casserole ingredients. To prepare, rinse the grains in a fine sieve under cold, running water. Place the desired amount of grains in a pot with the water called for on the package directions (usually 2 to 3 cups of water to 1 cup of grain). Cook according to the package directions. Spread the grains on a tray to cool, and then divide into individual or recipe-size amounts. Store in resealable plastic storage bags or plastic storage containers.

When you're roasting something in the oven, pop in a few herb-seasoned chicken breasts, a turkey breast half, or a pork tenderloin. Roast until done, then cool and slice for a convenient sandwich filling that's much lower in sodium and fat than deli cuts. Lean cooked meats are also wonderful to add to soups, salads, and casseroles.

Now you have all the building blocks for a nutritious eating plan, and the fun part begins. Turn to the next chapter to start putting together the WOW Diet that's just right for you!

Grain Guarantee

When scanning for whole grain packaged foods, one simple trick is to look for the whole grains stamp, which was created by the Whole Grains Council to make it easier for you to identify whole grains. There are two stamps: One is for foods containing at least half a serving, or 8 grams of whole grains, and the other is for foods made entirely with whole grains that contain at least 16 grams— a full serving.

PUTTING TOGETHER YOUR WOW DIET

IN TRUTH, IF YOU WANTED TO SKIP AHEAD to 28 Days of WOW Menus on page 182, you'd have all the information you need at your fingertips to nourish your body, satisfy your appetite, and meet your calorie-reduction goals for an entire month! But if you want to understand the techniques behind the magic, this chapter is definitely beneficial.

The first step to creating a tailored WOW Diet plan is to be aware of the nutritional guidelines and understand that they are recommendations, not rules. There may be days or meals where one or two nutrients are a bit higher than the number in the chart on the next page, and there may be days or meals where one or two nutrients may be lower, and that's fine. The goal is to aim to get as close to these guidelines as often as possible and not beat yourself up about minor differences sure to occur once in a while. This chapter will give you more ideas as to how you can stay on track, no matter what comes up in your life.

THE WOW DIET EATING PLAN

WE'VE GEARED THE WOW Diet eating plan to fit the needs of the average American woman. With three meals and one snack throughout the day, total calorie allotment is 1,600 calories. This is plenty to nourish and energize your body while simultaneously promoting weight loss.

But, just as eye and hair color vary among different people, so calorie requirements differ from one person to the next, depending on physical and lifestyle factors. If a 1,600-a-day calorie intake doesn't quell true hunger pangs or provide you with the energy you need, you may add a 200-calorie snack, which will bring you to a total intake of 1,800 calories.

NUTRIENT	DAILY	BREAKFAST	LUNCH	DINNER	SNACK/ DESSERT
Calories	1,600	375	475	550	200
Fat	53 g	12	16	18	7
Sat. fat	18 g	4	5	6	3
Fiber	20 g (or more)	6	6	8	2
Calcium	1,000 mg	330	330	210	130
Good fat	18 g (or more)	4	6	6	2
Protein	100 g	22	34	34	10
Sodium	2,400 mg	675	675	675	375

For some individuals, it may be advisable to start out on 1,800 calories a day. For example, if you're over 5'6" and/or you weigh more than 250 pounds, this slightly higher calorie allowance will serve your needs better. Again, if you're often hungry or fatigued at this calorie level, you may need to add another 200-calorie snack. In this case, you'll be eating three snacks a day and a total of 2,000 calories. Don't worry, you'll still lose weight, though probably more gradually.

In Chapter 2, you learned how many servings from each food group you should be eating each day, as well as just what constitutes a serving. Turning that long list of foods into meals for the day can be challenging for many. To make that task a bit easier, we've broken meals down into components and then plugged sample foods into each slot.

MEAL	FOOD SERVINGS	EXAMPLE
BREAKFAST	**Grains/Starches:** 2 servings	1 English muffin
	Fruits: 1 serving	½ grapefruit
	Dairy: 1 serving	1 cup yogurt
	Healthy Fats: 1 serving	1 tablespoon almond butter
	Lean Protein: 1 serving	1 large hard-cooked egg
LUNCH	**Grains/Starches:** 2 servings	1 small pita
	Fruits: 1 serving	1 medium apple
	Vegetables: 2 servings	½ cup lettuce; ½ cup cucumber; ½ cup raw baby carrots; ½ cup raw bell peppers
	Dairy: 1 serving	⅓ cup shredded Cheddar cheese
	Healthy Fats: 1 serving	⅓ avocado
	Lean Protein: 1 serving	3 ounces boneless, skinless chicken breast
SNACK	**Fruits:** 1 serving	½ cup grapes
	Dairy: 1 serving	1 slice American cheese
DINNER	**Grains/Starches:** 1 serving	½ cup pasta
	Vegetables: 2 servings	½ cup cooked mushrooms; ½ cup cooked onion
	Healthy Fats: 1 serving	2½ teaspoons olive oil
	Lean Protein: 1 serving	3 ounces lean ground beef
OPTIONAL SNACK*	**Grains/Starches:** 1 serving	3 cups popped light microwave popcorn
	Vegetables: 1 serving	½ cup carrot juice
	Healthy Fats: 1 serving	7 walnut halves
TOTAL	**Grains/Starches:** 6 servings	
	Fruits: 3 servings	
	Vegetables: 5 servings	
	Dairy: 3 servings	
	Healthy Fats: 4 servings	
	Lean Protein: 3 servings	

*If you still feel hungry on the 1,800 calorie plan, eat another optional snack for a total of 2,000 calories.

Susan Moyer, 51

LOST 17¼ POUNDS AND 11¾ INCHES

Susan Moyer had been a high school athlete and continued to play softball much of her adult life. But after she got divorced in 2002, she stopped playing and started gaining weight, which caused an old knee injury to flare up. The WOW program was challenging at first because her knee was sore and stiff. But she persevered, with her doctor's approval, modifying many of the moves and wearing a knee brace. After just a couple of weeks, she noticed that her knee pain was gone—and by the end of the 8-week program, she had not only lost 17½ pounds but gained her youthful energy, confidence, and independence. "The more physically fit I get, the more courageous and willing I am to take chances and do things that I haven't done before—all by myself!" she said. Three months after the official end of the program, Susan recorded an additional 7½-pound weight loss and shaved another 5¼ inches off her figure, for a grand total of 24¾ pounds and 17 inches lost in 5 months.

By using the food lists along with the chart on page 23, you should be able, with some practice, to rotate a variety of foods into each slot for endless meal possibilities based on your personal likes, dislikes, and lifestyle.

You'll notice the chart covers three daily meals plus two snacks, one optional. Think of these as wild-card foods. Perhaps you really want some veggies in your omelet at breakfast. Plug in an extra veggie serving instead of carrot sticks for a snack. Or if you'd like your Creamy Mac and Three Cheeses (page 155) for dinner to be even creamier, go ahead and plug that extra dairy serving in there. You're in charge.

As for timing your meals and snacks to segue best with your workouts, here are some tips to keep in mind. The optimal time for exercise/walking is several hours after a meal or 1 to 2 hours after a snack. Your digested food provides the energy for you to be at your peak, and you'll avoid any cramping that could occur if you walk shortly after eating.

Don't take the opposite tack, however. If you work out on an empty tummy, your staying power is likely to fizzle and your calorie burn to sputter. If you feel like you need a little boost before your workout, snack on about 150 calories of a quickly digested low-fat food, such as cottage cheese, dried cranberries, or peanut butter on half of a toasted whole wheat English muffin.

Postworkout noshing is also important for replenishing energy and helping your muscles recover so you're ready for your next workout. If your next meal is more than an hour away, have a 100- to 200-calorie snack that contains both carbohydrates and protein, such as an apple with cashew butter.

Establish your own rhythm to divide your current calories by breaking up meals and snacks that are spaced around your exercise schedule. And always remember to replenish your fluids with refreshing calorie-free water and green tea.

Just like all the guidelines in this book, this is not a hard-and-fast rule. If you'd rather have more pasta at dinner (perhaps two servings instead of one) and don't usually have many grains at lunch, skip the grains serving at lunch and add it to your dinner portion. Just try to keep the amount of food at each meal roughly the same. Having only one or two servings of food at breakfast and lunch and then 20 or so at dinner isn't healthy because it will set you up to be ravenous and overeat late in the day.

Which leads us to the importance of breakfast in setting the tone for a healthy eating day. Research shows that eating breakfast helps you eat less throughout the day.[1] Typical breakfast foods give you a big leg up on meeting your nutrient goals for the day. Breakfast often includes proteins such as eggs and peanut butter, low-fat dairy foods such as milk or yogurt, vitamin- and fiber-rich fruits, and whole grains such as cereal, toast, and oats. A recent study showed that eating breakfast cereal, specifically, is one of six healthy behaviors linked to a lower risk of heart failure.[2] The other heart-healthy habits: maintaining a normal body weight, not smoking, exercising regularly, moderating alcohol intake, and eating fruits and vegetables.

Breakfast can be as simple or as elaborate as you like. Whether you're already a breakfast eater and are looking for some new ideas or you're a breakfast skipper and don't know where to begin, check out the menus (starting on page 182) for some tasty ways to get your day started.

Here are some classic pairings for not only breakfast but lunch and dinner as well.

MEAL	RECIPE TYPE	PAIR WITH
BREAKFAST	Egg/protein-filled	Whole grain toast, English muffin, bagels, muffins
	Grain-based pancakes, waffles, cereal	Fruit, fat-free milk, yogurt
LUNCH/ DINNER	Veggie/salad-based	Whole grain crackers or roll, fruit, yogurt, cottage cheese, lean protein
	Grain-based—macaroni, spaghetti	Lean protein, cooked veggies, salad, raw veggies, fruit
	Protein—chicken, beef, seafood	Whole grain pasta or rice or other grain, cooked veggies, salad, fruit

These combos are the template for creating wonderful meals. If you're having grilled chicken, you can certainly steam up some broccoli and brown rice to go along with it, but why not flip through Salads & Sides (page 96) for recipes that will give your taste buds a real treat.

BANISH GUILT

ONE ISSUE THAT SHOULD BE addressed concerning dieting is guilt. You vow to eat certain foods a certain way. Everything is going fine. Then you slip. You eat one of the foods you swore not to touch. The guilt sets in. You feel terrible, and to deal with it, you eat, you feel guilty, and a vicious spiral ensues.

There are methods to cope with the "I should haves." First, don't set yourself up for guilt. Never say "never" about any food. Instead, give yourself permission to enjoy a few of your favorite high-calorie or high-fat foods in moderation *once in a while*—maybe a scoop of premium ice cream on a Friday afternoon or a small bag of potato chips with lunch on Wednesday.

If, despite your flexibility, some guilty feelings creep in, don't let them ruin all the good you've done. You slipped; it happens to everyone. The best thing you can do for yourself is to get right back on that healthy horse and continue your nutritious food choices and exercise. One goof doesn't amount to much in the big picture of a healthy lifestyle. Eat slightly fewer calories the next day or exercise a bit longer and you're back on track.

DINING OUT THE WOW WAY

WHETHER FOR BUSINESS, a celebration, or just getting together with friends, there are going to be lunches or dinners where you find yourself in a restaurant. If you're the kind of person who eats out only once or twice a year, a little splurge would be fine. On the other hand, if you're ordering off a menu several times a week, you should learn how to order the WOW way.

INCORPORATE AS MANY FOOD GROUPS AS POSSIBLE. Most restaurant entrées include a meat and a starch, so you'll probably need to order a salad (ask for dressing on the side) or a side of steamed vegetables.

SIZING UP PORTIONS

One of the most important parts in changing eating habits is understanding portion sizes. Knowing appropriate portion sizes and how to visualize them is a skill we can all master. Here are a few handy little tricks that can help.

PORTION SIZE	LOOKS LIKE
3 ounces of cooked meat	the palm of your hand (excluding your fingers) or a deck of cards
1 medium piece of fruit	a tennis ball
1 ounce of cheese	1 tube of lipstick
1 cup	a closed fist
1/2 cup	a computer mouse or half a baseball
1/4 cup	an egg or half a tennis ball
1 tablespoon	half a golf ball or the tip of your thumb (from last knuckle)
1 teaspoon	a die

KEEP AN EYE ON PORTIONS. Restaurants like to serve huge portions so customers feel they've gotten a good value. Consider ordering two appetizers and sharing with a friend, or take home half your meal for lunch the next day to truly get your money's worth.

CONSIDER ORDERING A BROTH-BASED SOUP AS AN APPETIZER. These types of soups are usually relatively low in calories but help fill you up before the entrée arrives, so you'll ultimately eat less.[3] Just avoid creamy or cheesy soups, which have a lot of fat.

PASS ON THE BREAD AND BUTTER, bread and olive oil, or fried chips with salsa. Asking the server to skip these starches will keep you from mindlessly munching and save you unnecessary fat and calories.

TAKEOUT WITHOUT BREAKING OUT

SOMETIMES THE BEST-LAID PLANS go awry. When the day just doesn't go as you anticipated and cooking your planned dinner is not an option, plan B is to make the best choice you can at your favorite take-out spot. With a few simple tenets in mind, you can get a fast meal without giving up your healthy eating principles entirely.

SIZE IT RIGHT. Skip the super-duper, deluxe, mega, and king-size menu versions. They are all code for "more than you need to be eating." A simple burger or sandwich can be the foundation of a great meal. One or two slices of a cheese or veggie-topped pizza can be the same.

ADD A SALAD OR FRESH FRUIT. These can round out the meal, satisfy your hunger, and offer vitamins and fiber with little fat and calories. Just go easy on the dressing.

OPT FOR WATER or fat-free milk to drink.

PARTY PLANNER

BIRTHDAY PARTIES, anniversaries, wedding, graduations—you have to face the fact that these events are a special part of life, and it's important to enjoy them. With preparation, you can have a good time and no regrets the next day.

EAT LIGHT MEALS THE DAY OF THE PARTY. While you may be inclined to eat nothing early in the day to allow for the higher-calorie food you'll be eating later, don't! It'll backfire. By the time you get to the restaurant or party, you'll be so hungry that you'll inhale everything you find and overeat for sure.

A wiser strategy is to eat small meals throughout the day to keep your calorie intake on the low side, but still keep something in your stomach so you're able to make smart decisions come party time.

MASTER THE BUFFET. So much food, so little time. There are two ways to go here. The first is to take miniportions of everything so you won't feel deprived of anything. Another option is to scan the buffet and pick two or three items (ideally, from different food groups) that look the best to you and dine on only those.

BE CAREFUL WITH ALCOHOL. Drinks are a double whammy. First, either the booze or the mixers or both will rack up the calories. Second, imbibing too much can hinder your ability to make good decisions. In this case, it can lead to unhealthy food choices and overeating. Try alternating alcoholic drinks with water, diluting wine to make spritzers, or choosing lower-calorie mixers, such as seltzer water. And always have some food in your stomach before you have a drink.

PRACTICE PLEASURE. Have you ever gone out to eat or to a party and found a certain dish just didn't taste very good but you ate it anyway? Well, stop doing that! No need to fill up on disappointing calories. At a buffet, select another item. At a restaurant, simply enjoy the rest of the meal without feeling like you're overindulging. Perhaps order a salad if you feel you need a bit more food.

KEEP IT STEADY

LOSING WEIGHT CAN certainly be challenging. Keeping the weight off can be even more difficult. Think about it: When you're losing weight, you're making big changes with big results. It's exciting when the pounds are dropping, the blood pressure's lowering, and your waist size is shrinking.

Keeping your weight steady for the long term may not provide quite the same rush, but the rewards are every bit as, if not more, gratifying. Bicycling with your kids or grandkids? Trail hiking on vacation? Digging in the garden? These are the wonderful life-affirming activities you'll breeze through when you keep your weight steady. Achieving balance is the key.

THE RECIPES

THE 150 RECIPES in the following chapters will provide delicious nourishment while you're on the WOW program—and, we hope, for months and years to come. We've developed streamlined versions of well-loved dishes so that the whole family can enjoy the same meal (no extra cooking for separate dieter's dishes).

We've kept ingredients to a minimum and procedures short. The recipes fall into two basic categories: dishes that cook really quickly start to finish, such as Hoisin Pork Stir-Fry on page 126, and dishes that require little active attention but cook unattended, such as the homey Beef Stew on page 119. This type is particularly welcome for leaner meat cuts that often need more cooking time to tenderize them.

Appetizers & Snacks includes easy first courses to incorporate into meals. Think Buffalo-Style Chicken Bites (page 42), Greek-Style Appetizer Cheesecake (page 41), or Cheesy Cornmeal Cakes with Salsa (page 40). Pack-and-go snacks, such as gooey Honey Nut Walking Stix (page 45) and yummy Banana Chocolate Chip Macadamia Muffins (page 46), will keep you energized on the run.

Breakfast recipes fit a variety of tastes and times frames: from fast Banana-Ginger Smoothie (page 69) to overnight Breakfast Strata (page 54).

Soups & Sandwiches offers versatile recipes that can serve as side dishes or light main courses. The appeal of Baked Potato Chowder (page 73), Chicken Tortilla Soup (page 75), and Turkey Apple Panini (page 93) is irresistible.

Salads & Sides provides options to make meals so much more interesting, with all the colors of the vegetable rainbow. Check out Mashed Sweet Potatoes and Carrots (page 112), Snow Peas with Basil (page 113), and Roasted Green Beans with Candied Walnuts (page 109).

Main Dishes includes Mexican Lasagna (page 152), Honey-Mustard Pork Tenderloin (page 125), Turkey Meatballs and Linguine (page 128), Stir-Fried Orange Chicken and Broccoli (page 131), and Seafood and Brown Rice Paella (page 142)—all are simple, satisfying, and filled with flavor.

Desserts is an especially welcome chapter. Peanut Butter Cup Sundaes (page 173), Chocolate Pudding Cake (page 170), Oatmeal-Date Bars (page 179), Banana Snack Cake (page 166), and other treats are included in the daily menus, so all you have to do is enjoy.

Geri Krempa, 46

LOST 11½ POUNDS AND 9½ INCHES

Geri Krempa thought she was a pretty hardy walker. "My girlfriends and I would look for the best hills and then go for an hour-long walk a few times a week," she said. "So I was surprised that just 30 minutes could kick my butt. I got a better workout in less time." The workouts also helped Geri shape up her eating habits. She stopped snacking mindlessly and lost her belly bloat. By the end of 8 weeks, she had also lowered her cholesterol by 10 points and her blood sugar by 11 points. And she reported that she no longer suffered from insomnia and had more energy during the day. "The weight came off easily . . . and I've been able to maintain it without being superstrict about my diet," she said. Three months after the official end of the program, Geri recorded an additional 4½-pound weight loss and shaved another 3¾ inches off her figure, for a grand total of 16 pounds and 13¼ inches lost in 5 months.

Q: It seems like it's much harder for me to lose weight than it was 10 or 20 years ago. Why is that?

A: There could be a number of factors for this. The first is simply that with age, the body tends to lose a bit of muscle mass. Less muscle means your body burns fewer calories, so you need fewer calories to maintain your weight. It's also quite common to become less active with age, which again, means fewer calories are needed. And years of dieting, weight gain, dieting, weight gain, and so on can slow down metabolism. That means—you guessed it—fewer calories needed to maintain your weight. The bottom line: To lose weight, you need to cut even more calories.

Q: I'd be thinner if someone prepared meals for me. Since I'm the one making dinner, it's a challenge. What suggestions do you have to overcome disaster this time of day?

A: This is a tough time for many of us. So take the offense by planning meals and preparing as much in advance as possible. First, if you find yourself ready to chow down the minute you walk in the door, start packing a snack to eat shortly before or right after you leave work. A simple cheese stick, a piece of fruit, or an ounce of nuts should be enough to tide you over so you don't devour everything in sight as you're cooking dinner. Second, try a slow cooker. If your mornings are busy, you can load up the pot the night before, cover it, and put it in the fridge. In the morning, pop it into the cooker, turn it on, and go. Even without a slow cooker, you can plan to measure out all your ingredients ahead of time. Cut and wash all your veggies, and trim and cut all your meat. With all of that done in advance, you'll simply have to throw it all together and cook when you get home in the evening.

Q: Is it possible to be slightly overweight and still be fit? How do you know when you weigh too much?

A: Yes, there are a number of factors that come into play when determining how healthy or fit someone is. They include body weight, activity level, blood pressure, blood sugar, blood cholesterol levels, and others. Since everyone's body is different, a registered dietitian or physician is the best person to talk to about what a healthy weight may be for you. However, here a few red flags that may point to health issues from excess weight:

- Is it affecting your ability to do normal everyday activities?
- Are the levels of the above-mentioned health indicators climbing?
- Is it difficult to exercise?
- Are you experiencing knee or back pain that could be due to your weight?

Q: Is the WOW diet family-friendly, or will I have to cook separate meals for my husband and children?

A: Definitely food for all to enjoy! While creating the recipes and menus, my husband and two young kids, along with family friends and relatives, were my personal test panel. Healthy food—as long as it tastes great—benefits everyone, no matter their age, size, or gender. Of course, hubbies may want a slightly larger portion, while young kids would eat a slightly smaller portion. In addition, it's never too early to model healthy eating for those you love the most.

Q: Help! I can't live without chocolate. Are there any ways to satisfy my chocolate tooth and not wreck my diet?

A: I can't live without it, either, and I don't. You can get your chocolate fix while still eating healthy. You could plan a small square of good-quality chocolate (the darker the chocolate, the higher the antioxidants) into your menu every day. For a snack, how about some chocolate pudding, chocolate milk, or hot chocolate made with fat-free milk? Dip fruit in a small amount of melted semisweet or dark chocolate.

Q: Is it okay to drink 2% milk instead of fat-free?

A: If you don't care for fat-free milk, 1% would be the next best choice. Here's a quick rundown of the calorie and fat differences in 1 cup (8 ounces) of the different kinds of milk.

- **Whole milk:** 150 calories, 8 g fat
- **2% milk:** 120 calories, 4.5 g fat
- **1% milk:** 100 calories, 2.5 g fat
- **Fat-free milk:** 80 calories, 0 g fat

You can see 2% is not significantly better than whole milk, but 1% cuts calories and fat. You may also want to try a brand of milk, such as Hood Simply Smart, that has a creamier mouthfeel than other low-fat milks.

Q: I know that nuts are high in fat. Will adding them to my diet raise my cholesterol?

A: While nuts are high in fat, it's a healthy fat. Not only will they not raise your cholesterol, research has shown that some nuts may help lower it.

Q: Is it true that people tend to crave carbs in the late afternoon? If so, what are some ways to deal with the craving?

A: It's hard to say what's "true" for everyone. Our bodies all work differently, and we have different inclinations. If you are one who does crave carbs in the afternoon, take preventive measures by eating a well-balanced lunch. Include whole grains, lean protein, some healthy fat, and fruits and/or veggies. Then plan a healthy snack about 3 hours after lunch, and you'll likely find your carb cravings abating.

THE
WOW
RECIPES

PART
two

Chapter

4

APPETIZERS
& SNACKS

Mushroom Spread

16 SERVINGS

55 MINUTES

1. COMBINE the dried mushrooms and water in a small bowl. Let stand for 15 minutes.

2. LINE a fine sieve with a coffee filter or paper towels. Set over a medium saucepan. Pour the mushroom liquid through the sieve. Set the mushrooms aside. Add the lentils to the pan and bring to a boil over high heat. Reduce the heat to medium-low. Cover the pan and simmer, stirring occasionally, for 20 minutes, or until tender and all the liquid has been absorbed.

3. SET a medium nonstick skillet coated with cooking spray over medium heat. Add the onion, button mushrooms, reconstituted mushrooms, garlic, and thyme. Cook, stirring occasionally, for 18 to 20 minutes, or until golden brown and very soft.

4. TRANSFER the lentils to a food processor. Puree until smooth. Add the mushroom mixture, walnuts, and salt. Pulse briefly just until combined.

5. SPOON into a serving bowl. Sprinkle with the parsley.

SERVING SUGGESTIONS: Serve Mushroom Spread with crackers, bread slices, or raw vegetables. Or stuff it into Belgian endive leaves or hollowed cherry tomatoes.

- 1 ounce dried mushrooms
- 2½ cups boiling water
- ½ cup brown lentils, picked over and rinsed
- 1 large onion, finely chopped
- 8 ounces button mushrooms, finely chopped
- 4 garlic cloves, chopped
- ½ teaspoon dried thyme
- ¼ cup finely chopped toasted walnuts
- ¼ teaspoon salt
- 2 tablespoons chopped fresh parsley

PER SERVING 48 calories, 1 g fat, 0 g saturated fat, 3 g protein, 6 g carbohydrates, 3 g fiber, 12 mg calcium, 40 mg sodium

Avocado-Peach Salsa with Multigrain Chips

1 tablespoon olive oil

1 tablespoon freshly squeezed lime juice

1 tablespoon sugar

1 tablespoon red wine vinegar

1 garlic clove, minced

½ teaspoon salt

1 peach, diced

1 avocado, diced

1 red bell pepper, diced

1 small red onion, finely chopped

6 ounces multigrain chips

8 SERVINGS

40 MINUTES

1. COMBINE the oil, lime juice, sugar, vinegar, garlic, and salt in a medium bowl. Whisk to blend. Add the peach, avocado, pepper, and onion and stir. Cover and refrigerate for 30 minutes to blend the flavors.

2. STIR the salsa before serving with the chips.

PER SERVING 178 calories, 10 g fat, 1 g saturated fat, 2 g protein, 20 g carbohydrates, 3 g fiber, 22 mg calcium, 249 mg sodium

Creamy Citrus Dip for Fruit

1 carton (6 ounces) fat-free vanilla yogurt

2 tablespoons honey

1½ teaspoons freshly grated lemon zest

4 SERVINGS (3 TABLESPOONS PER SERVING)

5 MINUTES

COMBINE the yogurt, honey, and lemon zest in a bowl. Mix well. Serve with your favorite cut-up fruit, such as apples, strawberries, pears, oranges, or pineapple.

PER SERVING 71 calories, 0 g fat, 0 g saturated fat, 2 g protein, 16 g carbohydrates, 0 g fiber, 78 mg calcium, 29 mg sodium

Pesto Dip

6 SERVINGS

5 MINUTES

COMBINE the basil, bread crumbs, cheese, almonds, and garlic in a blender or food processor. Process until smooth, scraping down the sides of the container as necessary. Add the mayonnaise and sour cream and process briefly to combine.

PER SERVING 116 calories, 3 g fat, 1 g saturated fat, 5 g protein, 18 g carbohydrates, 2 g fiber, 102 mg calcium, 268 mg sodium

2 cups chopped fresh basil

1 cup dried bread crumbs

3 tablespoons ($^3/_4$ ounce) grated Parmesan cheese

2 tablespoons chopped almonds

2 garlic cloves

$^1/_4$ cup fat-free mayonnaise

$^1/_4$ cup fat-free sour cream

Zesty Dill Spread on Whole Grain Crackers

6 SERVINGS

12 MINUTES

1. COMBINE the cottage cheese, horseradish, dill, and pepper in a bowl. Stir to mix.

2. SPREAD evenly on the crackers. Top each cracker with a piece of the tomato. Serve right away.

PER SERVING 52 calories, 1 g fat, 0 g saturated fat, 3 g protein, 7 g carbohydrates, 1 g fiber, 19 mg calcium, 123 mg sodium

$^1/_2$ cup 1% cottage cheese

1 teaspoon horseradish

$1^1/_2$ teaspoons minced fresh dill or $^3/_4$ teaspoon dried

Pinch of ground black pepper

24 seven-grain snack crackers

6 grape tomatoes, quartered

Crudités with Spicy Peanut Dipping Sauce

⅓ cup unsweetened peanut butter

2 small hot chile peppers (¾–1 ounce), seeded and chopped (wear plastic gloves when handling)

2 small garlic cloves, minced

3 tablespoons mango nectar or apple cider

¼ cup freshly squeezed lime juice

2 tablespoons low-sodium soy sauce

2 cups assorted raw vegetables

8 SERVINGS

8 MINUTES

COMBINE the peanut butter, peppers, garlic, nectar or cider, lime juice, and soy sauce in a blender. Process until a thick and smooth sauce forms, adding a little more nectar or cider as needed. Serve as a dip with the vegetables.

PER SERVING 80 calories, 5 g fat, 1 g saturated fat, 3 g protein, 6 g carbohydrates, 1 g fiber, 14 mg calcium, 190 mg sodium

Grilled Cumin Pita with White Bean Dip

8 SERVINGS	
13 MINUTES	

1. PREHEAT the grill or a grill pan.

2. COAT the pitas lightly with cooking spray and sprinkle with the cumin, paprika, and pepper. Grill, turning occasionally, for 3 to 4 minutes, or until lightly toasted and marked. Cut each pita into 6 wedges.

3. COMBINE the beans, lemon juice, oil, garlic, sage, and zest in the bowl of a food processor and puree. Transfer to a serving bowl and serve with the pita wedges.

4 whole grain pitas

½ teaspoon ground cumin

½ teaspoon ground paprika

⅛ teaspoon ground red pepper

1 can (15 ounces) no-salt-added cannellini beans, rinsed and drained

2 tablespoons freshly squeezed lemon juice

2 tablespoons extra-virgin olive oil

1 garlic clove, minced

1 teaspoon minced fresh sage

1 teaspoon freshly grated lemon zest

PER SERVING 160 calories, 5 g fat, 1 g saturated fat, 5 g protein, 25 g carbohydrates, 4 g fiber, 23 mg calcium, 190 mg sodium

Cheesy Cornmeal Cakes with Salsa

Salsa

- 1 small onion, minced
- 1 tomato, chopped (about 1 cup)
- 2 garlic cloves, minced
- 1 tablespoon minced fresh basil
- 1 teaspoon red-pepper flakes

Cornmeal Cakes

- 1 cup + 2 tablespoons stone-ground cornmeal
- 2 tablespoons ground flaxseed
- 1 cup cold water
- 2 tablespoons (½ ounce) grated Parmesan cheese
- ½ cup (2 ounces) shredded low-fat mozzarella cheese
- ½ cup (2 ounces) shredded low-fat extra-sharp Cheddar cheese

6 SERVINGS (2 CAKES EACH)

1 HOUR 18 MINUTES

1. **TO MAKE THE SALSA:** Combine the onion, tomato, garlic, basil, and red-pepper flakes in a small bowl. Mix well. Let stand for 30 minutes, stirring occasionally.

2. **TO MAKE THE CORNMEAL CAKES:** Combine the cornmeal, flaxseed, and water in a medium saucepan. Bring to a boil over medium-high heat. Cook, stirring frequently, for 12 to 15 minutes, or until the mixture is thick. Remove from the heat. Stir in the Parmesan.

3. **LINE** a baking pan with waxed paper. Spoon the cornmeal mixture onto the pan and spread to ½" thickness. Cover with plastic wrap and refrigerate for 20 minutes, or until firm.

4. **PREHEAT** the broiler. Cut the cornmeal mixture into 12 pieces and place on a large baking sheet. Coat the cakes with cooking spray. Broil 4" from the heat for 2 minutes, or until golden brown. Turn the cakes and coat the other side with spray. Top with the mozzarella and Cheddar. Broil for 2 minutes, or until the cheese melts. Top with the salsa.

PER SERVING 150 calories, 4 g fat, 2 g saturated fat, 9 g protein, 22 g carbohydrates, 3 g fiber, 202 mg calcium, 160 mg sodium

Greek-Style Appetizer Cheesecake

16 SERVINGS

1 HOUR

15 MINUTES

1. PREHEAT the oven to 325°F. Lightly coat a 9" springform pan with cooking spray.

2. PLACE the sun-dried tomatoes in a small bowl. Cover with boiling water. Soak for 10 minutes, or until very soft. Drain and coarsely chop.

3. COAT a medium nonstick skillet with cooking spray. Add the scallions and garlic. Cook over medium heat, stirring occasionally, for 2 to 3 minutes, or until tender. Add the artichokes and oregano. Cook for 2 minutes to evaporate any liquid.

4. COMBINE the ricotta, sour cream, egg, egg whites, and flour in a blender or food processor. Puree until smooth. Transfer to a medium mixing bowl. Add the artichoke mixture, Parmesan, feta, sun-dried tomatoes, and salt. Stir to mix. Pour into the prepared pan.

5. BAKE for 50 to 60 minutes, or until a toothpick inserted in the center comes out clean. Remove to a rack to cool completely. Cover and refrigerate for at least 3 hours. To serve, bring to room temperature. Remove the ring from the pan and cut the cheesecake into wedges.

- 1 ounce dry-packed sun-dried tomatoes
- 1 bunch scallions, sliced
- 2 garlic cloves, chopped
- 1 can (14 ounces) water-packed artichoke hearts, rinsed, drained, and coarsely chopped
- 1 teaspoon dried oregano
- 2 cups (16 ounces) fat-free ricotta cheese
- 3/4 cup (6 ounces) fat-free sour cream
- 1 egg
- 2 egg whites
- 2 tablespoons unbleached or all-purpose flour
- 1/3 cup (1 1/2 ounces) grated Parmesan cheese
- 1/2 cup (2 ounces) crumbled feta cheese
- 1/4 teaspoon salt

PER SERVING 81 calories, 2 g fat, 1 g saturated fat, 6 g protein, 9 g carbohydrates, 1 g fiber, 116 mg calcium, 351 mg sodium

Buffalo-Style Chicken Bites

8 ounces boneless, skinless chicken tenders, cut into 2" pieces

3½ tablespoons hot sauce

¼ cup reduced-fat sour cream

¼ cup (1 ounce) reduced-fat blue cheese crumbles

2 tablespoons low-fat buttermilk

½ tablespoon olive oil

1 tablespoon trans-free spreadable/tub margarine

½ tablespoon Asian chili garlic sauce

Dash of garlic powder

½ teaspoon cornstarch

1½ teaspoons cold water

1 cup baby carrots

4 SERVINGS

45 MINUTES

1. **COMBINE** the chicken and 1½ tablespoons of the hot sauce in a medium bowl. Toss to coat the chicken. Cover and marinate in the refrigerator for 45 to 60 minutes.

2. **COMBINE** the sour cream, blue cheese, and buttermilk in a small bowl. Mix well and set aside.

3. **HEAT** the oil in a skillet set over medium heat. Drain the chicken and add to the hot pan. Cook for 2 to 3 minutes on each side, or until golden brown on the outside and the juices run clear. Meanwhile, in a small saucepan, combine the margarine, chili garlic sauce, garlic powder, and remaining 2 tablespoons hot sauce over medium heat until melted together. Combine the cornstarch and water in a small bowl, whisking until smooth. Pour, whisking, into the sauce mixture. Cook for 2 to 3 minutes, or until the sauce thickens slightly.

4. **DRAIN** any excess oil from the cooked chicken. Pour the sauce on the chicken and toss. Serve with the blue cheese dip and carrots.

PER SERVING 159 calories, 9 g fat, 3 g saturated fat, 14 g protein, 5 g carbohydrates, 1 g fiber, 69 mg calcium, 525 mg sodium

Curried Snack Mix
with Golden Raisins

16
SERVINGS

1
HOUR

15
MINUTES

1. **PREHEAT** the oven to 400°F. Coat a baking sheet with cooking spray.

2. **SPREAD** the pita strips on a baking sheet and bake for 7 to 8 minutes, or until crisp. Remove from the oven, transfer to a bowl, and let cool 5 minutes. Stir in the cereal, pretzels, and almonds. Reduce the oven temperature to 200°F.

3. **COMBINE** the margarine, curry powder, sugar, Worcestershire sauce, garlic powder, paprika, coriander, and red pepper in a small saucepan over medium heat. Cook, stirring often, for 3 to 4 minutes, or until the margarine melts and the spices toast slightly. Stir into the cereal mixture and toss well to coat. Pour onto a baking sheet and bake for 40 to 45 minutes, or until crisp. Remove from the oven, stir in the raisins, and cool completely before serving.

1   multigrain pita, halved crosswise and thinly sliced

2   cups bite-size whole grain cereal squares, such as Wheat Chex

1   cup mini pretzels (about 2 ounces)

¼   cup whole roasted almonds

1   tablespoon trans-free spreadable/tub margarine

½   tablespoon curry powder

½   tablespoon sugar

¾   teaspoon Worcestershire sauce

½   teaspoon garlic powder

¼   teaspoon paprika

¼   teaspoon ground coriander

⅛   teaspoon ground red pepper

½   cup golden raisins

PER SERVING   90 calories, 2 g fat, 0 g saturated fat, 2 g protein, 16 g carbohydrates, 2 g fiber, 26 mg calcium, 150 mg sodium

Mustard-Glazed Snack Mix

4 cups bite-size whole grain cereal squares, such as Wheat Chex

1 cup broken whole wheat pretzel sticks (approximately 1" lengths)

½ cup unsalted almonds or peanuts

2 tablespoons yellow mustard

3 tablespoons honey

2 tablespoons trans-free stick margarine, cut into 4 pieces

2 teaspoons Worcestershire sauce

⅛ teaspoon ground red pepper

12 SERVINGS

46 MINUTES

1. PREHEAT the oven to 325°F. Line a jelly-roll pan with foil and coat with cooking spray. Toss together the cereal, pretzels, and nuts in a large bowl and set aside.

2. PLACE the mustard, honey, margarine, Worcestershire sauce, and red pepper in a medium microwaveable bowl. Cover with waxed paper and microwave on high for 45 to 60 seconds, or just until the margarine is melted. Stir together until smooth. Drizzle about one-third of the mustard mixture over the cereal mixture and toss, using a large spoon, until evenly coated. Repeat with the remaining mustard mixture. Spread the coated cereal mixture in a single layer on the prepared jelly-roll pan.

3. BAKE for 30 to 35 minutes, stirring halfway through, until evenly toasted. Set the pan on a rack to cool to room temperature, and store in an airtight container for up to 2 weeks.

PER SERVING 160 calories, 6 g fat, 1 g saturated fat, 5 g protein, 26 g carbohydrates, 5 g fiber, 92 mg calcium, 135 mg sodium

Honey-Nut Walking Stix

12
SERVINGS
(1 STICK PER SERVING)

45
MINUTES

1. COAT a 13" × 9" pan with cooking spray. Set aside.

2. COMBINE the popcorn, cereal, and raisins in a large bowl.

3. COMBINE the sugar and milk powder in a medium saucepan, off the heat. Whisk to blend. Add the honey and peanut butter. Cook over medium heat, stirring constantly, for 5 to 7 minutes, or until melted. Remove from the heat and pour over the popcorn mixture. Stir until well coated and, working quickly while the mixture is warm, spread evenly into the prepared pan. Allow to cool until set. Cut into 12 sticks.

4 cups plain popped popcorn

3 cups crispy brown rice cereal

½ cup golden raisins

¼ cup sugar

3 tablespoons fat-free milk powder

½ cup honey

½ cup creamy peanut butter

PER SERVING 181 calories, 6 g fat, 1 g saturated fat, 4 g protein, 30 g carbohydrates, 2 g fiber, 23 mg calcium, 88 mg sodium

Banana Chocolate Chip Macadamia Muffins

1 cup all-purpose flour

1 cup whole wheat pastry flour or whole wheat flour

1 teaspoon baking soda

½ teaspoon salt

½ teaspoon ground cinnamon

½ cup packed light brown sugar

¼ cup canola oil

2 large eggs

1 teaspoon vanilla extract

¾ cup fat-free plain or vanilla yogurt

2 very ripe bananas, mashed

¼ cup semisweet mini chocolate chips

¼ cup chopped unsalted macadamia nuts

12
SERVINGS
(1 MUFFIN
PER
SERVING)

1
HOUR

1. PREHEAT the oven to 400°F. Place 12 paper liners in a muffin pan.

2. COMBINE the flours, baking soda, salt, and cinnamon in a medium bowl. Stir to blend. Set aside.

3. COMBINE the sugar and oil in the bowl of an electric mixer. Beat until mixed. Add the eggs, one at a time, beating after each addition. Add the vanilla extract. Add one-third of the reserved flour mixture, then one-third of the yogurt, beating on low speed after each addition. Repeat 2 times until all of the dry ingredients and yogurt are incorporated. Add the bananas, chocolate chips, and nuts. Stir with a spatula to incorporate. Dollop the batter evenly into the muffin cups with an ice cream scoop or spoon.

4. BAKE for 18 to 22 minutes, or until a cake tester or toothpick inserted in the center of 1 muffin comes out clean.

NOTE: The batter can be prepared, put in the pan, refrigerated overnight, and baked in the morning.

PER SERVING 225 calories, 9 g fat, 2 g saturated fat, 4 g protein, 33 g carbohydrates, 2 g fiber, 38 mg calcium, 225 mg sodium

Fruit 'n' Nut Muffins

12 SERVINGS (1 MUFFIN PER SERVING)

40 MINUTES

1. **PREHEAT** the oven to 350°F.

2. **LINE** 12 muffin cups with paper liners and set aside.

3. **COMBINE** the flour, oats, sugar, bran, baking powder, cinnamon, allspice, and salt in a medium bowl and mix well. Add the grapes, carrot, milk, applesauce, oil, egg, and ¼ cup of the walnuts. Stir just until combined. Spoon the batter into the prepared muffin cups (they will be very full) and sprinkle with the remaining ¼ cup walnuts. Bake for 20 to 25 minutes, or until a toothpick inserted in the center comes out clean.

1¼ cups unbleached or all-purpose flour
¾ cup quick-cooking oats
½ cup packed light brown sugar
¼ cup wheat bran
1 tablespoon baking powder
½ teaspoon ground cinnamon
½ teaspoon ground allspice
¼ teaspoon salt
1 cup halved seedless grapes
½ cup grated carrot
½ cup fat-free milk
½ cup applesauce
3 tablespoons canola oil
1 egg, beaten
½ cup chopped walnuts

PER SERVING 207 calories, 8 g fat, 1 g saturated fat, 5 g protein, 31 g carbohydrates, 2 g fiber, 60 mg calcium, 100 mg sodium

BREAKFASTS

California-Style Eggs Benedict

2
SERVINGS

15
MINUTES

1. MASH the avocado with a fork in a small bowl. Add the sour cream, 1 tablespoon of the milk, and the lime juice. Mash until smooth, adding up to 2 tablespoons milk until the mixture is creamy. Set aside.

2. FILL a medium saucepan with about 2" of water. Place over high heat and bring to a boil. Meanwhile, toast the muffin.

3. CRACK the eggs into a small bowl one at a time. Slowly pour into the boiling water. Spoon some hot water over each yolk. Reduce the heat to medium and simmer for 2 to 3 minutes, or until the egg yolks are cooked to the desired consistency. With a slotted spoon, remove the eggs from the water and place on a towel-lined plate to absorb excess water.

4. PLACE a muffin half on each of 2 plates. Top each half with half of the spinach and 1 egg. Pour the reserved avocado cream on top.

¼ ripe avocado

¼ cup reduced-fat sour cream

1 to 3 tablespoons fat-free milk

¼ teaspoon freshly squeezed lime juice

1 whole wheat English muffin, split

2 large eggs

1 cup loosely packed baby spinach

PER SERVING 217 cal, 12 g fat, 4 g saturated fat, 11 g protein, 19 g carbohydrates, 4 g fiber, 175 mg calcium, 265 mg sodium

Cheese and Pepper Frittata

1 teaspoon olive oil

½ large red bell pepper, chopped

½ large green bell pepper, chopped

¾ cup (3 ounces) shredded reduced–fat Monterey Jack cheese

2 tablespoons chopped fresh basil

5 eggs, lightly beaten

2 egg whites, lightly beaten

1 tablespoon ground flaxseed

Ground black pepper

4 SERVINGS

45 MINUTES

1. PREHEAT the oven to 375°F. Coat a 9" oven-proof skillet with cooking spray and place over medium-high heat. Add the oil and heat for 30 seconds. Add the bell peppers and cook, stirring occasionally, for 5 minutes, or until just soft. Sprinkle the cheese and basil into the pan. Add the eggs, egg whites, flaxseed, and ground black pepper to taste.

2. BAKE for 30 minutes, or until the eggs are set. Let stand to cool slightly. Cut into wedges.

PER SERVING 190 calories, 12 g fat, 5 g saturated fat, 16 g protein, 6 g carbohydrates, 2 g fiber, 191 mg calcium, 290 mg sodium

Sunrise Casserole

6 SERVINGS

55 MINUTES

1. PREHEAT the oven to 350°F. Coat an 8" × 8" baking dish with cooking spray.

2. HEAT a large nonstick skillet coated with cooking spray over medium-high heat. Add the onion and bell pepper and cook for 3 to 4 minutes, or until almost soft. Add the sausage and sage. Cook, stirring often, for 5 minutes, or until the sausage is no longer pink.

3. COMBINE the milk, egg substitute, cheese, and flaxseed in a large bowl. Add the bread cubes and sausage mixture. Stir to mix, making sure that the bread cubes are moistened. Pour into the prepared baking dish. Press with the back of a spoon to pack the mixture.

4. BAKE for 35 to 40 minutes, or until browned and slightly puffed.

1 large onion, chopped

1 green or red bell pepper, chopped

6 ounces low-fat turkey sausage, cut into bite-size pieces

¼ teaspoon ground sage

2½ cups fat-free milk

¾ cup liquid egg substitute

½ cup (2 ounces) cubed low-fat Cheddar cheese

2 tablespoons ground flaxseed

4 slices whole wheat bread, crusts removed, cubed

PER SERVING 210 calories, 6 g fat, 2 g saturated fat, 18 g protein, 20 g carbohydrates, 3 g fiber, 308 mg calcium, 430 mg sodium

Spinach, Mushroom, and Mozzarella Omelet

2 eggs

2 egg whites

3 tablespoons water

1 teaspoon Italian seasoning

8 ounces mushrooms, sliced

1 onion, chopped

1 red bell pepper, chopped

1 garlic clove, minced

4 ounces (2 packed cups) fresh spinach leaves, chopped

¾ cup (3 ounces) shredded part-skim mozzarella cheese

4 SERVINGS

22 MINUTES

1. **PREHEAT** the oven to 200°F. Coat a baking sheet with cooking spray.

2. **WHISK** together the eggs, egg whites, water, and Italian seasoning in a medium bowl.

3. **HEAT** a large nonstick skillet coated with cooking spray over medium-high heat. Add the mushrooms, onion, pepper, and garlic and cook, stirring often, for 4 minutes, or until the pepper starts to soften. Add the spinach and cook for 1 minute, or until the spinach is wilted. Place in a small bowl and cover.

4. **WIPE** the skillet with a paper towel. Coat with cooking spray and place over medium heat. Pour in half of the egg mixture. Cook for 2 minutes, or until the bottom begins to set. Lift the edges with a spatula to allow the uncooked mixture to flow to the bottom of pan. Cook for 2 minutes longer, or until set. Sprinkle with half of the reserved vegetable mixture and half of the cheese. Cover and cook for 2 minutes, or until the cheese melts. Using a spatula, fold the omelet in half. Place on the prepared baking sheet and place in the oven to keep warm.

5. **COAT** a skillet with cooking spray. Repeat with the remaining egg mixture, vegetable mixture, and cheese to cook another omelet. To serve, halve each omelet.

PER SERVING 140 calories, 6 g fat, 3 g saturated fat, 13 g protein, 10 g carbohydrates, 3 g fiber, 213 mg calcium, 240 mg sodium

Ham and Vegetable Omelet Wrap

2
SERVINGS

18
MINUTES

1. **COMBINE** the egg whites and egg in a small bowl.

2. **HEAT** the oil in a medium nonstick skillet over medium-high heat. Add the onion and ham. Cook, stirring occasionally, for 2 to 3 minutes, or until the onion starts to soften. Stir in the peas, tomato, and pepper. Cook for 1 to 2 minutes, or until the tomato begins to wilt. Add the egg mixture and cook for 2 minutes, or until the bottom is set. Flip and cook for 2 minutes, or until the eggs are cooked through. Warm the wrap according to package directions, then place on a cutting board. Slide the egg onto the wrap, roll up jelly roll–style, then halve on an angle. Top each half with 2 teaspoons of the salsa.

3 egg whites, lightly beaten

1 egg, lightly beaten

1 teaspoon olive oil

1 small onion, chopped

1½ ounces deli-sliced ham, such as Healthy Choice, chopped

¼ cup frozen peas

1 small plum tomato, chopped (about ½ cup)

⅛ teaspoon ground black pepper

1 multigrain wrap

4 teaspoons jarred black bean and corn salsa

PER SERVING 170 calories, 6 g fat, 3 g saturated fat, 16 g protein, 19 g carbohydrates, 3 g fiber, 36 mg calcium, 450 mg sodium

Breakfast Strata

2 teaspoons olive oil

2 onions, chopped

4 cups broccoli florets

½ teaspoon dried basil

½ teaspoon dried oregano

⅓ cup water

12 slices multigrain bread, halved diagonally

½ cup (2 ounces) shredded reduced-fat Swiss cheese

½ cup (2 ounces) grated Parmesan cheese

5 eggs, lightly beaten

3 egg whites, lightly beaten

2 cups fat-free milk

1 tablespoon Dijon mustard

¼ teaspoon ground black pepper

8 SERVINGS

3 HOURS

30 MINUTES

1. HEAT the oil in a medium nonstick skillet over medium-high heat. Add the onion and cook, stirring occasionally, for 6 to 7 minutes, or until the onion browns. Add the broccoli, basil, and oregano. Cook, stirring occasionally, for 2 to 3 minutes, or until bright green. Pour in the water and cook 1 to 2 minutes longer, or until evaporated. Remove from the heat.

2. COAT an 11" × 7" baking dish with cooking spray and arrange half of the bread slices in the bottom, with all of the triangles facing same direction. Spread the broccoli mixture over the bread in a single layer, then top with the Swiss and Parmesan. Arrange the remaining bread in the dish with the triangles facing in the opposite direction. In a bowl, combine the eggs, egg whites, milk, mustard, and pepper. Pour over the bread. Press on the bread with a spatula to help absorb the milk mixture. Cover and refrigerate for 2 hours, or overnight.

3. PREHEAT the oven to 350°F. Bake the strata, uncovered, for 55 to 60 minutes, or until puffed, golden, and a knife inserted into the center comes out clean. Let stand for 10 minutes before serving.

PER SERVING 270 calories, 9 g fat, 3 g saturated fat, 19 g protein, 30 g carbohydrates, 8 g fiber, 468 mg calcium, 440 mg sodium

Huevos Rancheros Wrap

1
SERVING

10
MINUTES

1. PLACE a small nonstick skillet over medium heat. In a small bowl, combine the egg and egg whites and beat well. Pour the eggs into the pan and cook, stirring frequently, for 5 to 7 minutes, or until set.

2. LAY the tortilla on a plate. Spoon the eggs down the center of the tortilla. Sprinkle the cheese on the eggs. Top with the salsa and sour cream. Roll up and fold the ends under like a burrito.

1 large egg

2 large egg whites

1 whole wheat flour tortilla (8" diameter)

1 tablespoon (¼ ounce) shredded reduced-fat Cheddar cheese

2 tablespoons salsa

1 tablespoon reduced- fat sour cream

PER SERVING 257 calories, 9 g fat, 4 g saturated fat, 20 g pro, 33 g carbohydrates, 3 g fiber, 161 mg calcium, 716 mg sodium

Garlic and Tomato Frittata

1 red onion, chopped

2 large garlic cloves, minced

2 teaspoons olive oil

¼ cup fat-free, reduced-sodium chicken broth

2 tomatoes, chopped

1 small raw potato, shredded

½ small carrot, shredded

1 cup broccoli florets

½ teaspoon dried thyme

½ teaspoon salt

¼ teaspoon ground black pepper

4 eggs

4 egg whites

¼ cup (1 ounce) shredded low-fat sharp Cheddar cheese

4 sprigs fresh thyme (optional)

4 SERVINGS

30 MINUTES

1. PREHEAT the broiler. In a 10" nonstick, oven-proof skillet, combine the onion, garlic, oil, and broth. Cook over medium-high heat, stirring, for 5 minutes, or until the onion is soft but not browned. Add the tomatoes, potato, carrot, broccoli, and thyme. Cook, stirring, for 3 minutes. Add the salt and pepper.

2. COMBINE the eggs, egg whites, and cheese in a blender or food processor. Puree. Stir the egg mixture into the vegetable mixture. Reduce the heat to low and cook for 5 to 8 minutes, or until the underside is golden brown. Transfer to the broiler.

3. BROIL the frittata for 1 to 2 minutes, or until the top is puffed and golden brown. Cut into wedges and garnish with the fresh thyme (if using).

PER SERVING 200 calories, 8 g fat, 3 g saturated fat, 15 g protein, 18 g carbohydrates, 5 g fiber, 131 mg calcium, 290 mg sodium

Salmon Artichoke Hash

4 SERVINGS

45 MINUTES

1. **PREHEAT** the oven to 400°F. Line a baking sheet with foil. Spread the potatoes on the sheet and coat with cooking spray. Bake for 25 minutes, or until lightly browned. Set aside.

2. **HEAT** 1½ teaspoons of the oil in a large nonstick skillet over medium heat. Add the leek and cook for 3 to 4 minutes, or until softened. Transfer to a large bowl.

3. **CUT** the salmon into 1" pieces and add to the bowl. Stir in the artichoke hearts, reserved potatoes, and pepper.

4. **WARM** the remaining 1½ teaspoons oil over medium-high heat in the same skillet used for the leeks. Add the salmon mixture and shape into a shallow mound with back of a spatula. Cover and cook for 3 to 4 minutes, or until lightly browned and crisp on bottom. Using the spatula, cut the hash into 4 sections. Flip the sections and cook for 3 to 4 minutes on the other side.

5. **SERVE** sprinkled with the tomato and dill (if using).

1 pound new potatoes, cut into ½" cubes

1 tablespoon olive oil

1 large leek, chopped (white and light-green parts only)

6 ounces smoked salmon, skin removed

1 package (10 ounces) frozen quartered artichoke hearts, thawed and patted dry

½ teaspoon ground black pepper

1 tomato, seeded and finely chopped

4 sprigs fresh dill (optional)

PER SERVING 314 calories, 9 g fat, 2 g saturated fat, 29 g protein, 31 g carbohydrates, 7 g fiber, 85 mg calcium, 485 mg sodium

Ricotta and Fig Breakfast Sandwich

8 slices German-style dark wheat bread

½ cup reduced-fat ricotta cheese

½ cup sliced stemmed dried figs

½ cup thinly sliced hulled strawberries

1 tablespoon honey

4 SERVINGS

5 MINUTES

1. SPREAD each slice of the bread with 1 tablespoon of the ricotta.

2. ARRANGE the figs and strawberries on 4 slices and drizzle with honey.

3. TOP each slice with one of the remaining slices of bread and halve diagonally.

PER SERVING 279 calories, 4 g fat, 1 g saturated fat, 11 g protein, 49 g carbohydrates, 8 g fiber, 124 mg calcium, 310 mg sodium

Breakfast Bread Pudding

2 cups fat-free evaporated milk

1 cup fat-free egg substitute

⅔ cup sugar

1 teaspoon vanilla extract

½ teaspoon ground cinnamon

½ cup chopped mixed dried fruit

⅓ cup dried currants

4 cups cubed multigrain bread, lightly toasted

8 SERVINGS

1 HOUR

15 MINUTES

1. PREHEAT the oven to 350°F. Coat a 1½-quart baking dish with cooking spray.

2. WHISK together the milk, egg substitute, sugar, vanilla extract, cinnamon, dried fruit, and currants in a large bowl. Add the bread cubes and stir to coat. Transfer to a baking dish, making sure that the dried fruit is evenly distributed.

3. BAKE for 1 hour, or until puffed and a knife inserted in the center of the pudding comes out clean. Serve warm.

PER SERVING 205 calories, 2 g fat, 0 g saturated fat, 11 g protein, 38 g carbohydrates, 2 g fiber, 229 mg calcium, 220 mg sodium

Banana Pancakes
with Maple-Walnut Syrup

1. **PLACE** a large nonstick skillet over medium heat or preheat an electric griddle to 350°F.

2. **COMBINE** the baking mix, milk, banana, egg, and cinnamon in a mixing bowl. Stir just until mixed. Combine the syrup and nuts in a small saucepan. Cook over low heat for 5 minutes, or until warm.

3. **POUR** the batter onto the pan or griddle using a ¼-cup measure. Cook for 3 minutes, or until large bubbles appear on the pancake tops. Flip and cook for 2 minutes, or until golden brown on the bottoms. Serve the pancakes with Maple Walnut Syrup.

NOTE: To toast walnuts, heat a small dry skillet over medium-high heat. Add the nuts and stir frequently for 3 to 5 minutes, or until toasted. Take care not to cook too long because they burn easily.

- 1 cup reduced-fat baking mix, such as Bisquick Heart Smart
- ½ cup fat-free milk
- 1 ripe banana, mashed
- 1 large egg, beaten
- ½ teaspoon ground cinnamon
- ½ cup reduced-calorie maple syrup
- 3 tablespoons chopped toasted walnuts

PER SERVING 330 calories, 9 g fat, 1 g saturated fat, 8 g protein, 57 g carbohydrates, 3 g fiber, 275 mg calcium, 504 mg sodium

Orange French-Toasted English Muffins

2 large eggs

¼ cup + 2 tablespoons fat-free milk

¼ teaspoon vanilla extract

¼ teaspoon ground cinnamon

Freshly grated zest of 1 orange

3 whole wheat English muffins, split and toasted

2 SERVINGS

20 MINUTES

1. PLACE a nonstick skillet over medium heat or preheat an electric griddle to 350°F.

2. BEAT the eggs with a fork or whisk in a shallow bowl. Add the milk, vanilla, cinnamon, and orange zest. Whisk lightly to combine. Submerge the muffins into the egg mixture and let them soak for a few minutes. Transfer the muffins to the heated pan or griddle.

3. COOK for 2 to 3 minutes, or until golden brown on the bottom. Flip and cook for 2 to 3 minutes more, or until golden brown on the bottom.

PER SERVING 291 calories, 7 g fat, 2 g saturated fat, 17 g protein, 43 g carbohydrates, 7 g fiber, 351 mg calcium, 557 mg sodium

Whole Grain French Toast with Nutmeg-Scented Fruit

4
SERVINGS

40
MINUTES

1. TO MAKE FRUIT: Combine the all-fruit spread, water, lemon juice, and nutmeg in a large skillet over medium heat. Bring to a boil.

2. ADD the pears and apricots. Reduce the heat to low, cover, and simmer, stirring occasionally, for 10 minutes, or until the pears are tender. Cover to keep warm.

3. TO MAKE THE FRENCH TOAST: Preheat the oven to 425°F. Coat a large baking sheet with cooking spray.

4. BEAT the eggs, egg whites, vanilla extract, and nutmeg with a fork in a shallow bowl. Beat in the milk.

5. DIP the bread slices, one at a time, into the egg mixture, letting the slices soak briefly. Arrange on the prepared baking sheet, fitting them together tightly if necessary. Spoon any remaining egg mixture over the bread.

6. BAKE without turning for 20 to 25 minutes, or just until the slices are lightly golden.

7. SERVE with the fruit.

Fruit

- $1/2$ cup apricot all-fruit spread
- $1/4$ cup water
- 2 teaspoons freshly squeezed lemon juice
- $1/2$ teaspoon ground nutmeg
- 3 pears (about $1^1/4$ pounds), unpeeled, cored, and cut into 1" slices
- $1/3$ cup dried apricot halves, halved

French Toast

- 2 eggs
- 2 egg whites
- 1 teaspoon vanilla extract
- $1/4$ teaspoon ground nutmeg
- $1/4$ cup fat-free milk
- 8 slices whole wheat or multigrain bread, halved diagonally

PER SERVING 372 calories, 5 g fat, 1 g saturated fat, 14 g protein, 71 g carbohydrates, 9 g fiber, 112 mg calcium, 336 mg sodium

Cocoa-Espresso Waffles

1½ cups whole wheat pastry flour

½ cup unsweetened cocoa powder

2 teaspoons baking powder

¼ teaspoon baking soda

1 cup 1% milk

½ cup packed light brown sugar

2 teaspoons espresso powder

3 tablespoons canola oil

3 egg whites

⅛ teaspoon salt

2 tablespoons mini chocolate chips (optional)

Maple syrup

5 SERVINGS

35 MINUTES

1. PREHEAT the oven to 250°F.

2. WHISK together the flour, cocoa, baking powder, and baking soda in a large bowl until combined. Make a well in the center of the flour mixture and add the milk, sugar, espresso powder, and oil. Whisk until blended.

3. PREHEAT a waffle iron for 4 minutes, or according to the manufacturer's instructions. (A drop of water should sizzle and bounce when dropped on the iron.) Meanwhile, beat the egg whites and salt with an electric mixer at high speed just until they form soft peaks. Fold the whites into the chocolate batter in 3 additions, folding in the chocolate chips (if using) with the last addition of whites. Fold just until combined.

4. COAT the heated waffle grids with cooking spray right before using. Add enough batter to almost cover the grids (¾ cup) and cook for 3 to 4 minutes. Repeat with the remaining batter. (To keep warm, place a single layer of waffles on a foil-lined baking sheet in the oven.) Serve with maple syrup.

PER SERVING 306 calories, 11 g fat, 2 g saturated fat, 9 g protein, 50 g carbohydrates, 6 g fiber, 204 mg calcium, 346 mg sodium

Cornmeal Flapjacks with Berries

6 SERVINGS

25 MINUTES

1. **PREHEAT** the oven to 200°F. Coat a baking sheet with cooking spray.

2. **COMBINE** the cornmeal, flour, baking soda, and salt in a large bowl.

3. **COMBINE** the buttermilk, egg, oil, and maple syrup in a medium bowl. Add to the flour mixture and stir just until blended.

4. **HEAT** a large nonstick skillet coated with cooking spray over medium heat. Pour the batter by scant ¼ cupfuls into the skillet. Cook for 2 minutes, or until tiny bubbles appear on the surface and the edges begin to look dry. Flip and cook for 2 minutes, or until golden. Place the flapjacks on the prepared baking sheet and place in the oven to keep warm.

5. **RECOAT** the skillet with cooking spray. Repeat with the remaining batter to make a total of 18 flapjacks.

6. **SERVE** the flapjacks with berries.

1 cup stone-ground cornmeal

¾ cup whole wheat pastry flour

1 teaspoon baking soda

¼ teaspoon salt

1¼ cups low-fat buttermilk

1 egg

1 tablespoon canola oil

2 tablespoons maple syrup

2 cups berries, such as blueberries, raspberries, and blackberries

PER SERVING 210 calories, 5 g fat, 1 g saturated fat, 6 g protein, 37 g carbohydrates, 4 g fiber, 89 mg calcium, 380 mg sodium

Lemon-Blueberry Clafouti

2 cups fresh or frozen and thawed blueberries

4 eggs

¾ cup 1% milk

3 tablespoons honey

2 tablespoons trans-free spreadable/tub margarine, melted

1 teaspoon vanilla extract

3 teaspoons freshly grated lemon zest

Pinch of salt

½ cup whole wheat pastry flour

6 SERVINGS

40 MINUTES

1. PREHEAT the oven to 350°F. Coat a 9" pie plate with cooking spray. Scatter the blueberries in the pie plate and set aside.

2. WHISK the eggs, milk, honey, margarine, vanilla extract, lemon zest, and salt in a bowl. Stir in the flour until blended. Pour the batter over the blueberries.

3. BAKE for 30 to 35 minutes, or just until the clafouti is set in the center. Serve hot.

NOTE: If using frozen blueberries, thaw and drain on paper towels before using.

PER SERVING 180 calories, 7 g fat, 2 g saturated fat, 7 g protein, 24 g carbohydrates, 2 g fiber, 64 mg calcium, 90 mg sodium

German Apple Pancake

8 SERVINGS

35 MINUTES

1. PREHEAT the oven to 375°F.

2. TO PREPARE THE APPLES: In an ovenproof, 10" nonstick skillet, melt the margarine over medium-high heat. Add the apples, brown sugar, and apple pie spice. Cover and cook, tossing occasionally, for 4 minutes, or until softened. Remove from the heat.

3. TO PREPARE THE PANCAKE: While the apples are cooking, place the egg whites and salt in the bowl of an electric mixer. Beat on low speed for 1 minute, or until foamy.

4. INCREASE the mixer speed to high. Beat, adding 1 tablespoon of the confectioners' sugar, for 1 to 2 minutes, or until soft peaks form. Set aside.

5. COMBINE the flours, flaxseed, and baking powder in a mixing bowl. Stir with a fork to mix. Set aside. In a separate small bowl, combine the milk, egg yolks, and lemon extract and use a fork to beat. Add to the dry ingredients and stir to blend. Transfer the whites to the bowl and fold to mix. Dollop the batter over the apples in the skillet.

6. BAKE for 15 minutes, or until puffed and golden. Dust lightly with confectioners' sugar. Cut into wedges.

Apples

- 2 tablespoons trans-free spreadable/tub margarine
- 3 Golden Delicious apples, sliced (about 1 pound)
- 2 tablespoons packed light brown sugar
- 1 teaspoon apple pie spice

Pancake

- 2 eggs, separated
  Pinch of salt
- 1 tablespoon confectioners' sugar + extra for dusting
- 3/4 cup whole wheat pastry flour
- 1/4 cup soy flour
- 1 tablespoon ground flaxseed
- 1 teaspoon baking powder
- 3/4 cup whole milk
- 1 1/2 teaspoons lemon extract

PER SERVING 170 calories, 5 g fat, 2 g saturated fat, 5 g protein, 25 g carbohydrates, 4 g fiber, 82 mg calcium, 120 mg sodium

Multigrain Cereal

2 cups rolled oats

2 cups rolled wheat flakes, such as Bob's Red Mill

2 cups rolled barley flakes, such as Bob's Red Mill

2 cups rolled rye flakes, such as Bob's Red Mill

1 box (1 pound) dark or golden raisins

1½ cups ground flaxseed

¾ cup sesame seeds

Salt

36 SERVINGS

30 MINUTES

1. **COMBINE** the oats, wheat flakes, barley flakes, rye flakes, raisins, flaxseed, and sesame seeds in an airtight container. Store in the freezer until ready to use.

2. **TO COOK:** For 1 serving, bring 1 cup of water to a boil in a small saucepan. Add a pinch of salt. Add ⅓ cup cereal, cover, and cook, stirring occasionally, for 25 minutes, or until thickened and creamy.

NOTE: For 4 servings, use 3 cups water, ¼ teaspoon salt, and 1½ cups cereal. Cook for 25 to 30 minutes.

PER SERVING 144 calories, 3 g fat, 0 g saturated fat, 5 g protein, 27 g carbohydrates, 5 g fiber, 43 mg calcium, 13 mg sodium

Apple Pie Oatmeal

½ cup quick-cooking oats

1 cup fat-free milk, divided

2 teaspoons packed light brown sugar

¼ teaspoon ground cinnamon

Pinch of ground nutmeg

Dash of salt

½ apple, diced

1 SERVING

5 MINUTES

1. **COMBINE** the oats, ¾ cup of the milk, the sugar, cinnamon, nutmeg, and salt in a high-sided microwaveable bowl. Stir to mix. Cook on high power for 1 minute. Stir and cook for 1 minute longer.

2. **ADD** the apple. Cook in 30-second increments until the mixture reaches the desired consistency. Serve with the remaining ¼ cup milk.

PER SERVING 335 calories, 3 g fat, 0 g saturated fat, 15 g protein, 63 g carbohydrates, 7 g fiber, 356 mg calcium, 397 mg sodium

Date-Walnut Pudding

8 SERVINGS

1 HOUR

15 MINUTES

PREHEAT the oven to 325°F. Coat an 8" × 8" glass or ceramic baking dish with cooking spray. Place the oats, milk, dates, walnuts, vanilla extract, and apple pie spice in the dish. Stir to mix. Cover with foil. Bake for 1 hour, or until thickened and bubbling. Let stand for 10 minutes.

1½ cups quick-cooking oats
3 cups low-fat plain soy milk
½ cup (3 ounces) chopped dates
½ cup (3 ounces) chopped walnuts
2 teaspoons vanilla extract
½ teaspoon apple pie spice

PER SERVING 230 calories, 7 g fat, 1 g saturated fat, 8 g protein, 34 g carbohydrates, 5 g fiber, 104 mg calcium, 35 mg sodium

Apricot-Currant Scones

12 SERVINGS (1 SCONE PER SERVING)

30 MINUTES

1. PREHEAT the oven to 425°F. Coat a baking sheet with cooking spray.

2. COMBINE the flours, sugar, baking powder, and salt in a large bowl. Cut in the margarine and oil until the mixture resembles fine meal. Add the apricots and currants and toss to combine. Stir in the yogurt and milk.

3. TRANSFER to a lightly floured surface and pat out to an 8" circle. Cut into 12 wedges and place on the prepared baking sheet, being careful not to let the pieces touch. Bake for 12 to 15 minutes, or until lightly browned on top. Cool slightly on a wire rack and serve warm.

1 cup all-purpose flour
1 cup whole wheat pastry flour
⅓ cup sugar
1 tablespoon baking powder
¼ teaspoon salt
2 tablespoons cold trans-free stick margarine, cut into small pieces
1 tablespoon canola oil
½ cup dried apricots, slivered
½ cup dried currants
½ cup fat-free plain yogurt
3 tablespoons fat-free milk

PER SERVING 160 calories, 3 g fat, 0 g saturated fat, 3 g protein, 30 g carbohydrates, 2 g fiber, 87 mg calcium, 170 mg sodium

Orange Bran Muffins

2 cups shredded all-bran cereal

¾ cup hot water

¼ cup canola oil

1 tablespoon freshly grated orange zest

½ cup freshly squeezed orange juice

¾ cup low-fat buttermilk

2 tablespoons light molasses

2 tablespoons honey

1 egg

1¼ cups whole wheat pastry flour

⅓ cup + 2 teaspoons rolled oats

2 teaspoons baking soda

½ teaspoon salt

1 cup raisins

¼ cup chopped toasted walnuts (optional)

¼ cup sugar

12 SERVINGS (1 MUFFIN PER SERVING)

35 MINUTES

1. PREHEAT the oven to 400°F. Coat a 12-cup muffin pan with cooking spray.

2. COMBINE the cereal, water, and oil in a medium bowl. Stir until the cereal is softened.

3. COMBINE the orange zest, ¼ cup of the juice, the buttermilk, molasses, honey, and egg in another bowl. Stir until well blended. Stir the orange mixture into the cereal mixture.

4. COMBINE the flour, ⅓ cup of the oats, the baking soda, and salt in a large bowl. Add the cereal mixture and stir just until blended. Stir in the raisins and walnuts (if using).

5. DIVIDE the batter evenly among the prepared muffin cups. Sprinkle with the remaining 2 teaspoons oats. Bake for 15 minutes, or until a toothpick inserted in the center of a muffin comes out clean. Place the pan on a rack.

6. COMBINE the sugar and the remaining ¼ cup orange juice in a small saucepan. Bring to a boil over medium heat and stir until the sugar dissolves. Using a toothpick, poke holes in the muffin tops. Brush with the orange syrup.

7. COOL on a rack for 5 minutes. Remove to the rack to cool completely.

PER SERVING 210 calories, 8 g fat, 1 g saturated fat, 5 g protein, 35 g carbohydrates, 5 g fiber, 92 mg calcium, 310 mg sodium

Parfait Presto

1 SERVING
5 MINUTES

ASSEMBLE the parfait using a parfait, pilsner, or tall wine glass. Spoon a small handful of berries into the bottom of the glass. Top with about ¼ cup of the yogurt, one-third of the granola, and half of the banana and kiwifruit slices, followed by the remaining ¼ cup yogurt, one-third of the granola, and the remaining banana and kiwifruit. Sprinkle with the remaining granola.

½ cup fresh raspberries
½ cup fat-free plain yogurt
1 tablespoon granola
½ small banana, sliced
½ kiwifruit, sliced

PER SERVING 180 calories, 3 g fat, 0 g saturated fat, 8 g protein, 35 g carbohydrates, 7 g fiber, 176 mg calcium, 70 mg sodium

Banana–Ginger Smoothie

2 SERVINGS
5 MINUTES

COMBINE the banana, yogurt, honey, and ginger in a blender. Blend until smooth.

1 banana, sliced
¾ cup (6 ounces) low-fat vanilla yogurt
1 tablespoon honey
½ teaspoon freshly grated ginger

PER SERVING 157 calories, 1 g fat, 1 g saturated fat, 5 g protein, 34 g carbohydrates, 2 g fiber, 149 mg calcium, 57 mg sodium

SOUPS &
SANDWICHES

Creamy Broccoli Soup
with Parmesan Crisps

4 SERVINGS

40 MINUTES

1. FILL a large pot with 1" of water. Place a steamer rack in the pot. Cover and set over high heat until the water boils. Place the broccoli evenly on the rack. Cover the pot and cook for 5 minutes, or until the broccoli is bright green and crisp-tender. Remove the broccoli from the steamer and set aside.

2. HEAT the oven to 400°F. Place the wrap on a baking sheet and sprinkle with the cheese, spreading it out until near the edges. Bake for 8 to 10 minutes, or until the cheese is melted and the wrap is crisp. Immediately cut into 8 wedges. Set aside.

3. HEAT the broth, water, and milk in a small saucepan until almost simmering. Meanwhile, heat the oil in a large saucepan over medium heat. Add the onion and garlic and cook for 3 to 5 minutes, or until translucent. Add the flour and cook, stirring, for 1 minute. Add the hot broth mixture and simmer, constantly stirring with a whisk, for 5 minutes, or until the mixture thickens. Add the reserved broccoli and cook for 5 minutes, or until tender. Remove from the heat and cool slightly.

4. TRANSFER the mixture to a blender or food processor. Add the parsley, thyme, and pepper. Puree until smooth, in batches if necessary.

5. RETURN the soup to the saucepan and reheat just to boiling. Serve with Parmesan Crisps.

- 6 cups chopped broccoli florets and peeled stems
- 1 multigrain wrap (8" diameter)
- 1/3 cup (1 1/2 ounces) grated Parmesan cheese
- 1 cup fat-free, reduced-sodium chicken broth
- 1 cup water
- 1 cup fat-free milk
- 2 teaspoons olive oil
- 1 onion, chopped
- 2 garlic cloves, minced
- 3 tablespoons flour
- 1/2 packed cup fresh parsley, chopped
- 1 tablespoon fresh thyme, chopped
- 1/2 teaspoon ground black pepper

PER SERVING 170 calories, 5 g fat, 2 g saturated fat, 11 g protein, 26 g carbohydrates, 5 g fiber, 238 mg calcium, 360 mg sodium

Superfast Herbed White Bean Soup

2 cans (15.5 ounces each) no-salt-added cannellini beans, rinsed and drained

1 cup fat-free, reduced-sodium chicken broth

¾ cup water

¼ cup chopped fresh parsley

¾ teaspoon minced fresh rosemary

¼ teaspoon ground black pepper

1 tablespoon freshly squeezed lemon juice

4 teaspoons extra-virgin olive oil

4 SERVINGS

15 MINUTES

1. COMBINE 1 can of the beans, the broth, water, parsley, rosemary, and pepper in a blender. Puree until smooth.

2. TRANSFER to a small saucepan and add the second can of beans. Bring to a boil. Remove from the heat, stir in the lemon juice, and spoon into 4 bowls. Drizzle each with 1 teaspoon of the oil.

PER SERVING 200 calories, 6 g fat, 1 g saturated fat, 10 g protein, 26 g carbohydrates, 8 g fiber, 66 mg calcium, 100 mg sodium

Baked Potato Chowder

<table>
<tr><td>4
SERVINGS</td></tr>
<tr><td>30
MINUTES</td></tr>
</table>

1. PLACE the potatoes in a large microwaveable bowl. Cook on high power, stirring halfway through the cooking time, for 5 minutes. Add the stock or broth, milk, salt, and pepper. Cook on high power, stirring halfway through the cooking time, for 10 minutes, or until the potatoes are very tender. With a slotted spoon, remove about one-third of the potatoes to a bowl and set aside.

2. MASH the potatoes and liquid in the bowl until creamy, using a wand blender or electric mixer. (The mixture may also be mashed in the bowl of a food processor fitted with a metal blade.) Stir in the reserved potatoes and ½ cup of the cheese. Serve topped with the bacon, sour cream, chives, and the remaining 2 tablespoons cheese.

3 large baking potatoes, peeled and cubed

2 cups chicken stock or fat-free, reduced-sodium chicken broth

1 cup fat-free milk

¼ teaspoon salt

¼ teaspoon ground black pepper

½ cup + 2 tablespoons (4½ ounces) shredded reduced-fat Cheddar cheese

2 slices reduced-sodium bacon, cooked and crumbled

¼ cup reduced-fat sour cream

2 tablespoons chopped fresh chives or 1 tablespoon dried

PER SERVING 340 calories, 7 g fat, 4 g saturated fat, 16 g protein, 55 g carbohydrates, 4 g fiber, 380 mg calcium, 592 mg sodium

Tortellini Corn Chowder

2 slices turkey
  bacon, coarsely
  chopped

1 onion, chopped

1 celery rib,
  chopped

1 small red bell
  pepper, chopped

1½ cups fresh or
  frozen corn
  kernels

½ cup rinsed and
  drained no-salt-
  added canned
  navy beans

2 cups fat-free,
  reduced-sodium
  chicken broth

⅓ cup unbleached
  or all-purpose
  flour

3 cups 1% milk

⅓ cup chopped
  fresh basil or
  1 teaspoon dried

8 ounces low-fat
  fresh or frozen
  cheese tortellini,
  cooked and
  drained

8
SERVINGS

36
MINUTES

1. SET a Dutch oven over medium heat. Add the bacon. Cook for 1 minute, or until it releases some moisture. Add the onion, celery, and pepper. Cook for 5 minutes, or until the vegetables soften. Add the corn, beans, and broth. Bring to a boil over high heat. Reduce the heat to medium. Simmer for 15 minutes.

2. PLACE the flour in a medium bowl. Gradually add the milk, whisking until smooth. Pour into the Dutch oven. Stir until well blended. Add the basil. Cook, stirring occasionally, for 3 minutes, or until thickened. Add the tortellini. Cook for 2 minutes, or until heated through.

PER SERVING 210 calories, 4 g fat, 2 g saturated fat, 11 g protein, 34 g carbohydrates, 3 g fiber, 181 mg calcium, 350 mg sodium

Chicken Tortilla Soup

8 SERVINGS

40 MINUTES

1. **HEAT** the oil over medium-high heat in a large pot. Add the tortillas, onion, and garlic. Cook for 5 minutes, or until the onion and garlic are tender.

2. **ADD** the stock or broth, scraping the bottom of the pan to loosen any browned bits. Add the corn, salsa, beans, tomatoes, pepper, and cumin. Heat to a boil; reduce the heat to medium and simmer for 25 to 30 minutes, or until the flavors blend.

3. **ADD** the chicken to the pot and stir. Cook for 5 minutes, or until the chicken is heated. Remove from the heat and stir in the half-and-half. Serve each portion topped with 1 tablespoon of the sour cream.

3 tablespoons olive oil

6 corn tortillas (5" diameter), roughly chopped

$\frac{1}{2}$ onion, chopped

3 garlic cloves, minced

4 cups chicken stock or fat-free reduced-sodium chicken broth

$2\frac{1}{2}$ cups frozen corn kernels

2 cups salsa

1 can (15 ounces) reduced-sodium black beans, rinsed and drained

1 can (14 ounces) low-sodium petite diced tomatoes, drained

1 red bell pepper, diced

2 tablespoons ground cumin

2 cups leftover cooked, chopped chicken or 2 (6-ounce) boneless, skinless chicken breasts, cooked and chopped

1 cup fat-free half-and-half

$\frac{1}{2}$ cup reduced-fat sour cream

PER SERVING 263 calories, 9 g fat, 2 g saturated fat, 13 g protein, 34 g carbohydrates, 5 g fiber, 97 mg calcium, 407 mg sodium

Chicken Chili with Black Beans

12 ounces boneless, skinless chicken breasts, cubed

2 garlic cloves, minced

1 can (28 ounces) diced tomatoes

1 can (15 ounces) black beans, rinsed and drained

1 onion, coarsely chopped (about 1 cup)

2 large celery ribs, sliced (about 1 cup)

1 green bell pepper, chopped (about 1 cup)

1 jalapeño chile pepper, seeded and minced (wear plastic gloves when handling)

4 teaspoons mild chili powder

$1/2$ teaspoon dried oregano

8 ounces yellow summer squash, halved lengthwise and cut into $1/2$" slices

5 SERVINGS

30 MINUTES

1. **HEAT** a pot coated with cooking spray over medium-high heat for 1 minute. Add the chicken and garlic and cook for 3 minutes, or until the chicken is lightly browned.

2. **ADD** the tomatoes, beans, onion, celery, peppers, chili powder, and oregano. Bring to a boil. Reduce the heat to low. Cover and simmer, stirring occasionally, for 15 minutes. Add the squash. Cover and simmer, stirring occasionally, for 10 minutes, or until the squash is tender.

PER SERVING 213 calories, 2 g fat, 0 g saturated fat, 23 g protein, 28 g carbohydrates, 10 g fiber, 82 mg calcium, 287 mg sodium

Chunky Tilapia and Tomato Soup

2 SERVINGS

20 MINUTES

1. **COMBINE** the carrots, onion, oil, and thyme in a large saucepan. Cook, stirring over medium heat, for 5 minutes, or until softened.

2. **ADD** the broth and water. Bring almost to boiling. Add the tilapia, broccoli, tomatoes (with juice), and pepper. Reduce the heat and simmer, stirring occasionally, for 8 minutes, or until the tilapia is cooked.

- 6 baby carrots, thinly sliced (about ⅓ cup)
- 1 small red onion, cut in slivers (about ⅓ cup)
- 2 teaspoons olive oil
- ½ teaspoon dried thyme
- 1 cup fat-free, reduced-sodium chicken broth
- 2 cup water
- 8 ounces tilapia fillets, cut into large chunks
- 1½ cups chopped broccoli florets
- 1 cup canned no-salt-added diced tomatoes
- ½ teaspoon ground black pepper

PER SERVING 210 calories, 7 g fat, 2 g saturated fat, 26 g protein, 10 g carbohydrates, 4 fiber, 55 calcium, 360 mg sodium

Summer Clam Chowder

2 cans
(6.5 ounces
each) minced
clams

2 strips bacon,
chopped

1 large onion,
chopped

3 celery ribs,
chopped

2 cups water

1 can
(14.5 ounces)
fat-free
reduced-sodium
chicken broth

1 teaspoon dried
thyme

1 bay leaf

1 pound red
potatoes, with
skin, cut into
½" chunks

¼ cup unbleached
or all-purpose
flour

2 cups 1% milk

1½ cups frozen corn
kernels

¼ cup chopped
fresh parsley

8
SERVINGS

1
HOUR

3
MINUTES

1. DRAIN the clams and reserve the juice. Set aside.

2. COOK the bacon in a Dutch oven over medium heat, stirring often, for 3 minutes. Add the onion and celery. Cook for 5 minutes, or until the onion is soft. Add the water, broth, thyme, bay leaf, and reserved clam juice. Bring to a boil and stir well. Add the potatoes.

3. COOK for 20 to 25 minutes, or until the potatoes are tender. Meanwhile, place the flour in a small bowl. Gradually add 1½ cups of the milk, whisking until smooth. Add to the pot along with the corn, parsley, and reserved clams. Cook, stirring frequently, for 10 minutes, or until thickened. Add up to ½ cup more milk for a thinner chowder, if desired. Remove and discard the bay leaf.

PER SERVING 170 calories, 2 g fat, 1 g saturated fat, 12 g protein, 26 g carbohydrates, 3 g fiber, 120 mg calcium, 240 mg sodium

Pepper Steak Soup

4 SERVINGS

45 MINUTES

1. **THINLY** slice the beef on the diagonal into ¼"-thick slices. Cut large pieces in half. Sprinkle with the pepper and ¼ teaspoon of the salt. Set aside.

2. **STIR** together the broth, wine (if using), tomato sauce, and thyme in a large saucepan. Cover and bring to a boil over high heat. Reduce the heat to low and simmer, covered, for 10 minutes.

3. **WARM** the oil over medium-high heat in a large nonstick skillet until hot but not smoking. Add half of the reserved beef slices and cook, turning once, for 2 minutes, or until browned. Transfer to a clean bowl. Cook the remaining beef.

4. **ADD** the onion, bell peppers, garlic, and remaining ¼ teaspoon salt to skillet. Toss to mix well and add 2 tablespoons of the water. Lower the heat to medium and cook, stirring often, for 10 minutes, or until the vegetables are tender. If the pan gets dry, add the remaining 1 tablespoon water. Add the tomatoes and cook, stirring often, for 5 minutes, or until softened.

5. **ADD** the beef, any juices, and vegetables to the broth mixture. Warm through but don't boil.

12 ounces well-trimmed lean, boneless beef top round

½ teaspoon ground black pepper

½ teaspoon salt

4 cups fat-free, no-salt-added beef broth

½ cup dry red wine (optional)

½ cup no-salt-added tomato sauce

¼ teaspoon dried thyme

1 tablespoon olive oil

1 sweet white onion, halved and thinly sliced

2 green bell peppers, cut into strips

4 garlic cloves, minced

3 tablespoons water

1½ cups halved cherry tomatoes

PER SERVING 220 calories, 8 g fat, 2 g saturated fat, 23 g protein, 14 g carbohydrates, 3 g fiber, 52 mg calcium, 340 mg sodium

Hearty Country Vegetable Soup

1 tablespoon olive oil

1/2 large onion, thinly sliced

3 celery ribs, thinly sliced

1 small head green cabbage, coarsely chopped

2 carrots, sliced into 1/2" thick rounds

2 garlic cloves, minced

3/4 cup (4 ounces) dried white beans, soaked overnight and drained

5 1/2 cups low–sodium vegetable broth

1/2 teaspoon dried thyme

1/2 teaspoon dried savory or sage

6 ounces green beans, cut into 1/2" lengths

1 zucchini, (6 ounces), coarsely chopped

1/2 teaspoon ground black pepper

3 tablespoons chopped fresh basil or dill (optional)

8 SERVINGS

2 HOURS

35 MINUTES

1. HEAT the oil in a soup pot over medium-low heat. Stir in the onion, celery, cabbage, carrots, and garlic. Cover the pot and cook, stirring occasionally, for 12 to 15 minutes, or until the vegetables soften. Add the white beans and 5 cups of the broth. Bring to a boil. Reduce the heat to medium-low and stir in the thyme and savory or sage. Cover and cook for 1 to 1 1/2 hours, or until the beans are almost tender, adding more of the remaining 1/2 cup broth if the soup becomes too thick.

2. STIR in the green beans and zucchini. Partially cover and cook for 20 to 30 minutes, or until the green beans are tender. Season with the pepper and basil (if using). Divide among bowls.

PER SERVING 120 calories, 2 g fat, 0 g saturated fat, 5 g protein, 22 g carbohydrates, 4 g fiber, 86 mg calcium, 135 mg sodium

Onion and Roasted Garlic Soup

4 SERVINGS	
1 HOUR	
55 MINUTES	

1. TO MAKE THE GARLIC PASTE: Preheat the oven to 400°F. Cut a thin slice from the top of the garlic to expose the cloves. Place the head cut side up on a large piece of foil. Seal the top and sides of the foil tightly. Place in the oven and roast for 45 to 60 minutes, or until the cloves are very soft and lightly browned. Remove and set aside until cool enough to handle. Squeeze the cloves into a medium bowl. With the back of a large metal spoon, mash the garlic to a smooth paste. Set aside.

2. TO MAKE THE SOUP: Heat the oil in a large heavy saucepan or Dutch oven over medium-low heat. Add 4 cups of the onions and sprinkle with the salt. Cook, stirring often, for 20 to 25 minutes, or until the onions are very tender and lightly browned. Stir in the bay leaf, thyme, rosemary, pepper, and remaining 2 cups onions. Cook, stirring often, for 6 minutes longer, or just until the onions have softened slightly.

3. ADD the broth, water, and sherry (if using). Increase the heat, cover, and bring to a boil. Lower the heat and let simmer, covered, for 20 minutes. Stir in the reserved garlic paste, cover, and let simmer for 10 minutes longer. Remove from the heat. Discard the bay leaf.

4. PREHEAT the broiler. Place 4 broilerproof onion soup crocks on a jelly-roll pan. Ladle the soup evenly into the bowls and place a slice of the toast on top of each. Sprinkle evenly with the Swiss and Parmesan. Broil about 6" from the heat source for 2 minutes, or until the cheese is melted and bubbly. Serve at once.

NOTE: Start the roasted garlic before you begin slicing and cooking the onions. You could also roast it a day before and keep it tightly wrapped in a small bowl in the refrigerator.

PER SERVING	230 calories, 6 g fat, 2 g saturated fat, 10 g protein, 35 g carbohydrates, 6 g fiber, 173 mg calcium, 310 mg sodium

Roasted Garlic Paste (See Note)

- 1 large head garlic

Soup

- 1 tablespoon olive oil
- 6 onions, sliced (about 6 cups)
- 1/8 teaspoon salt
- 1 bay leaf
- 1/4 teaspoon dried thyme, crumbled
- 1/4 teaspoon dried rosemary, crumbled
- 1/4 teaspoon ground black pepper
- 3 cups fat-free, no-salt-added beef broth
- 1 cup water
- 1/4 cup dry sherry (optional)
- 4 small slices crusty whole grain bread, toasted (cut to fit the shape of your bowls)
- 3 tablespoons (3/4 ounce) shredded low-fat Swiss cheese
- 2 tablespoons (1/2 ounce) freshly grated Parmesan cheese

Maple Squash Soup with Apple

6 SERVINGS

31 MINUTES

Ingredients

- 2 large Granny Smith apples (1 pound), peeled and cored
- 1 tablespoon olive oil
- 1 large onion, coarsely chopped
- ¼ teaspoon ground cinnamon
- ⅛ teaspoon ground cumin
- ⅛ teaspoon salt
- ⅛ teaspoon ground black pepper
- 1 package (12 ounces) frozen winter squash, thawed
- 2½ cups fat-free, reduced-sodium chicken broth
- ¾ cup 1% milk
- ¼ cup pure maple syrup

1. **CUT** the apples into large chunks. Chop about ¼ cup of the chunks into small pieces. Set aside.

2. **HEAT** the oil in a Dutch oven over medium heat. Add the onion and apple chunks and cook, stirring often, for about 8 minutes, or until tender. Stir in the cinnamon, cumin, salt, and pepper.

3. **ADD** the squash and broth. Cover and bring to a boil over high heat. Reduce the heat to low and simmer, covered, stirring occasionally, for 15 minutes.

4. **PUREE** the soup in batches in a food processor or blender. Return to the saucepan and stir in the milk and syrup. Bring to a boil over medium heat, stirring often. Allow it to cool slightly, ladle into bowls, and garnish each with a little of the reserved chopped apple.

PER SERVING 160 calories, 3 g fat, 1 g saturated fat, 3 g protein, 34 g carbohydrates, 4 g fiber, 75 mg calcium, 453 mg sodium

Tomato Avocado Open-Faced Sandwiches

4
SERVINGS

10
MINUTES

SPREAD each slice of toast with 1 tablespoon of the hummus. Layer each with the avocado and tomato slices and sprinkle with pepper. Halve each slice on an angle.

8   slices whole grain bread, toasted

8   tablespoons prepared hummus

1   large ripe avocado, halved, peeled, pitted, and thinly sliced

2   tomatoes (about 6 ounces each), sliced

    Pinch of ground black pepper

PER SERVING — 59 calories, 10 g fat, 2 g saturated fat, 10 g protein, 34 g carbohydrates, 8 g fiber, 79 mg calcium, 328 mg sodium

Portobello Swiss Cheese Burgers with Caramelized Onions

2 teaspoons olive oil

1 onion, thinly sliced (about 1 cup)

1 teaspoon sugar

1 tablespoon balsamic vinegar

4 portobello mushroom caps (about 3½–4 ounces each)

⅛ teaspoon salt

¼ teaspoon ground black pepper

4 slices reduced-fat Swiss cheese (about 2 ounces total)

4 light multigrain English muffins, (100 calories each), such as Thomas', split

4 SERVINGS

29 MINUTES

1. **PREHEAT** the grill.

2. **HEAT** 1 teaspoon of the oil in a small nonstick skillet over medium-high heat. Add the onion and sugar and cook, stirring occasionally, for 5 to 6 minutes, or until lightly browned. Remove from the heat.

3. **COMBINE** the vinegar and remaining 1 teaspoon oil in a small bowl. Brush over the mushroom caps and sprinkle with the salt and pepper. Grill, covered, turning occasionally, for 9 to 11 minutes, or until tender. Top each with 1 slice of the cheese and grill for 1 to 2 minutes longer, or until the cheese melts. Transfer to a plate and keep warm.

4. **TOAST** the English muffins. Place the bottom half of each muffin on a plate and top with 1 portobello cap and one-fourth of the onion. Top with the remaining muffin halves.

PER SERVING 210 calories, 6 g fat, 2 g saturated fat, 11 g protein, 31 g carbohydrates, 5 g fiber, 251 mg calcium, 210 mg sodium

French Roasted Vegetable Sandwiches

8
SERVINGS
1
HOUR
27
MINUTES

1. PREHEAT the oven to 400°F. Coat a large baking sheet with cooking spray. Arrange the eggplant, pepper, tomato, and onion on the sheet. Brush with the oil. Sprinkle with the garlic and rosemary. Bake for 45 minutes, or until golden brown and tender.

2. SPLIT the bread horizontally and scoop out the interior, leaving a 1" shell. (Reserve the bread for another use.) Spread the yogurt over the bottom of the shell, then sprinkle with the vinegar. Arrange the vegetables in the bottom of the shell. Sprinkle with the cheese. Top with the spinach. Place the top of the bread over the filling. Wrap tightly in plastic wrap and refrigerate for 30 minutes, or until chilled. Cut into 8 wedges.

1 small eggplant, peeled and cut into thick slices

1 red bell pepper, quartered

1 tomato, halved

1 onion, cut into thick slices

2 tablespoons olive oil

2 teaspoons minced garlic

$\frac{1}{2}$ teaspoon crushed dried rosemary

1 round loaf Italian bread (8" diameter)

2 tablespoons fat-free plain yogurt

3 tablespoons balsamic vinegar

2 teaspoons grated Parmesan cheese

$\frac{1}{2}$ cup tightly packed spinach leaves

PER SERVING	220 calories, 6 g fat, 1 g saturated fat, 7 g protein, 36 g carbohydrates, 4 g fiber, 71 mg calcium, 346 mg sodium

Sicilian Tuna
on Whole Grain Bread

1 can (6 ounces) solid white tuna in water, drained

3 tablespoons chopped carrot

3 tablespoons chopped celery

2 tablespoons chopped red onion

2 tablespoons chopped fresh parsley

2 teaspoons capers, drained

2½ teaspoons olive oil

1½ teaspoons freshly squeezed lemon juice

⅛ teaspoon crushed fennel seeds

⅛ teaspoon salt

⅛ teaspoon ground black pepper

4 slices multigrain bread

2 SERVINGS

10 MINUTES

COMBINE the tuna, carrot, celery, onion, parsley, and capers in a medium bowl . Mix well to combine. Stir in the oil, lemon juice, fennel seeds, salt, and pepper. Place 2 slices of the bread on a work surface and top each with half of the tuna mixture. Top with the remaining bread slices.

PER SERVING 210 calories, 8 g fat, 2 g saturated fat, 15 g protein, 24 g carbohydrates, 6 g fiber, 61 mg calcium, 410 mg sodium

Veracruz Shrimp Tacos

4 SERVINGS

35 MINUTES

1. TOSS the shrimp, scallions, oil, and oregano in a bowl. Let stand for 15 minutes.

2. COMBINE the tomatoes, avocado, cilantro, flaxseed, lime juice, and salt in another bowl. Set aside.

3. PREHEAT a perforated grill rack set over the grill. Wearing a protective mitt, brush the grill rack with oil and wipe off the excess. Place the reserved shrimp and scallions on the grill rack. Cook for 2 minutes, or until the shrimp are browned on the bottom. Flip and cook for 2 minutes longer, or until opaque. Remove to a plate.

4. PLACE the tortillas directly on the grill. Cook for 1 minute on each side, or until warm and starting to puff. Place 2 tortillas on each of 4 plates. Divide the shrimp and scallions evenly on the tortillas. Top with the reserved salsa and sprinkle with the hot-pepper sauce.

8 ounces medium shrimp, peeled

12 scallions, trimmed, cut in 1" pieces

2 teaspoons canola oil

1 teaspoon dried oregano

1 cup grape tomatoes, halved

¼ ripe avocado, sliced

¼ cup chopped fresh cilantro

2 tablespoons ground flaxseed

Juice of 1 lime

Pinch of salt

8 corn tortillas (6" diameter)

Hot-pepper sauce

PER SERVING 260 calories, 8 g fat, 1 g saturated fat, 17 g protein, 33 g carbohydrates, 6 g fiber, 174 mg calcium, 170 mg sodium

California Club Sandwiches

4 slices country-style multigrain bread

1 teaspoon Dijon mustard

½ small cucumber, thinly sliced

½ avocado, sliced (about 3 ounces)

½ tomato, sliced

1 ounce soft goat cheese, crumbled (about 2 tablespoons)

¼ cup alfalfa sprouts

2 SERVINGS

10 MINUTES

PLACE 2 slices of the bread on a work surface. Spread 1 side of each with some of the mustard. Top each with half of the cucumber, avocado, tomato, cheese, and sprouts and 1 of the remaining bread slices. Cut each sandwich in half.

PER SERVING 200 calories, 9 g fat, 3 g saturated fat, 8 g protein, 26 g carbohydrates, 8 g fiber, 70 mg calcium, 350 mg sodium

Almond, Tarragon, and Chicken Salad Sandwiches

4 SERVINGS

35 MINUTES

1. **CUT** the chicken into ¼" cubes and transfer to a medium bowl.

2. **HEAT** a small skillet over medium heat. Add the almonds and cook, shaking the pan often, for 5 to 6 minutes, or until lightly browned. Add to the bowl with the chicken and stir in the bell pepper, scallions, mayonnaise, honey, tarragon, and black pepper. Mix well.

3. **TOAST** the bread and top 4 slices with ½ cup of the chicken mixture. Top with the remaining bread slices and cut each sandwich in half on an angle.

3 boneless, skinless chicken breast halves (4 ounces each), cooked and cooled

3 tablespoons sliced almonds

¼ red bell pepper, chopped (about ⅓ cup)

2 scallions, chopped (about ¼ cup)

¼ cup fat-free mayonnaise

1 tablespoon honey

1 tablespoon chopped fresh tarragon

⅛ teaspoon ground black pepper

8 slices low-calorie, high-fiber multigrain bread

PER SERVING 240 calories, 5 g fat, 1 g saturated fat, 25 g protein, 29 g carbohydrates, 7 g fiber, 65 mg calcium, 410 mg sodium

Chicken Salad Roll-Ups

1 can (8 ounces) mandarin oranges

¼ cup Asian plum sauce

1 tablespoon rice wine vinegar or wine vinegar

1 teaspoon grated fresh ginger

8 ounces cold cooked boneless, skinless chicken breast, cut into small strips

1 red bell pepper, chopped

½ small cucumber, seeded and chopped

2 scallions, thinly sliced

2½ cups packed chopped romaine

4 whole wheat tortillas (8" diameter)

4 SERVINGS

15 MINUTES

1. **DRAIN** the oranges, reserving 2 tablespoons of the juice.

2. **COMBINE** the plum sauce, vinegar, ginger, and reserved orange juice in a large bowl. Add the chicken, pepper, cucumber, scallions, romaine, and oranges. Toss to coat.

3. **PLACE** the tortillas on a work surface. Divide the salad evenly among the tops. Roll into cylinders. Slice in half diagonally.

PER SERVING 211 calories, 2 g fat, 0 g saturated fat, 18 g protein, 37 g carbohydrates, 4 g fiber, 47 mg calcium, 319 mg sodium

63 Cornmeal Flapjacks with Berries

67 Apricot-
Currant Scones

84 Portobello Swiss Cheese
Burgers with Caramelized Onions

46 **Banana Chocolate Chip
Macadamia Muffins**

155 Creamy Mac and
Three Cheeses

128 **Turkey Meatballs and Linguine**

36 **Avocado-Peach Salsa with Multigrain Chips**

75 Chicken Tortilla Soup

142 Seafood and Brown Rice Paella

173 **Peanut Butter Cup Sundae**

Mediterranean Pockets

1. COMBINE the yogurt, lemon juice, and oregano in a small bowl. Mix well and set aside.

2. PLACE the pitas in the microwave oven. Cook on high power for 15 to 20 seconds, or until soft and warm. Cut in half and open to form pockets. Spread equal amounts of the reserved yogurt mixture inside each pocket. Fill each with equal amounts of the chicken, spinach, cheese, and olives.

$\frac{1}{4}$ cup fat-free plain yogurt

$\frac{1}{2}$ teaspoon freshly squeezed lemon juice

$\frac{1}{4}$ teaspoon dried oregano

2 whole wheat pitas (6$\frac{1}{2}$" diameter)

3 ounces reduced-sodium deli chicken

1 cup baby spinach leaves

2 tablespoons ($\frac{1}{2}$ ounce) crumbled reduced-fat feta cheese

$\frac{1}{3}$ cup pitted black olives, chopped

PER SERVING 278 calories, 6 g fat, 1 g saturated fat, 20 g protein, 41 g carbohydrates, 6 g fiber, 102 mg calcium, 952 mg sodium

Chapter 6 Soups & Sandwiches

91

Tex-Mex Turkey, Mango, and Pineapple Wraps

1 multigrain wrap (10" diameter)

4 teaspoons reduced-fat mayonnaise

¼ cup (1 ounce) shredded reduced-fat Cheddar cheese

4 ounces deli-sliced salt-free turkey breast

½ cup chopped romaine

⅓ cup chopped fresh pineapple

¼ cup chopped fresh mango

1 tablespoon pickled jalapeño chile pepper slices (optional)

2 SERVINGS

14 MINUTES

1. PLACE the wrap on a work surface and spread the side facing you with the mayonnaise. Spread the cheese across the center of the wrap (so that the line is parallel to the edge of the counter closest to you), leaving a 1½" border at each end. Top with the turkey, romaine, pineapple, mango, and pepper (if using). Fold right and left sides of the wrap so that they just cover the very edges of the filling, then fold the bottom over and roll up jelly roll–style.

2. HEAT a small nonstick skillet over medium heat. Add the wrap and cook for 1 to 2 minutes per side, or until lightly browned on the outside. Transfer to a cutting board and cut in half on an angle.

PER SERVING 226 calories, 5 g fat, 2 g saturated fat, 24 g protein, 27 g carbohydrates, 3 g fiber, 228 mg calcium, 404 mg sodium

Turkey Apple Panini

1 SANDWICH

15 MINUTES

1. **PLACE** a panini press or small nonstick skillet over medium heat, or preheat an electric panini press.

2. **COMBINE** the cranberry sauce and mayonnaise in small bowl. Stir until blended. Spread 1 side of each bread slice with the cranberry mixture. On 1 slice, layer the turkey and apple. Top with the second slice of bread, cranberry side down. Brush 1 side of the sandwich with ½ teaspoon of the olive oil.

3. **PLACE** the sandwich oil side down on the panini press or skillet. Brush the top with the remaining ½ teaspoon olive oil. Close the press or, if using a skillet, top with a heavy plate wrapped in aluminum foil. Press down to flatten. Cook for about 3 minutes, or until the bottom is golden brown. Flip and cook for 3 minutes, or until the bottom is golden.

2 tablespoons jellied cranberry sauce

2 teaspoons reduced-fat mayonnaise

2 slices whole grain bread

2 ounces reduced-sodium deli turkey

¼ apple, thinly sliced

1 teaspoon olive oil, divided

PER SERVING 328 calories, 9 g fat, 1 g saturated fat, 16 g protein, 48 g carbohydrates, 12 g fiber, 203 mg calcium, 592 mg sodium

Roast Beef and Charred Vegetable Sandwiches

¼ cup low-fat buttermilk or fat-free plain yogurt

2 tablespoons reduced-fat mayonnaise

¼ cup (1 ounce) crumbled blue cheese

2 tablespoons chopped fresh chives or scallion greens

4 plum tomatoes, halved lengthwise

1 small red onion, cut into 4 slices

¾ pound thinly sliced cooked lean roast beef

4 leaves lettuce

4 whole wheat buns, toasted

4 SERVINGS

14 MINUTES

1. COMBINE the buttermilk, mayonnaise, cheese, and chives in a small bowl.

2. HEAT a large nonstick skillet coated with cooking spray over medium-high heat. Add the tomatoes and onion and cook for 3 minutes per side, or until lightly charred.

3. LAYER the roast beef, onion, tomatoes, and lettuce on the bottoms of the buns. Drizzle with the blue cheese dressing. Cover with the bun tops.

PER SERVING 190 calories, 6 g fat, 3 g saturated fat, 10 g protein, 24 g carbohydrates, 3 g fiber, 107 mg calcium, 380 mg sodium

Cuban-Style Sandwich

1 SANDWICH

15 MINUTES

1. **PLACE** a panini press or small nonstick skillet over medium heat, or preheat an electric panini press.

2. **COMBINE** the mustard and relish in a small bowl. Spread on 1 side of each slice of bread. Top with the ham, turkey, cheese, and remaining bread slice. Brush 1 side of the sandwich with ½ teaspoon of the oil.

3. **PLACE** the sandwich oil side down on the panini press or skillet. Brush the top with the remaining ½ teaspoon oil. Close the press or, if using a skillet, top the sandwich with a heavy plate wrapped in aluminum foil. Press down to flatten. Cook for 5 minutes, or until the sandwich is golden brown on the bottom. Flip the sandwich and cook for 3 to 5 minutes, or until the bottom is golden brown and the cheese melts.

1 tablespoon mustard

1 teaspoon dill pickle relish

2 slices (1 ounce each) Hawaiian or challah bread

1 ounce reduced-sodium deli-style ham

1 ounce reduced-sodium deli-style turkey breast

1 slice (¾ ounce) reduced-fat Swiss cheese

1 teaspoon canola oil, divided

PER SERVING 339 calories, 13 g fat, 3 g saturated fat, 25 g protein, 32 g carbohydrates, 2 g fiber, 271 mg calcium, 969 mg sodium

Chapter
7

SALADS
& SIDES

Fruited Spinach Salad with Ham and Toasted Walnuts

4 SERVINGS

18 MINUTES

1. TO MAKE THE DRESSING: Whisk the buttermilk, mayonnaise, vinegar, mustard, and pepper in a salad bowl.

2. TO MAKE THE SALAD: Add the spinach, apple, pear, ham, onion, pumpkin seeds, raisins, and walnuts to the bowl. Toss until well coated with dressing.

Dressing

- $1/2$ cup low-fat buttermilk
- 2 tablespoons reduced-fat mayonnaise
- 1 tablespoon cider vinegar
- $1^{1}/_{2}$ teaspoons grainy Dijon mustard
- $1/2$ teaspoon ground black pepper

Salad

- 1 package (6 ounces) prewashed baby spinach
- 1 large Granny Smith apple, quartered, cored, and thinly sliced crosswise
- 1 large ripe pear, quartered, cored, and thinly sliced crosswise
- 4 ounces sliced lean 42% lower-sodium ham, cut into 2" × $1/2$" strips
- 1 small red onion, thinly sliced ($1/4$ cup)
- 2 tablespoons pumpkin seeds
- 2 tablespoons golden raisins
- 2 tablespoons coarsely chopped walnuts, toasted

PER SERVING 190 calories, 5 g fat, 1 g saturated fat, 9 g protein, 30 g carbohydrates, 6 g fiber, 85 mg calcium, 430 mg sodium

Roasted Beet Salad

4 beets (about 1 pound), stems trimmed to 1"

2 tablespoons apricot all-fruit spread

1 tablespoon white balsamic vinegar

1½ teaspoons olive oil

1½ teaspoons flaxseed oil

2 tablespoons snipped fresh chives or thinly sliced scallion greens

½ teaspoon salt

¼ teaspoon ground black pepper

2 navel oranges, peeled

4 cups mixed bitter salad greens, such as arugula, watercress, endive, and escarole

4
SERVINGS

1
HOUR

55
MINUTES

1. PREHEAT the oven to 400°F. Coat a 9" round baking pan with cooking spray.

2. PLACE the beets in the prepared baking pan and cover tightly with foil. Roast for 1 hour, or until very tender. Uncover and let the beets stand until cool enough to handle.

3. WHISK the all-fruit spread, vinegar, oils, chives or scallions, salt, and pepper in a bowl.

4. SLIP the skins off the beets and discard the skins. Chop the beets. Section the oranges into the bowl with the dressing. Add the beets and toss to coat well. Let stand for at least 15 minutes to allow the flavors to blend.

5. ARRANGE the greens on a serving plate just before serving, Top with the beet mixture.

PER SERVING 145 calories, 4 g fat, 1 g saturated fat, 3 g protein, 27 g carbohydrates, 5 g fiber, 82 mg calcium, 395 mg sodium

Cheesy Broccoli Salad

6 SERVINGS

45 MINUTES

1. STEAM the broccoli in a microwaveable or stove-top steamer for 6 minutes, or until tender. Let cool.

2. COMBINE the yogurt, vinegar, sugar, and pepper in a large bowl. Whisk to blend. Add the cheese, onion, and broccoli. Stir to coat the ingredients with the dressing. Cover and refrigerate for at least 30 minutes, or as long as 2 days.

6 cups small broccoli florets

²⁄₃ cup fat-free plain yogurt

3 tablespoons red wine vinegar

2 tablespoons sugar

½ teaspoon ground black pepper

1 cup (4 ounces) shredded reduced-fat Cheddar cheese

½ red onion, diced (about ½ cup)

PER SERVING 100 calories, 4 g fat, 2 g saturated fat, 8 g protein, 11 g carbohydrates, 2 g fiber, 338 mg calcium, 188 mg sodium

Easy Couscous Salad

1¼ cups whole wheat couscous

⅓ cup freshly squeezed lemon juice

2 teaspoons olive oil

1 red bell pepper, chopped

1 orange bell pepper, chopped

1 can (15 ounces) chickpeas, rinsed and drained

½ cup (2 ounces) crumbled 50% less–fat feta cheese

1 tablespoon minced fresh basil, cilantro, or parsley

4 SERVINGS

13 MINUTES

1. BRING 1¾ cups of hot water to a boil in a medium saucepan. Add the couscous, cover, and turn off the heat. Let stand for 5 minutes, then fluff with a fork or salad tongs and transfer to a large bowl.

2. ADD the lemon juice to the couscous and toss. Add the oil and toss again to coat. Mix in the peppers, chickpeas, and cheese. Sprinkle with the basil, cilantro, or parsley. Serve immediately, at room temperature, or chill.

PER SERVING 260 calories, 5 g fat, 1 g saturated fat, 12 g protein, 44 g carbohydrates, 8 g fiber, 63 mg calcium, 350 mg sodium

Onion, Caper, and Orange Salad

4
SERVINGS

5
MINUTES

WHISK the vinegar, oil, and honey or sugar in a salad bowl. Add the romaine, oranges, onion, and capers. Toss well. Season with ground black pepper to taste.

¼ cup balsamic vinegar

1½ tablespoons olive oil

2 tablespoons honey or sugar

5 cups torn romaine

2 cans (8 ounces each) mandarin orange slices, drained

1 small red onion, minced (about ¼ cup)

1 tablespoon drained capers

PER SERVING 160 calories, 6 g fat, 1 g saturated fat, 2 g protein, 27 g carbohydrates, 4 g fiber, 69 mg calcium, 75 mg sodium

Potato Salad with Warm Bacon Dressing

2 pounds red potatoes, cut into large chunks

2 strips bacon, chopped

1 small red onion, chopped

1 garlic clove, chopped

3 tablespoons cider vinegar

3 tablespoons apple juice

1 tablespoon stone-ground mustard

¼ cup chopped fresh parsley

⅛ teaspoon salt

6 SERVINGS

35 MINUTES

1. SET a vegetable steamer in a medium saucepan. Fill with water to just below the steamer. Place the potatoes in the steamer. Cover and bring to a boil over high heat. Reduce the heat to medium-high. Cook for 15 to 20 minutes, or until tender. Transfer to a large bowl and allow to cool for 10 minutes.

2. COOK the bacon in a medium nonstick skillet over medium heat for 3 minutes, or until the fat starts to melt. Add the onion and garlic. Cook, stirring, for 3 minutes, or until the onion is soft and the bacon is crisp. Reduce the heat to low. Add the vinegar, apple juice, mustard, parsley, and salt. Cook for 2 minutes, or until heated through. Pour over the potatoes. Toss to evenly coat.

PER SERVING 129 calories, 1 g fat, 0 g saturated fat, 4 g protein, 27 g carbohydrates, 3 g fiber, 24 mg calcium, 141 mg sodium

Honey-Grilled Chicken Salad

2 SERVINGS

25 MINUTES

1. **PREHEAT** a grill or grill pan to medium-high heat. Brush the grill rack with oil or coat with cooking spray.

2. **BRUSH** the chicken with the honey. Place on the grill and cook for 5 to 8 minutes per side, or until a thermometer inserted sideways in the thickest part registers 170° F and the juices run clear. Remove from the grill and set aside to cool.

3. **COMBINE** the mayonnaise, yogurt, and rosemary in a bowl. Stir to blend. Cube or shred the chicken. Add to the bowl, along with the apple and walnuts. Toss to coat the ingredients with the dressing. Serve right away or cover and refrigerate for up to 24 hours before serving.

1 boneless, skinless chicken breast (8 ounces), pounded to $3/4$" thickness

$1\frac{1}{2}$ tablespoons honey

2 tablespoons reduced-fat mayonnaise

2 tablespoons fat-free plain yogurt

$\frac{1}{4}$ teaspoon dried rosemary

$\frac{1}{2}$ apple, diced

2 tablespoons chopped walnuts

PER SERVING 297 calories, 12 g fat, 2 g saturated fat, 25 g protein, 23 g carbohydrates, 2 g fiber, 41 mg calcium, 184 mg sodium

Creamy Macaroni Salad

8 ounces macaroni

½ cup fat-free sour cream

¼ cup reduced-fat mayonnaise

1½ tablespoons red wine vinegar or cider vinegar

½ teaspoon salt

4 celery ribs, sliced

3 scallions, sliced

½ cup frozen peas, thawed

1 jar (4 ounces) diced pimientos, drained

2 hard-cooked eggs, coarsely chopped

2 tablespoons chopped fresh parsley

8 SERVINGS
1 HOUR
15 MINUTES

1. BRING a medium saucepan full of water to a boil. Add the macaroni and cook according to package directions until al dente. Drain and rinse under cold running water.

2. COMBINE the sour cream, mayonnaise, vinegar, and salt in a large bowl. Add the macaroni, celery, scallions, peas, pimientos, eggs, and parsley. Toss to coat. Cover and refrigerate for at least 1 hour.

PER SERVING   160 calories, 3 g fat, 1 g saturated fat, 7 g protein, 28 g carbohydrates, 2 g fiber, 46 mg calcium, 280 mg sodium

Southwest Cobb Salad

1. ARRANGE the lettuce on a large platter. Arrange the corn, beans, tomato, celery, bell pepper, onion, cheese, and bacon crosswise in strips over the romaine.

2. COMBINE the avocado, buttermilk, lime juice, and hot-pepper sauce in a food processor or blender. Process until smooth. Drizzle over the salad or pass at the table.

1   large head romaine, chopped

1   package (10 ounces) frozen corn kernels, thawed

1   can (15 ounces) no-salt-added black beans, rinsed and drained

1   large tomato, chopped

2   celery ribs, chopped

1   green bell pepper, chopped

1   red onion, chopped

1   cup (4 ounces) shredded fat-free Monterey Jack cheese

4   slices turkey bacon, cooked and crumbled

½   ripe avocado, cut into chunks

1   cup low-fat buttermilk

2   tablespoons freshly squeezed lime juice

½   teaspoon hot-pepper sauce

PER SERVING 210 calories, 5 g fat, 1 g saturated fat, 15 g protein, 30 g carbohydrates, 8 g fiber, 316 mg calcium, 550 mg sodium

Pork and Corn Salad
with Tomato Basil Dressing

1 small pork tenderloin (10 ounces), well trimmed, cut into ½"-thick slices, each slice halved crosswise

½ cup slivered fresh basil

1½ tablespoons olive oil

2 garlic cloves, minced

½ teaspoon ground black pepper

⅛ teaspoon salt

¾ cup canned diced tomatoes

2 teaspoons red wine vinegar

1½ cups frozen corn kernels

2 red bell peppers, chopped (about 2 cups)

3 tablespoons water

4 cups colorful mixed baby greens

4 SERVINGS

23 MINUTES

1. PLACE the pork in a medium bowl. Add ¼ cup of the basil, 1 tablespoon of the oil, the garlic, black pepper, and ¹⁄₁₆ teaspoon of the salt. Toss to coat the pork well. Set aside while preparing the rest of the salad.

2. PLACE the tomatoes in a large salad bowl. Stir in the vinegar and the remaining ¼ cup basil, ½ tablespoon oil, and ¹⁄₁₆ teaspoon salt.

3. PLACE the corn, bell peppers, and water in a large nonstick skillet. Cover and cook over medium-high heat, stirring often, for 3 to 4 minutes, or until the corn is tender. Stir into the tomato mixture.

4. DRY the skillet. Place the reserved pork in the same skillet and cook over medium heat, turning often, for 5 minutes, or until no longer pink in thickest part.

5. ADD the pork and pan juices to the tomato-corn mixture. Add the mixed greens and toss to blend the ingredients and wilt the greens slightly. Serve immediately.

PER SERVING 220 calories, 7 g fat, 2 g saturated fat, 19 g protein, 21 g carbohydrates, 5 g fiber, 55 mg calcium, 230 g sodium

Green and White Bean Salad

4 SERVINGS

41 MINUTES

1. BRING a pot of water to a boil. Add the green beans. Cook for 30 seconds, or until the beans turn bright green. Rinse under cold water and transfer to a medium bowl.

2. ADD the great Northern beans, vinegar, onion, parsley, basil, oil, and mustard. Stir well. Let the salad marinate at room temperature for 30 minutes. Add the salt and ground black pepper to taste.

3 cups diagonally sliced green beans

1 cup canned great Northern beans, rinsed and drained

1/3 cup balsamic vinegar

1 small sweet or red onion, minced (about 1/4 cup)

1/4 cup minced fresh parsley

1/4 cup minced fresh basil

2 teaspoons olive oil

2 teaspoons honey mustard

1/2 teaspoon salt
Ground black pepper

PER SERVING 149 calories, 3 g fat, 1 g saturated fat, 7 g protein, 25 g carbohydrates, 7 g fiber, 83 mg calcium, 25 mg sodium

Pan-Seared Salmon Salad

3 tablespoons chopped, dry-packed, sun-dried tomatoes

3 tablespoons balsamic vinegar

2 teaspoons olive oil

$1\frac{1}{2}$ teaspoons dried basil

1 teaspoon Dijon mustard

$\frac{1}{8}$ teaspoon salt

1 roasted red pepper, cut into small strips

1 pound mixed salad greens

6 ounces button or shiitake mushrooms, sliced

1 small onion, minced

8 ounces salmon fillets, skin removed

1 teaspoon Italian seasoning

4 SERVINGS

26 MINUTES

1. PLACE the sun-dried tomatoes in a small bowl. Cover with boiling water. Allow to soak for 10 minutes, or until soft. Drain and discard the liquid.

2. WHISK the vinegar, oil, basil, mustard, and salt in a large bowl until smooth. Place the pepper, sun-dried tomatoes, and greens in the bowl but do not toss. Set aside.

3. COAT a medium nonstick skillet lightly with cooking spray. Add the mushrooms and onion. Coat lightly with cooking spray. Cook over medium-high heat for 5 to 7 minutes, or until soft. Remove to a plate to cool.

4. WIPE the skillet with a paper towel. Coat the skillet with cooking spray and set over high heat. Lightly coat the salmon with cooking spray. Sprinkle with the Italian seasoning. Add the salmon to the skillet and cook for 3 minutes on each side, or until the fish flakes easily. Check by cutting into 1 fillet.

5. ADD the mushrooms and onion to the reserved bowl. Toss and transfer to 4 plates. Top each with a salmon fillet.

PER SERVING 190 calories, 9 g fat, 2 g saturated fat, 15 g protein, 12 g carbohydrates, 4 g fiber, 93 mg calcium, 220 mg sodium

Roasted Green Beans
with Candied Walnuts

4
SERVINGS

50
MINUTES

1. PREHEAT the oven to 375°F.

2. COOK the walnuts in a medium skillet over medium-low heat, stirring occasionally, for about 5 minutes, or until toasted. Add the butter and cook, stirring constantly, for 2 minutes, or until the butter is golden brown. Stir in the sugar and pepper and cook for 30 seconds. Remove from the heat and set aside.

3. PUT the green beans in a large rimmed baking pan and toss with the oil and salt to coat well. Place the pan in the oven.

4. ROAST for 10 minutes. With oven mitts, cover the pan with aluminum foil. Roast for 30 minutes, or until the beans are tender and lightly browned.

5. ADD the nut mixture to the beans. Toss and serve.

¼ cup chopped walnuts

2 teaspoons unsalted butter

1 teaspoon packed brown sugar

¼ teaspoon ground black pepper

1½ pounds green beans, trimmed

2 teaspoons olive oil

¼ teaspoon kosher salt

PER SERVING 130 calories, 9 g fat, 2 g saturated fat, 3 g protein, 12 g carbohydrates, 7 g fiber, 91 mg calcium, 121 mg sodium

Apple and Sweet Potato Hash Browns

1 teaspoon +
2 tablespoons
canola oil

1 large Granny
Smith apple,
peeled and sliced
into matchsticks

1 onion, thinly
sliced (about
$\frac{1}{2}$ cup)

3 sweet potatoes,
cut into
matchsticks
(about 2 cups)

Pinch of ground
cinnamon

8 SERVINGS

28 MINUTES

1. **HEAT** 1 teaspoon of the oil in a large skillet over medium-high heat. Add the apple and onion and cook for 4 minutes, or until soft. Set aside in a covered bowl. Add 1 tablespoon of the oil to the skillet. Heat until sizzling. Spread the potatoes in the pan in an even layer and press them down lightly with a spatula. Cook for 5 minutes, or until golden brown on the bottom. Drizzle with remaining oil and flip the potatoes. Cook for 5 minutes longer.

2. **ADD** the apple-and-onion mixture to the potatoes and heat through. Sprinkle with the cinnamon.

PER SERVING 90 calories, 4 g fat, 0 g saturated fat, 1 g protein, 14 g carbohydrates, 3 g fiber, 16 mg calcium, 27 mg sodium

Buttermilk-Smashed Red Potatoes with Scallions

4 SERVINGS

18 MINUTES

1. PLACE the potatoes, broth, and enough water to barely cover in a large heavy saucepan. Bring to a boil over high heat. Reduce the heat to low, partially cover, and simmer for 12 to 15 minutes, or until the potatoes are very tender.

2. RESERVE ¼ cup cooking water. Drain the potatoes and return them to the pot. With a potato masher, mash until fairly smooth.

3. BEAT in buttermilk and enough reserved cooking water with a wooden spoon, a bit at a time, to make the potatoes moist but with a chunky texture. Stir in the salt and pepper, and sprinkle with the scallions.

1½ pounds small red potatoes, scrubbed and halved

1 cup fat-free, reduced-sodium chicken or vegetable broth

½ cup low-fat buttermilk

¼ teaspoon salt

¼ teaspoon ground black pepper

2 scallions, thinly sliced

PER SERVING 156 calories, 0 g fat, 0 g saturated fat, 5 g protein, 32 g carbohydrates, 2 g fiber, 43 mg calcium, 311 mg sodium

Mashed Sweet Potatoes and Carrots

2 sweet potatoes, peeled and cubed

4 carrots, peeled and cubed

2 tablespoons trans-free spreadable/tub margarine

2 tablespoons apple cider

2 teaspoons packed brown sugar

$\frac{1}{2}$ teaspoon ground cinnamon

4
SERVINGS

45
MINUTES

1. COMBINE the potatoes and carrots in a large saucepan. Cover with cold water. Set over high heat and bring to a boil. Reduce the heat and simmer for 20 minutes, or until tender.

2. DRAIN the potatoes and carrots and return to the pan. Mash with a potato masher. Add the margarine, cider, brown sugar, and cinnamon. Stir to blend.

PER SERVING 139 calories, 6 g fat, 1 g saturated fat, 2 g protein, 21 g carbohydrates, 4 g fiber, 36 mg calcium, 125 mg sodium

Roasted Brussels Sprouts and Onions with Thyme

$1\frac{1}{2}$ pounds fresh Brussels sprouts, trimmed, halved or quartered into equal pieces

1 large sweet white onion, quartered and cut into $\frac{1}{2}$"-thick slices

1 tablespoon olive oil

4 teaspoons fresh thyme

$\frac{1}{4}$ teaspoon salt

$\frac{1}{8}$ teaspoon ground black pepper

4
SERVINGS

39
MINUTES

1. PREHEAT the oven to 400°F. Set out a rimmed baking sheet.

2. PLACE the Brussels sprouts on a baking sheet and toss with the onion, oil, thyme, salt, and pepper.

3. ROAST for 20 to 25 minutes, stirring 2 or 3 times, until the vegetables are tender and lightly browned.

PER SERVING 120 calories, 4 g fat, 1 g saturated fat, 6 g protein, 19 g carbohydrates, 7 g fiber, 85 mg calcium, 192 mg sodium

Snow Peas with Basil

4 SERVINGS

11 MINUTES

1. **COMBINE** the vinegar, basil, and 2 teaspoons of the oil in a large bowl.

2. **HEAT** a 10" nonstick skillet coated with cooking spray over medium-high heat. Add the remaining 1 teaspoon oil. Add the bell peppers and corn. Cook, stirring, for 4 minutes, or until the peppers soften slightly. Sprinkle with the salt and black pepper.

3. **ADD** the snow peas. Cook, stirring, for 3 minutes, or until the snow peas are crisp-tender. Transfer to a bowl. Toss well to coat with the vinegar mixture.

- 2 teaspoons cider vinegar
- 2 teaspoons chopped fresh basil
- 3 teaspoons olive oil
- 1 red bell pepper, chopped
- 1/4 cup frozen corn kernels
- 1/4 teaspoon salt
- 1/4 teaspoon ground black pepper
- 3 cups snow peas

PER SERVING 80 calories, 4 g fat, 1 g saturated fat, 2 g protein, 10 g carbohydrates, 3 g fiber, 35 mg calcium, 147 mg sodium

Sweet-and-Sour Broccoli

4 SERVINGS

11 MINUTES

1. **COMBINE** the onion, oil, garlic, oregano, and salt in a skillet. Cook, stirring, over low heat for 3 minutes, or until fragrant.

2. **ADD** the broccoli and stir to coat. Cook for 2 minutes, or until sizzling. Add the tomatoes and raisins. Cook for 1 to 2 minutes, or until the broccoli is crisp-tender.

- 1 small red onion, minced (about 1/4 cup)
- 1 tablespoon + 1 teaspoon olive oil
- 2 garlic cloves, minced
- 3/4 teaspoon dried oregano
- 1/16 teaspoon salt
- 2 1/2 cups small broccoli florets
- 2/3 cups canned diced tomatoes with juice
- 2 tablespoons raisins

PER SERVING 90 calories, 5 g fat, 1 g saturated fat, 2 g protein, 9 g carbohydrates, 2 g fiber, 26 mg calcium, 150 mg sodium

Asian-Style Asparagus

1 tablespoon reduced-sodium soy sauce

2 teaspoons rice wine vinegar

1/2 teaspoon toasted sesame oil

1/2 teaspoon chopped fresh ginger

1 garlic clove, minced

1/8 teaspoon crushed red-pepper flakes

1 1/4 pounds thin asparagus spears, ends trimmed

4 SERVINGS

16 MINUTES

1. COMBINE soy sauce, vinegar, oil, ginger, garlic, and red-pepper flakes in a small bowl. Stir well to blend. Set aside.

2. PLACE a large skillet coated with cooking spray over medium-high heat. Add the asparagus. Cover and cook, shaking the pan frequently to turn the asparagus, for 4 to 5 minutes, or until crisp-tender and lightly charred. Add the reserved soy mixture. Cook, shaking the pan, for 1 minute, or until the liquid is reduced to a glaze.

PER SERVING 40 calories, 2 g fat, 0 g saturated fat, 3 g protein, 6 g carbohydrates, 3 g fiber, 36 mg calcium, 135 mg sodium

Sesame Spinach

1 teaspoon sesame seeds

2 teaspoons canola oil

1 small garlic clove, minced

1 pound baby spinach leaves

2 tablespoons water

1 1/2 teaspoons reduced-sodium soy sauce

4 SERVINGS

8 MINUTES

1. PLACE the sesame seeds in a skillet. Cook over medium-high heat, stirring frequently, for 2 minutes, or until golden. Remove to a bowl.

2. RETURN the skillet to medium-low heat. Add the oil and garlic. Cook for 30 seconds, or until fragrant. Add the spinach, water, and soy sauce to the pan. Toss with tongs. Cover for 1 minute, or until the spinach wilts. Sprinkle with the sesame seeds.

PER SERVING 75 calories, 3 g fat, 0 g saturated fat, 3 g protein, 12 g carbohydrates, 5 g fiber, 88 mg calcium, 256 mg sodium

Roasted Vegetable Medley

4 SERVINGS

1 HOUR

1. PREHEAT the oven to 425°F.

2. COMBINE the potatoes, carrots, parsnips, oil, butter, salt, and pepper on a 13" × 9" baking pan or baking sheet with sides. Toss until the vegetables are well coated. Spread the vegetables in a single layer on the bottom of the pan.

3. ROAST, stirring occasionally, for 20 minutes. Remove the pan from the oven. Stir the garlic with the vegetables.

4. RETURN the pan to the oven. Roast, stirring occasionally, for 20 minutes, or until golden brown and tender.

PER SERVING 161 calories, 6 g fat, 2 g saturated fat, 3 g protein, 26 g carbohydrates, 4 g fiber, 39 mg calcium, 184 mg sodium

1 pound small, red-skinned potatoes, quartered
4 carrots, peeled and cut into sticks
2 parsnips, peeled and cut into sticks
1 tablespoon olive oil
2 teaspoons butter, melted
$\frac{1}{4}$ teaspoon kosher salt
$\frac{1}{4}$ teaspoon ground black pepper
2 garlic cloves, minced

Cajun-Blackened Zucchini

4 SERVINGS

24 MINUTES

1. PREHEAT the oven to 400°F. Coat a large baking sheet with sides with cooking spray.

2. SPREAD the zucchini on the prepared baking sheet. Coat lightly with olive oil, then sprinkle with half of the Cajun seasoning and the salt. Flip the slices and repeat. Spread them out in a single layer.

3. BAKE for 10 minutes, or until starting to sizzle. Flip the zucchini. Scatter the scallions over the pan, pressing with a spatula to coat them with the oil and seasoning. Bake for 10 minutes, or until the scallions are wilting.

PER SERVING 27 calories, 1 g fat, 0 g saturated fat, 2 g protein, 5 g carbohydrates, 2 g fiber, 26 mg calcium, 86 mg sodium

1 pound zucchini, halved, then cut into $\frac{1}{4}$" lengthwise slices
Olive oil in a spray bottle
2 teaspoon salt-free Cajun seasoning
$\frac{1}{8}$ teaspoon salt
4 scallions, sliced (about $\frac{1}{2}$ cup)

Cauliflower, Green Bean, and Tomato Gratin

½ bag (16 ounces) frozen cauliflower florets

1 cup (¼ of 14-ounce bag) frozen cut Italian green beans, cut green beans, or sugar snap peas

1 cup cherry tomatoes, rinsed and stemmed

¼ cup dried whole wheat bread crumbs

2½ tablespoons (1½ ounces) grated Pecorino Romano cheese

½ tablespoon olive oil

1 small garlic clove, grated or crushed

4 SERVINGS

30 MINUTES

1. PREHEAT the oven to 400°F. Coat a 13" × 5" × 9" baking dish with cooking spray.

2. BRING 1 cup water to a boil in a large saucepan. Add the cauliflower and beans or peas, cover, and cook for 3 minutes, then drain. Distribute the cauliflower, beans or peas, and tomatoes evenly in the prepared dish.

3. COMBINE the bread crumbs, cheese, oil, and garlic in a small bowl. Stir with a fork until blended. Sprinkle the mixture evenly over the vegetables.

4. BAKE for 20 minutes, or until the crumbs are golden brown.

PER SERVING 89 calories, 3 g fat, 1 g saturated fat, 4 g protein, 10 g carbohydrates, 3 g fiber, 82 mg calcium, 131 mg sodium

Braised Burgundy Cabbage

6 SERVINGS

37 MINUTES

1. HEAT the oil in a large nonstick skillet over medium heat. Add the onion, walnuts, and garlic. Cook, stirring often, for 5 to 7 minutes, or until the onion is softened and the walnuts are toasted. Add the cabbage, vinegar, and oregano. Cover and cook, stirring occasionally, for 12 to 15 minutes, or until the cabbage is soft and tender. Season with the salt and pepper.

2. REMOVE from the heat and add the apple and cheese. Toss to combine.

2 teaspoons canola oil

1 red onion, thinly sliced (about 1 cup)

$\frac{1}{4}$ cup chopped walnuts

1 garlic clove, minced

1 small head red cabbage, shredded (about 4 cups)

2 tablespoons balsamic vinegar

2 tablespoons chopped fresh oregano

$\frac{1}{4}$ teaspoon salt

$\frac{1}{4}$ teaspoon ground black pepper

1 McIntosh apple, cut into $\frac{1}{2}$" pieces

$2\frac{1}{2}$ ounces goat cheese, crumbled (about $\frac{1}{4}$ cup + 2 tablespoons)

PER SERVING 130 calories, 8 g fat, 2 g saturated fat, 4 g protein, 12 g carbohydrates, 3 g fiber, 76 mg calcium, 160 mg sodium

MAIN DISHES

Beef Stew

1. HEAT a large saucepan coated with cooking spray over medium heat. Add the beef and cook, turning as needed, for 10 minutes, or until browned on all sides. Add the onion and garlic and cook, stirring frequently, for 4 minutes, or until the onion is soft.

2. ADD the broth, water, and bay leaf. Cover and bring to a boil. Reduce the heat to low and simmer for 1¼ hours.

3. ADD the carrots, celery, turnips, potatoes, and pepper. Cover and return to a boil. Reduce the heat to low and simmer for 30 minutes, or until the vegetables are tender. Skim off any visible fat from the surface of the stew. Remove and discard the bay leaf.

4. REMOVE about 1 cup of the liquid. In a small bowl, whisk the liquid and flour until the mixture is smooth and free of lumps. Stir into the stew. Add the marjoram. Cook and stir over medium heat until the stew thickens and begins to gently boil. Cook and stir for 1 minute longer.

¾ pound boneless beef chuck arm steak, trimmed of all visible fat and cut into 1" cubes

1 onion, chopped

2 garlic cloves, minced

3 cups fat-free, reduced-sodium beef broth

2 cups water

1 bay leaf

2 large carrots, sliced (about 2 cups)

2 large celery ribs, sliced (about 1 cup)

2 turnips, peeled and cubed (about 1½ cups)

2 red or white-skinned potatoes, peeled and cubed (about 1½ cups)

½ teaspoon ground black pepper

¼ cup unbleached or all-purpose flour

2 teaspoons dried marjoram

PER SERVING 270 calories, 6 g fat, 2 g saturated fat, 23 g protein, 31 g carbohydrates, 5 g fiber, 77 mg calcium, 490 mg sodium

Beef Cottage Pie

6
SERVINGS

55
MINUTES

1½ pounds lean
ground beef
(95% lean or
greater)

1 cup soft bread
crumbs

1 small onion,
finely chopped

1 small green bell
pepper, finely
chopped

1 egg white

3 tablespoons no-
salt-added
ketchup

1¼ cups low-fat
buttermilk

¼ teaspoon salt

2½ pounds russet
potatoes, peeled
and cut into
1" cubes

1 cup (4 ounces)
shredded low-
fat Cheddar
cheese

1. PREHEAT the oven to 350°F. Lightly coat a 9"
pie pan with cooking spray.

2. COMBINE the beef, bread crumbs, onion,
pepper, egg white, ketchup, ¼ cup of the
buttermilk, and ⅛ teaspoon of the salt in a
large bowl. Mix with a wooden spoon or your
hands. Press into the bottom and up the sides
of the prepared pan, creating a 1"-thick shell.

3. BAKE for 25 minutes, or until no longer pink. Drain any
accumulated juices. Pat dry with a paper towel.

4. SET a steamer rack in a large pot filled with 2" of boiling
water. Place the potatoes on the rack. Cover and cook
over high heat for 15 minutes, or until fork-tender.
Remove to a bowl. Mash with a potato masher. Add the
remaining 1 cup buttermilk and ⅛ teaspoon salt. Mash
until smooth.

5. SPRINKLE ½ cup of the cheese over the bottom of the pie
shell. Spread half of the potatoes over the top. Dollop the
remaining potatoes around the edge. Sprinkle the
remaining ½ cup cheese in the center.

6. INCREASE the oven temperature to 400°F. Bake for 15
minutes, or until heated through.

PER SERVING 400 calories, 7 g fat, 3 g saturated fat, 34 g protein, 51 g carbohydrates, 4 g fiber, 163 mg calcium, 400 mg sodium

Old-Fashioned Meat Loaf

5 SERVINGS
1 HOUR
10 MINUTES

1. PREHEAT the oven to 350°F. Combine the beef, oats, tomato juice, cheese, egg, oregano, onion powder, salt, and pepper in a medium bowl. With clean hands or 2 forks, mix well. Place in a nonstick 8½" × 4¼" × 3" loaf pan. Pat the surface down to make an even loaf. Place in the oven. Bake for 30 minutes.

2. COMBINE the ketchup and vinegar in a small bowl. Whisk to blend. Pour the mixture evenly over meat loaf. Bake for 30 minutes, or until a thermometer inserted in the thickest part registers 165°F.

1 pound lean ground beef (95% lean or greater)

¾ cup quick-cooking oats

1 can (5.5 ounces) low-sodium tomato juice

¼ cup (1 ounce) grated Romano cheese

1 egg, beaten

1 teaspoon dried oregano

1 teaspoon onion powder

Dash of salt

Dash of ground black pepper

½ cup no-salt-added ketchup

½ cup balsamic vinegar

PER SERVING 265 calories, 8 g fat, 3 g saturated fat, 24 g protein, 21 g carbohydrates, 2 g fiber, 104 mg calcium, 552 mg sodium

Beef and Black Bean Picadillo over Brown Rice

1 cup instant brown rice, such as Uncle Ben's

¾ pound lean ground beef (95% lean or greater)

2 teaspoons olive oil

1 red bell pepper, coarsely chopped

1 red onion, chopped (about 1 cup + 2 tablespoons)

2 garlic cloves, minced

2½ teaspoons ground cumin

½ teaspoon sugar

¼ teaspoon salt

½ teaspoon crushed red-pepper flakes

1 can (15–16 ounces) black beans, rinsed and drained

1 can (14½ ounces) no-salt-added diced tomatoes in juice

½ cup dark raisins

2 tablespoons pimiento-stuffed olives

4 SERVINGS

47 MINUTES

1. **COOK** the rice according to package directions. Set aside.

2. **HEAT** a large nonstick skillet coated with cooking spray over medium-high heat. Crumble in the ground beef and cook, stirring to break up any chunks, for 5 minutes, or until no longer pink. Drain and set aside.

3. **HEAT** the oil over medium heat in the same skillet. Add the bell pepper, 1 cup of the onion, and the garlic. Cook, stirring often, for 5 minutes, or until tender. Return the beef to the skillet and stir in the cumin, sugar, salt, and red-pepper flakes. Cook and stir for 1 minute. Stir in the beans, tomatoes (with juice), and raisins. Bring to a simmer. Reduce the heat to low, cover, and simmer, stirring once or twice, for 15 minutes, or until the flavors have blended.

4. **SPRINKLE** the picadillo with the olives and the remaining 2 tablespoons onion and serve with rice.

PER SERVING 410 calories, 8 g fat, 3 g saturated fat, 28 g protein, 56 g carbohydrates, 9 g fiber, 95 mg calcium, 250 mg sodium

Braised Pork Cutlets
with Cider Sauce

4
SERVINGS

25
MINUTES

1. **POUR** the oil into a large skillet set over medium-high heat. When the oil is hot, place the chops in the pan. Cook for 3 minutes, or until seared on the bottom. Flip and add the cider and broth. Cover the pan and reduce the heat to medium-low. Simmer for 8 to 10 minutes, or until a thermometer inserted in the thickest part registers 160°F. Remove the chops to a plate. Cover with aluminum foil to keep warm.

2. **ADD** the garlic to the pan juices. Adjust the heat to medium and cook for 10 minutes, or until the mixture is reduced by half. Combine the cornstarch and water in a small bowl. Whisk until smooth. Pour into the pan, whisking, and cook for 1 to 2 minutes, or until the sauce thickens slightly. Spoon the sauce over the chops.

- 1 tablespoon olive oil
- 4 boneless pork loin chops (4 ounces each), trimmed of fat, pounded to $1/4$" thickness
- $1\frac{1}{2}$ cups apple cider
- $3/4$ cup fat-free, reduced-sodium chicken broth
- 2 garlic cloves, minced
- 2 teaspoons cornstarch
- 2 tablespoons cold water

PER SERVING 238 calories, 13 g fat, 4 g saturated fat, 18 g protein, 12 g carbohydrates, 0 g fiber, 19 mg calcium, 134 mg sodium

Grilled Pork Chops

2 tablespoons fat-free, reduced-sodium chicken broth

3 tablespoons balsamic vinegar

3 garlic cloves, minced

1 tablespoon dried oregano

2 teaspoons olive oil

¼ teaspoon salt

4 bone-in center-cut pork chops (6 ounces each), trimmed of all visible fat

4
SERVINGS

55
MINUTES

1. COMBINE the broth, vinegar, garlic, oregano, oil, and salt in a shallow baking dish. Add the chops. Turn several times to coat both sides. Cover and marinate in the refrigerator for 30 minutes, or up to 4 hours. Turn the chops several times as they marinate.

2. COAT a grill rack or broiler pan with cooking spray. Preheat the grill or broiler. Grill or broil the chops, turning once, for about 4 or 5 minutes per side, or until a thermometer inserted in the center of a chop registers 160°F and the juices run clear.

PER SERVING 182 calories, 8 g fat, 2 g saturated fat, 22 g protein, 4 g carbohydrates, 1 g fiber, 46 mg calcium, 206 mg sodium

Honey-Mustard Pork Tenderloin

4 SERVINGS

29 MINUTES

1 pound pork tenderloin, cut into 4 pieces (4 ounces each) and trimmed of all visible fat

1 teaspoon canola oil

1 onion, finely chopped (about ½ cup)

½ cup fat-free reduced-sodium chicken broth

1 tablespoon honey mustard

1. **PRESS** the tenderloins to ½" thickness using your palm or the flat side of a large knife.

2. **HEAT** a large nonstick skillet coated with cooking spray over medium-high heat for 2 minutes. Sear the pork for 2 minutes per side, or until browned. Remove from the skillet and set aside.

3. **HEAT** the oil over medium heat in the same skillet. Add the onion and cook, stirring frequently, for 4 to 5 minutes, or until soft. Add the broth and cook at a brisk simmer for 2 to 3 minutes, or until slightly reduced. Whisk in the mustard.

4. **RETURN** the pork to the skillet, spooning some of the mustard glaze over the top. Reduce the heat to low and cook for 4 to 5 minutes, or until the pork is hot and only slightly pink in the center (check by inserting the tip of a sharp knife into 1 tenderloin). Serve the pork topped with the mustard glaze.

PER SERVING 169 calories, 5 g fat, 1 g saturated fat, 24 g protein, 5 g carbohydrates, 0 g fiber, 13 mg calcium, 142 mg sodium

Hoisin Pork Stir-Fry

1 pound pork tenderloin, trimmed of all visible fat

2 tablespoons reduced-sodium soy sauce

1 tablespoon dry sherry

1 tablespoon cornstarch

1 tablespoon toasted sesame oil

3 cups broccoli florets

1 carrot, peeled and sliced on an angle

1/4 teaspoon red-pepper flakes

1 tablespoon grated fresh ginger

2 garlic cloves, minced

1/2 cup orange juice

3 tablespoons hoisin sauce

4 SERVINGS

25 MINUTES

1. **CUT** the pork into 1½" × ¼" strips with a sharp knife. Place in a bowl and add the soy sauce, sherry, and cornstarch, tossing to combine.

2. **HEAT** the oil in a large nonstick skillet over medium-high heat. Add the broccoli, carrot, and red-pepper flakes. Cook, stirring often, for 3 to 4 minutes, or until crisp-tender. Remove to a plate. Add the ginger and garlic to the pan and cook for 1 minute. Stir in the pork and cook for 4 minutes, or until the pork is no longer pink. Add the broccoli mixture to the pan and toss for 1 minute. Add the orange juice and hoisin sauce and bring to a boil. Cook for 1 minute longer, stirring to coat, until the mixture thickens slightly.

PER SERVING 246 calories, 8 g fat, 2 g saturated fat, 27 g protein, 16 g carbohydrates, 3 g fiber, 48 mg calcium, 543 mg sodium

Tandoori Turkey Kebabs

4 SERVINGS

27 MINUTES

1. **SOAK** 8 wooden skewers in a bowl of water and set aside. Coat the grill grates with cooking spray and preheat the grill.

2. **COMBINE** the yogurt, garam masala, garlic, and ginger in a medium bowl. Add the turkey and marinate for at least 10 minutes.

3. **PREPARE** the couscous according to package directions, adding the dried fruit during cooking.

4. **SLIDE** the turkey onto the reserved skewers. Place the kebabs on the hot grill and cook, turning frequently, for 10 to 12 minutes, or until the turkey is cooked through.

5. **PLACE** ½ cup of the couscous onto each of 4 plates. Top each with 2 kebabs.

1 cup fat-free plain yogurt

2 tablespoons garam masala (an Indian spice mix found in the ethnic-food aisle of most grocery stores)

2 garlic cloves, chopped

½ teaspoon ground ginger (optional)

1 pound turkey tenderloin, cut into 2" pieces

¾ cup dry whole wheat couscous

⅓ cup dried-fruit mix, chopped (any variety)

PER SERVING 276 calories, 3 g fat, 0 g saturated fat, 34 g protein, 32 g carbohydrates, 4 g fiber, 94 mg calcium, 112 mg sodium

Turkey Meatballs and Linguine

1 pound lean ground turkey breast (7% fat or less)

3 garlic cloves, minced

1 egg white

⅓ cup dried whole wheat bread crumbs

½ teaspoon salt

½ teaspoon ground black pepper

1 tablespoon olive oil

1 onion, chopped (about 1 cup)

1 teaspoon dried basil

1 teaspoon dried oregano

1 can (28 ounces) no-salt-added diced tomatoes, with juice

2 tablespoons no-salt-added tomato paste

12 ounces whole wheat linguine

6 SERVINGS

45 MINUTES

1. PREHEAT the oven to 400°F. Coat a baking sheet with cooking spray.

2. COMBINE the turkey, 1 clove of the garlic, the egg white, bread crumbs, ¼ teaspoon of the salt, and ¼ teaspoon of the pepper in a bowl. With slightly damp hands, form the mixture into eighteen 1½" balls and set them about 1" apart on the prepared baking sheet. Bake, turning once, for 23 to 25 minutes, or until the meatballs are browned, firm, and no longer pink inside.

3. HEAT the oil in a large saucepan over medium-high heat. Add the onion, basil, oregano, and the remaining 2 cloves of garlic. Cook, stirring occasionally, for 2 to 3 minutes, or until the onion begins to soften. Stir in the tomatoes (with juice), tomato paste, and the remaining ¼ teaspoon salt and ¼ teaspoon pepper. Bring to a boil. Reduce the heat to medium-low and simmer, partially covered, for 12 to 15 minutes, or until the sauce starts to thicken. Add the meatballs and simmer for 5 minutes, or until the sauce has thickened and the meatballs are hot.

4. COOK the linguine according to package directions. Drain. To serve, divide the linguine among 6 shallow bowls and top each with 3 meatballs and some sauce.

PER SERVING 390 calories, 5 g fat, 0 g saturated fat, 31 g protein, 55 g carbohydrates, 12 g fiber, 29 mg calcium, 350 mg sodium

Home-Style
Turkey Pot Pie

6 SERVINGS

1 HOUR

5 MINUTES

1. HEAT a nonstick skillet coated with cooking spray over medium-high heat. Add the onion, garlic, and tarragon. Cook, stirring occasionally, for 3 to 4 minutes, or until starting to soften. Combine the broth and flour and pour into the skillet. Add the sweet potatoes and mustard. Bring to a boil, reduce the heat to medium-low, cover, and simmer for 15 minutes, or until the sweet potatoes are tender. Stir in the turkey, peas and carrots, corn, parsley, and salt.

2. PREHEAT the oven to 375°F. Coat a 9" deep-dish pie pan with cooking spray.

3. POUR the filling into the prepared pie pan. Unroll the crust and top the pie pan. Roll any excess dough that hangs over the edge and crimp. Cut a decorative opening in the crust, and bake for 23 to 25 minutes, or until the top is browned and the filling is hot and bubbly.

1 onion, chopped (about 1 cup)

2 garlic cloves, minced

2 teaspoons dried tarragon

1 can (14 1/2 ounces) fat-free, reduced-sodium chicken broth

3 tablespoons whole wheat flour

2 sweet potatoes, peeled and cut into 1/2" pieces

1 tablespoon Dijon mustard

2 1/2 cups cubed leftover roast turkey breast (about 12 ounces)

1 cup frozen peas and carrots

1/2 cup frozen corn kernels

1/4 cup chopped fresh parsley

1/2 teaspoon salt

1 refrigerated pie crust (7 1/2 ounces)

PER SERVING 356 calories, 12 g fat, 5 g saturated fat, 23 g protein, 39 g carbohydrates, 4 g fiber, 50 mg calcium, 493 mg sodium

Turkey Stuffed with Mushrooms and Spinach

1 turkey London broil (about 1½ pounds)

2 teaspoons olive oil + additional for misting

1 cup sliced brown or white mushrooms, chopped (about 3 ounces)

1 cup (1 ounce) lightly packed baby spinach leaves

4 scallions, sliced

2 tablespoons ground flaxseed

½ teaspoon poultry seasoning

⅛ teaspoon salt
Ground black pepper

2 tablespoons (½ ounce) shredded Swiss cheese

½ cup water

6 SERVINGS

1 HOUR

15 MINUTES

1. PREHEAT the oven to 350°F. Set the turkey on a work surface. With a sharp knife, cut through the middle to create a pocket. Set aside.

2. HEAT 2 teaspoons of the oil over medium heat in an ovenproof skillet. Add the mushrooms, spinach, scallions, flaxseed, poultry seasoning, salt, and ground black pepper to taste. Cook, stirring, for 3 minutes, or until the spinach wilts. Spoon the mixture into the pocket in the reserved turkey. Cover the stuffing with the cheese. Press the open edge down to seal. Fasten with toothpicks, if desired.

3. ADD the water to the skillet. Cook over medium heat, scraping with a spatula to release the browned bits on the pan bottom. Bring to a boil. Turn off the heat. Place the turkey in the skillet. Mist lightly with olive oil.

4. ROAST the turkey for 45 minutes, or until an instant-read thermometer inserted in the center registers 165°F. Remove to a cutting board. Let stand for 15 minutes, or until the internal temperature rises to 170°F. Slice the turkey. Reheat the juices in the skillet to drizzle over the turkey.

PER SERVING 160 calories, 4 g fat, 1 g saturated fat, 30 g protein, 3 g carbohydrates, 2 g fiber, 29 mg calcium, 125 mg sodium

Stir-Fried Orange Chicken and Broccoli

<table>
<tr><td>

4
SERVINGS

27
MINUTES

</td></tr>
</table>

1. **CUT** the broccoli into small florets. Trim and discard about 2" of the tough stems. Thinly slice the remaining stems.

2. **COMBINE** the orange juice, soy sauce, cornstarch, and orange marmalade in a small bowl. Stir until blended. Set aside.

3. **HEAT** the oil in a wok or large nonstick skillet over high heat. Add the chicken and cook, stirring frequently, for 2 to 3 minutes, or until no longer pink and the juices run clear. Add the scallions, garlic, ginger, and red-pepper flakes. Stir to combine. With a slotted spoon, remove the chicken to a plate.

4. **ADD** the broth and broccoli to the wok and reduce the heat to medium. Cover and cook for 2 minutes. Increase the heat to high and add the bell pepper. Cook, stirring frequently, for 2 minutes, or until the broth evaporates and the vegetables are crisp-tender. Stir the reserved sauce and add to the wok along with the chicken. Cook, stirring constantly, for 1 to 2 minutes, or until the sauce thickens and the chicken is hot.

1 large bunch broccoli (about 1½ pounds)
½ cup orange juice
2 tablespoons reduced-sodium soy sauce
2 teaspoons cornstarch
2 tablespoons orange marmalade
1 tablespoon canola oil
1 pound chicken tenders, trimmed and cut into 1" pieces
3 scallions, sliced
3 large garlic cloves, minced
1 tablespoon minced fresh ginger
Pinch of red-pepper flakes
⅓ cup fat-free, reduced-sodium chicken broth
1 red bell pepper, thinly sliced

PER SERVING 261 calories, 5 g fat, 0 g saturated fat, 32 g protein, 27 g carbohydrates, 6 g fiber, 104 mg calcium, 386 mg sodium

Chicken Parmesan

½ cup dried bread crumbs

½ cup flour

2 eggs, beaten

4 boneless, skinless chicken breasts (3 ounces each), pounded to ¼" thickness

1½ tablespoons olive oil

1 cup low-sodium spaghetti sauce

¼ cup (1 ounce) shredded reduced-fat mozzarella cheese

2 tablespoons (½ ounce) grated Parmesan cheese

4 SERVINGS

30 MINUTES

1. PREHEAT the oven to 400°F.

2. PLACE the bread crumbs in a shallow bowl. Place the flour in another shallow bowl. Place the eggs in a third shallow bowl. One at a time, dip the chicken breasts into the flour, then into the egg, and then into the bread crumbs. Set aside until all the breasts are coated.

3. HEAT a large skillet over medium heat. Add the oil. When the oil is hot, place the chicken in the pan. Cook over medium-low heat for 2 minutes on each side, or until browned. Place the chicken on a baking sheet.

4. BAKE for 10 minutes, or until a thermometer inserted in the thickest part registers 165°F and the juices run clear.

5. REMOVE from the oven. Pour ¼ cup of the sauce on each breast. Top each with 1 tablespoon of the mozzarella and ½ tablespoon of the Parmesan. Return to the oven to bake for 5 minutes, or until the cheese bubbles.

PER SERVING 366 calories, 14 g fat, 4 g saturated fat, 28 g protein, 31 g carbohydrates, 3 g fiber, 190 mg calcium, 283 mg sodium

Chicken Roulade

1. **PLACE** the spinach in a large nonstick skillet with water clinging to the leaves or a tablespoon or two of water if dried. Cover and cook for 2 minutes, tossing occasionally, or until wilted. Drain and press firmly with the back of a spoon or squeeze to remove excess moisture. Wipe out the skillet.

2. **COMBINE** the onion, 1 teaspoon of the oil, the garlic, red-pepper flakes, and the water in a medium nonstick skillet. Turn the heat to medium. Cook for 2 minutes, or until the onion sizzles. Reduce the heat to low. Cover and cook, stirring once, for 3 minutes, or until softened. Combine the onion mixture, hummus, cheese, and spinach in a small bowl. Stir to mix. Set aside.

3. **SPRINKLE** the tomatoes evenly on the smooth side of the cutlets.

4. **DIVIDE** the spinach mixture among the cutlets. Spread to the edges of 3 sides, leaving about 1" at the narrow tip free of the spinach mixture. Loosely roll up the chicken, ending with the narrow tip, and secure with toothpicks.

5. **ADD** the remaining 1 teaspoon oil to a large skillet and set over medium heat. Place the chicken in the pan. Cook, turning, for 10 minutes, or until golden brown on all sides. Add the broth or wine, cover, and cook over low heat for 7 minutes. Uncover and transfer the chicken to a serving platter. Cover with foil to keep warm.

6. **BOIL** the skillet juices for 5 minutes, or until reduced to a glaze. Diagonally slice the chicken into 1"-thick pieces. Drizzle with the pan juices and serve.

2 cups (2 ounces) baby spinach

1 small onion, finely chopped (about ¼ cup)

2 teaspoons olive oil

1 garlic clove, minced

⅓ teaspoon red-pepper flakes

1 tablespoon water

¼ cup prepared hummus

¼ cup (1 ounce) grated Parmesan cheese

2 tablespoons chopped dry-packed sundried tomatoes

4 chicken cutlets (about 4 ounces each) or chicken breast halves, trimmed and pounded thin into cutlets

½ cup fat-free, reduced-sodium chicken broth or dry white wine

PER SERVING 190 calories, 6 g fat, 2 g saturated fat, 30 g protein, 6 g carbohydrates, 2 g fiber, 76 mg calcium, 250 mg sodium

Rosemary Roast Chicken

1 broiler-fryer chicken (3 pounds)

3 teaspoons dried rosemary, crushed

¼ teaspoon salt

1 lemon, sliced

1 small onion, chopped

2 cans (14½ ounces each) fat-free, reduced-sodium chicken broth

1 tablespoon cornstarch

⅓ cup Madeira or alcohol-free white wine

6 SERVINGS

1 HOUR

30 MINUTES

1. **PREHEAT** the oven to 450°F. Coat a roasting rack and roasting pan with cooking spray.

2. **WASH** the chicken and pat it dry with paper towels. (Reserve the giblets for another use.) Season the cavity with 1 teaspoon of the rosemary and the salt. Place the lemon slices inside the cavity. Place the chicken, breast side up, on a prepared roasting rack. Rub 1 teaspoon of the remaining rosemary over the breast meat under the skin of the chicken. Scatter the onion around the bottom of the pan. Pour in 1 can of broth.

3. **ROAST** the chicken for 20 minutes. Baste with the pan juices and lower the heat to 350°F. Roast, basting every 15 minutes, for 45 to 50 minutes, or until a thermometer inserted in a breast registers 180°F and the juices run clear. Transfer the chicken to a cutting board and loosely cover with foil.

4. **WHISK** the cornstarch with ¼ cup of the remaining broth in a small bowl until smooth. Set aside.

5. **PLACE** the roasting pan on the stove top over medium-high heat. Add the wine. Boil for 2 to 3 minutes, scraping the bottom of the pan to remove the browned bits, or until reduced to ¼ cup. Add the remaining broth. Bring to a boil. Skim off and discard any fat that rises to top. Pour in the reserved cornstarch mixture and the remaining 1 teaspoon rosemary. Cook, stirring constantly, for 2 to 3 minutes, or until slightly thickened.

6. **CARVE** the chicken. Remove and discard the skin before eating. Serve with the gravy.

PER SERVING — 167 calories, 3 g fat, 1 g saturated fat, 25 g protein, 5 g carbohydrates, 1 g fiber, 26 mg calcium, 486 mg sodium

Instant Chicken and White Bean Stew

4 SERVINGS

20 MINUTES

1. COOK the onion and garlic in oil in a nonstick skillet over medium heat until soft. Add the broth, zucchini, beans, and pepper. Heat just to boiling. Boil for 2 minutes.

2. ADD the chicken, return just to boiling, and remove from the heat. Add the pesto. Let stand for 2 to 3 minutes to blend the flavors.

1 onion, chopped

2 garlic cloves, minced

2 teaspoons olive oil

2 cups fat-free, reduced-sodium chicken broth

2 zucchini, halved lengthwise and thinly sliced

1 can (19 ounces) no-salt-added cannellini beans, rinsed and drained

$\frac{1}{8}$ teaspoon ground black pepper

$1\frac{1}{2}$ cups diced skinless leftover roasted chicken

2 tablespoons prepared pesto

PER SERVING 280 calories, 9 g fat, 2 g saturated fat, 27 g protein, 24 g carbohydrates, 7 g fiber, 283 mg calcium, 430 mg sodium

Southwestern Chicken Sauté

1 tablespoon chili powder

1¼ teaspoons ground cumin

¼ teaspoon salt

⅛ teaspoon ground red pepper

4 boneless, skinless chicken breast halves (4 ounces each)

2 teaspoons olive oil

½ cup fat-free, reduced-sodium chicken broth

1 tablespoon cider vinegar

2 plum tomatoes, diced

1 cup frozen corn kernels

½ cup rinsed and drained no-salt-added black beans

1 can (4 ounces) mild green chiles, drained

¼ cup chopped fresh cilantro

4 SERVINGS

33 MINUTES

1. **COMBINE** the chili powder, cumin, salt, and pepper in a cup. Rub both sides of the chicken breasts with 1 tablespoon of the spice mixture.

2. **HEAT** the oil in a large nonstick skillet over medium-high heat. Add the chicken and cook, turning once, for 6 minutes, or until the spice coating is browned and the surface of the chicken is opaque. Place the chicken on a plate and keep warm.

3. **ADD** the broth, vinegar, and remaining spice mixture to the skillet. Bring to a boil over high heat, stirring to loosen the browned bits from the pan. Boil for 2 minutes, or until the liquid is slightly reduced.

4. **RETURN** the chicken to the skillet, adding any juices that have collected on the plate. Add the tomatoes, corn, beans, and chiles and bring to a boil. Reduce the heat to medium, cover, and simmer for 5 minutes, or until a thermometer inserted in the thickest portion of the chicken registers 160°F and the juices run clear. Sprinkle with the cilantro.

PER SERVING 240 calories, 5 g fat, 1 g saturated fat, 30 g protein, 19 g carbohydrates, 5 g fiber, 58 mg calcium, 380 mg sodium

Seafood and Okra Jambalaya

6 SERVINGS

1 HOUR

5 MINUTES

1. **HEAT** the oil in a large pot over medium-high heat. Add the chorizo and cook for 2 minutes, or until starting to brown. Stir in the okra, onion, pepper, and celery. Cook, stirring occasionally, for 8 to 10 minutes, or until softened. Add the Creole seasoning and cook for 30 seconds.

2. **STIR** in the tomatoes, water, broth, and rice. Bring to a boil, reduce the heat to medium-low, cover, and simmer for 25 minutes. Stir in the shrimp and catfish and cook for 5 minutes, or until the liquid is absorbed, the fish flakes easily, and the shrimp are opaque. Remove from the heat and let stand for 5 to 10 minutes, or until the seafood is cooked through.

2 teaspoons olive oil

1 cured chorizo sausage (1¾ ounces), finely chopped

1 package (10 ounces) frozen, cut okra

1 onion, chopped (about 1 cup)

1 red bell pepper, chopped (about 1 cup)

3 celery ribs, chopped (about 1 cup)

1½ teaspoons salt-free Creole seasoning

1 can (14.5 ounces) diced no-salt-added tomatoes

1 cup water

1 cup fat-free, reduced-sodium chicken broth

1 cup brown rice (cooks in 30 minutes)

1¼ pounds peeled and deveined medium shrimp

½ pound catfish fillet, cut into chunks

PER SERVING 300 calories, 10 g fat, 3 g saturated fat, 31 g protein, 22 g carbohydrates, 3 g fiber, 114 mg calcium, 530 mg sodium

Flounder and Broccoli Roll-Ups

3 cups small broccoli florets

2 slices multigrain bread

4 ounces fat-free cream cheese, softened

1 egg white

2 tablespoons (½ ounce) grated Parmesan cheese

4 skinless flounder fillets (6 ounces each)

¼ teaspoon salt

¼ teaspoon ground black pepper

2 teaspoons olive oil

3 garlic cloves, sliced

2 tomatoes, chopped (about 2 cups)

2 tablespoons chopped fresh basil

4 SERVINGS

45 MINUTES

1. PREHEAT the oven to 350°F. Coat an 8" × 8" baking dish with cooking spray.

2. BRING a large saucepan of lightly salted water to a boil. Add the broccoli, return to a boil, and cook for 2 minutes. Drain, rinse under cold water, and drain again well. Transfer the broccoli to a cutting board and finely chop.

3. PLACE the bread into the bowl of a food processor and pulse into bread crumbs. Transfer to a bowl and add the broccoli, cream cheese, egg white, and cheese. Stir to mix well.

4. PLACE the flounder on a work surface and sprinkle with ⅛ teaspoon of the salt and ⅛ teaspoon of the pepper. Top 1 end of each fillet with one-fourth of the broccoli mixture. Roll up jelly roll–style and secure the ends with toothpicks. Place in the prepared dish, seam side down. Cover with foil and bake for 25 minutes, or until the fish flakes easily.

5. HEAT the oil in a medium nonstick skillet over medium-high heat. Add the garlic and cook for 45 seconds, or until starting to brown. Add the tomatoes and cook for 2 to 3 minutes, or until softened. Remove from the heat and stir in the basil and the remaining ⅛ teaspoon salt and ⅛ teaspoon pepper. Serve over the flounder.

PER SERVING 290 calories, 6 g fat, 2 g saturated fat, 43 g protein, 16 g carbohydrates, 5 g fiber, 228 mg calcium, 500 mg sodium

Herb and Crumb–Topped Tilapia

4 SERVINGS

20 MINUTES

1. PREHEAT the oven to 375°F.

2. COAT a small baking pan with cooking spray. Combine the bread crumbs, flaxseed, oregano, garlic, and salt in a small bowl. Drizzle half of the oil over the tilapia. Rub to coat. Sprinkle with the bread crumb mixture. Rub to coat evenly. Place in the prepared baking pan and drizzle with the remaining oil.

3. BAKE for 10 minutes, or until the tilapia is cooked through. Serve with the lemon wedges.

2 tablespoons whole wheat bread crumbs

2 tablespoons ground flaxseed

1 teaspoon dried oregano

$\frac{1}{2}$ teaspoon minced garlic

$\frac{1}{16}$ teaspoon salt

$1\frac{1}{2}$ tablespoons olive oil

4 tilapia fillets (5 ounces each)

4 lemon wedges for garnish

PER SERVING — 190 calories, 7 g fat, 2 g saturated fat, 26 g protein, 4 g carbohydrates, 2 g fiber, 19 mg calcium, 90 mg sodium

Mediterranean Flounder

4 flounder fillets
(4 ounces each)

1 teaspoon dried
oregano

¼ teaspoon salt

½ cucumber,
halved, peeled,
seeded, and
sliced

½ cup rinsed and
drained no-salt-
added canned
chickpeas

3 plum tomatoes,
sliced

⅓ cup (1½ ounces)
crumbled feta
cheese

1 tablespoon
chopped pitted
kalamata olives

6 tablespoons fat-
free, reduced-
sodium chicken
broth or water

4
SERVINGS

25
MINUTES

1. PREHEAT the oven to 350°F. Arrange 4 sheets of foil (12" × 12" each) on a work surface.

2. PLACE 1 fillet in the center of each piece of foil. Season with the oregano and salt. Bring the sides of the foil pieces up slightly to cup each fillet.

3. TOP each fillet with equal amounts of the cucumber, chickpeas, tomatoes, cheese, and olives. Add 1½ table-spoons of the broth or water to each packet. Bring the edges of each piece of foil together and crimp to seal. Place the packets on a baking sheet.

4. BAKE for 15 minutes, or until the fish flakes easily. Check for doneness by opening 1 packet very carefully (steam will be released). To serve, transfer the contents of each packet to a plate.

PER SERVING 190 calories, 5 g fat, 3 g saturated fat, 26 g protein, 9 g carbohydrates, 2 g fiber, 104 mg calcium, 470 mg sodium

Main-Dish Seafood Salad

4 SERVINGS

34 MINUTES

1. COMBINE the vinegar, water, sugar, and ginger in a small saucepan. Bring to a boil over medium-high heat. Reduce the heat to medium and cook for 20 minutes, or until reduced to ¼ cup. Strain into a large bowl. Whisk in the soy sauce and oils. Set aside.

2. COAT a grill rack or broiler pan with cooking spray. Preheat the grill or broiler.

3. THREAD the shrimp and/or scallops onto metal skewers. Season with salt. Place on the prepared rack or pan. Grill or broil for 2 to 3 minutes per side, or until lightly browned and opaque.

4. DIVIDE the greens, pepper, snow peas, and scallions evenly among 4 plates. Drizzle with the vinaigrette. Top with the shrimp and/or scallops, removing from the skewers, if desired.

½ cup rice wine vinegar or white wine vinegar

¼ cup water

1½ tablespoons sugar

1 tablespoon grated fresh ginger

2 teaspoons reduced-sodium soy sauce

2 teaspoons vegetable oil

1½ teaspoons toasted sesame oil

1 pound large peeled and deveined shrimp and/or sea scallops

⅛ teaspoon salt

1 pound mixed greens

1 red bell pepper, cut into strips

1 cup snow peas

4 scallions, thinly sliced on the diagonal

PER SERVING 210 calories, 6 g fat, 1 g saturated fat, 24 g protein, 14 g carbohydrates, 4 g fiber, 126 mg calcium, 370 mg sodium

Seafood and Brown Rice Paella

5 teaspoons olive oil

¾ pound peeled and deveined medium shrimp

¾ pound sea scallops

1 large onion, chopped (about 1½ cups)

4 garlic cloves, minced

¼ teaspoon saffron threads, lightly crushed

1 cup quick-cooking brown rice, such as Uncle Ben's

1 cup fat-free, reduced-sodium chicken broth

1 cup water

1 cup frozen peas

6 pimiento-stuffed manzanilla olives

1 tablespoon drained capers

1 package (9 ounces) frozen artichoke hearts, thawed

1 tomato, chopped (about 1 cup)

2 tablespoons chopped fresh cilantro

6 SERVINGS

50 MINUTES

1. HEAT 2 teaspoons of the oil in a large nonstick skillet over medium-high heat. Add the shrimp and cook, turning once, for 2 to 3 minutes, or until opaque. Transfer to a plate. Heat 1 teaspoon of the remaining oil, add the scallops and cook, turning once, for 3 to 4 minutes, or until opaque. Transfer to the plate with the shrimp. Return the skillet to the stove and heat the remaining 2 teaspoons oil over medium-high heat. Add the onion and garlic. Cook, stirring occasionally, for 2 to 3 minutes, or until the onion begins to soften. Stir in the saffron and cook for 30 seconds. Add the rice and cook, stirring, for 1 minute. Pour in the broth, water, peas, olives, and capers. Bring to a boil, reduce the heat to medium-low, cover, and simmer for 20 minutes, or until the liquid is almost completely absorbed and the rice is tender.

2. INCREASE the heat to medium-high and stir in the artichoke hearts and tomato. Cook, stirring occasionally, for 3 to 4 minutes, or until the tomato begins to wilt. Stir in the shrimp and scallops and cook for 1 to 2 minutes, or until heated through. Remove from the heat and stir in the cilantro.

PER SERVING 270 calories, 7 g fat, 1 g saturated fat, 26 g protein, 26 g carbohydrates, 5 g fiber, 95 mg calcium, 370 mg sodium

Red Snapper
with Fruit Sauce

4
SERVINGS
33
MINUTES

1. COAT a grill rack or broiler pan with cooking spray. Preheat the grill or broiler.

2. PLACE the snapper in a shallow dish. Pour ½ cup of the orange juice over the fillets, turning them to coat. Cover and refrigerate for 15 minutes.

3. COMBINE the nectarines, banana, kiwi, onion, pepper, cilantro, the remaining 2 tablespoons orange juice, the sugar, and salt in a medium bowl. Toss gently to mix.

4. REMOVE the snapper from the orange juice. Discard the juice. Place on the prepared rack or pan. Grill or broil for 4 to 5 minutes per side, or until the fish flakes easily. Serve topped with the nectarine mixture. Sprinkle with the almonds.

4 red snapper fillets (5 ounces each)

½ cup + 2 tablespoons orange juice

2 nectarines, cut into small pieces

1 banana, cut into small pieces

1 kiwifruit, cut into small pieces

½ small red onion, finely chopped

1 serrano or jalapeño chile pepper, seeded and minced (wear plastic gloves when handling)

2 tablespoons chopped fresh cilantro

1 tablespoon packed light brown sugar

⅛ teaspoon salt

¼ cup slivered almonds

PER SERVING — 270 calories, 6 g fat, 1 g saturated fat, 32 g protein, 24 g carbohydrates, 4 g fiber, 82 mg calcium, 170 mg sodium

Grilled Grouper with Chili-Lime Sauce

2 tablespoons trans-free spreadable/tub margarine

Freshly grated zest of 1 lime

1 teaspoon chili powder

¼ teaspoon salt

4 grouper fillets (6 ounces each), each ¾" thick

2 teaspoons chopped fresh cilantro (optional)

4 SERVINGS

25 MINUTES

1. PLACE the margarine, lime zest, chili powder, and salt in a small microwaveable bowl. Microwave on medium power for 1 minute, or until the margarine is melted.

2. COAT a grill rack with cooking spray. Preheat the grill. Brush the fish on both sides with the chili-lime sauce. Sprinkle with the cilantro (if using).

3. PLACE the fish on the rack, rounded side down and grill for 5 to 6 minutes, or until golden. Turn and brush again with the sauce. Cook for 3 to 4 minutes more, or until the flesh is completely opaque but still juicy. Drizzle any remaining sauce evenly over the fish.

PER SERVING 200 calories, 6 g fat, 1 g saturated fat, 33 g protein, 1 g carbohydrates, 0 g fiber, 49 mg calcium, 280 mg sodium

Broiled Orange Roughy with Sun-Dried Tomatoes

4
SERVINGS

18
MINUTES

1. PREHEAT the broiler. Combine the diced tomatoes, broth, nuts, sun-dried tomatoes, and garlic in a 10" skillet. Bring to a boil over medium-high heat. Cook and stir for 3 minutes. Add the parsley and basil. Stir well and remove from the heat.

2. PLACE the orange roughy on a nonstick broiler pan. Sprinkle with the oil, salt, and pepper. Broil 6" from heat source for 3 to 5 minutes, or until the fish is lightly browned and flakes easily when lightly pressed with a fork. Spoon some of the sauce over each portion before serving.

2 cups diced tomatoes

$\frac{1}{4}$ cup fat-free, reduced-sodium chicken broth

$\frac{1}{4}$ cup pine nuts, chopped

4 dry-packed sun-dried tomatoes, chopped

2 garlic cloves, minced

$\frac{1}{4}$ cup chopped fresh parsley

2 tablespoons minced fresh basil

4 orange roughy fillets (4 ounces each)

1 teaspoon olive oil
Dash of salt
Dash of ground black pepper

PER SERVING 190 calories, 8 g fat, 1 g saturated fat, 23 g protein, 9 g carbohydrates, 3 g fiber, mg calcium, 420 mg sodium

South of France Baked Cod

3 onions, chopped (about 1½ cups)

1 green bell pepper, chopped

1 red bell pepper, chopped

¼ cup apple juice

4 tomatoes, chopped (about 4 cups)

4 red potatoes, cubed (about 2 cups)

¼ cup chopped fresh parsley

1 garlic clove, minced

1 tablespoon capers, rinsed

2 teaspoons packed brown sugar

1 teaspoon chopped pitted black olives

4 cod fillets (4 ounces each)

4 SERVINGS

42 MINUTES

1. PREHEAT the oven to 400°F.

2. PLACE a 10" nonstick skillet coated with cooking spray over medium-high heat until hot. Add the onions, peppers, and apple juice. Cook, stirring, for 5 minutes, or until the peppers are soft. Add the tomatoes, potatoes, parsley, and garlic. Cook, stirring occasionally, for 10 minutes, or until the sauce thickens slightly. Add the capers, sugar, and olives. Stir well.

3. SPREAD half of the sauce in the bottom of a 13" × 9" baking dish. Place the cod on top. Cover with the remaining sauce.

4. COVER and bake for 15 minutes, or until the fish is opaque in center. Check by inserting tip of a sharp knife into the center of 1 fillet.

PER SERVING 238 calories, 2 g fat, 0 g saturated fat, 25 g protein, 33 g carbohydrates, 6 g fiber, 75 mg calcium, 153 mg sodium

Haddock Stew with Shallots and Dill

4 SERVINGS

48 MINUTES

1. **HEAT** the oil in a large saucepan over medium-high heat. Add the shallots and cook, stirring occasionally, for 5 minutes, or just until soft. Add the broth, water, potatoes, carrots, celery, mustard, salt, and pepper. Bring to a boil. Reduce the heat to low, cover, and simmer for 15 minutes, or until the vegetables are tender.

2. **ADD** the haddock. Simmer, covered, for 5 minutes, or until the fish is opaque. Stir in the milk, dill, and parsley. Simmer for 3 minutes, or until heated through.

- 1½ tablespoons olive oil
- 5 shallots, thinly sliced
- 1 cup fat-free, reduced-sodium chicken broth
- 1 cup water
- 2 potatoes, cut into ½" cubes
- 2 carrots, thinly sliced
- 2 celery ribs, sliced
- ½ teaspoon dry mustard
- ¼ teaspoon salt
- ¼ teaspoon ground black pepper
- 1 pound skinless haddock fillet, cut into 2" pieces
- 1 cup 1% milk
- ¼ cup finely chopped fresh dill
- 2 tablespoons minced fresh parsley

PER SERVING 280 calories, 7 g fat, 2 g saturated fat, 28 g protein, 27 g carbohydrates, 3 g fiber, 164 mg calcium, 320 mg sodium

Seared Salmon with Mango Salsa

Salsa

- 1 ripe mango, peeled and cut into small cubes (about 1½ cups)
- ½ red bell pepper, chopped (about ¾ cup)
- ½ red onion, chopped (about ¾ cup)
- 3 tablespoons freshly squeezed lime juice
- 2 tablespoons chopped fresh mint
- 1 tablespoon finely chopped jalapeño chile pepper (wear plastic gloves when handling)
- ¼ teaspoon salt

Salmon

- Juice of 1 lemon (about ¼ cup)
- ½ teaspoon paprika
- Freshly ground black pepper
- 6 salmon fillets (4 ounces each)
- 2 teaspoons olive oil

6 SERVINGS

1 HOUR 25 MINUTES

1. **TO PREPARE THE SALSA:** Toss together the mango, bell pepper, onion, lime juice, mint, chile pepper, salt, and black pepper in a small bowl. Cover and chill for at least 1 hour to blend the flavors.

2. **TO PREPARE THE SALMON:** Combine the lemon juice and paprika in a large shallow baking dish. Season with black pepper. Place the salmon in the dish and flip to cover both sides. Marinate, covered, for up to 1 hour in the refrigerator.

3. **REMOVE** the fillets from the marinade. Discard the marinade. Heat the oil in a large nonstick skillet over medium-high heat. Sear the fillets for 15 minutes, turning once, or until just opaque. Serve with the salsa.

PER SERVING 270 calories, 14 g fat, 3 g saturated fat, 23 g protein, 12 g carbohydrates, 2 g fiber, 268 mg calcium, 170 mg sodium

Salmon and Onions Baked in Foil

4 SERVINGS

30 MINUTES

1. **PREHEAT** the oven to 400°F.

2. **COAT** a 10" nonstick skillet with cooking spray. Add the wine and bring to a boil over medium-high heat. Add the onions, bell pepper, garlic, thyme, and sage. Cook, stirring, for 10 to 12 minutes, or until the onions are very soft.

3. **PLACE** four 12" × 12" pieces of foil on a work surface. Place 1 fillet on each piece of foil. Divide the vegetables evenly over the fillets. Sprinkle with the salt and pepper. Fold the sides of the foil over the fish to create sealed packets. Place the packets on a large baking sheet.

4. **BAKE** for 10 to 12 minutes, or until the fish is opaque in the center. Check by carefully opening 1 packet and inserting the tip of a sharp knife into 1 fillet.

$\frac{1}{4}$ cup white wine or nonalcoholic white wine

2 onions, sliced (about 2 cups)

1 green or red bell pepper, chopped (about 1 cup)

3 garlic cloves, minced

$\frac{1}{2}$ teaspoon dried thyme

$\frac{1}{8}$ teaspoon dried sage

4 salmon fillets (4 ounces each)

$\frac{1}{4}$ teaspoon salt

$\frac{1}{4}$ teaspoon ground black pepper

PER SERVING 264 calories, 13 g fat, 3 g saturated fat, 24 g protein, 11 g carbohydrates, 2 g fiber, 46 mg calcium, 218 mg sodium

Seafood Kebabs

¼ cup apple juice
1 tablespoon hoisin sauce
1 tablespoon reduced-sodium soy sauce
1 teaspoon sugar
1 teaspoon cider vinegar
1 cup broccoli florets
1 cup frozen pearl onions
1 small red bell pepper, cut into 1" cubes
4 ounces halibut steak, cut into 1" cubes
4 ounces uncooked peeled medium shrimp
4 scallops, quartered

4
SERVINGS

46
MINUTES

1. COMBINE the apple juice, hoisin sauce, soy sauce, sugar, and vinegar in a small bowl. Mix well.

2. THREAD the broccoli, onions, pepper, halibut, shrimp, and scallops alternately onto four 12" metal skewers. Place the skewers in a 13" × 9" baking dish. Drizzle with the apple-juice mixture. Cover and refrigerate for 30 minutes, brushing frequently with the marinade.

3. PREHEAT the broiler. Broil the kebabs 4" from the heat, basting frequently with the marinade, for 3 minutes, or until brown. Turn and broil for 3 minutes, or until the halibut and shrimp are opaque in the center. Check by inserting the tip of a sharp knife into 1 cube of the halibut and 1 shrimp.

PER SERVING 136 calories, 2 g fat, 0 g saturated fat, 16 g protein, 15 g carbohydrates, 1 g fiber, 52 mg calcium, 310 mg sodium

Shrimp-and-Crab Cakes

4 SERVINGS

29 MINUTES

1. **TOAST** the bread and allow to cool. Crumble into fine crumbs and set aside.

2. **COMBINE** the egg white, mayonnaise, and seasoning blend in a large bowl. Whisk to blend. Add the shrimp, crabmeat, celery, scallions, flaxseed, parsley, and one-third of the reserved bread crumbs. Toss to mix.

3. **SHAPE** into 8 cakes, each about ½" thick. Spread the remaining bread crumbs on a shallow plate. Dip the cakes into the crumbs, pressing lightly to adhere.

4. **COAT** a large nonstick skillet with cooking spray. Place the cakes in the skillet. Cook over medium heat for 2 to 3 minutes, or until lightly browned on the bottom. Remove the pan from the heat and coat the cakes lightly with cooking spray. Return the pan to the heat. Carefully turn the cakes. Cook for 2 minutes, or until lightly browned on the bottom. Turn the cakes 2 more times, coating with cooking spray each time. Cook for 2 minutes longer per side, or until cooked through.

- 2 slices white bread
- 1 egg white
- 2 tablespoons reduced-fat mayonnaise
- 1½ teaspoons sodium-free seasoning blend
- ½ pound peeled and deveined large shrimp, finely chopped
- ½ pound lump crabmeat, picked over for shells and flaked
- 1 celery rib, finely chopped
- 3 scallions, white parts only, chopped
- 1 tablespoon ground flaxseed
- 2 tablespoons chopped fresh parsley

PER SERVING 220 calories, 5 g fat, 1 g saturated fat, 26 g protein, 15 g carbohydrates, 2 g fiber, 123 mg calcium, 480 mg sodium

Mexican Lasagna

1 pound lean ground beef (95% lean or greater)

1 jar (24 ounces) salsa

5 to 6 corn tortillas (8" diameter)

2 cups fat-free sour cream

9 ounces (2¼ cups) shredded reduced-fat Cheddar/Jack cheese combo or shredded reduced-fat Cheddar cheese

1 bag (10 ounces) frozen corn kernels

10 SERVINGS

1 HOUR

10 MINUTES

1. PREHEAT the oven to 375°F. Coat a 13" × 9" (3-quart) baking dish with cooking spray.

2. SET a large nonstick skillet over medium heat. Add the ground beef and cook, stirring frequently, for 8 minutes, or until the meat is browned and cooked through. Drain any excess fat and discard it. Stir in the salsa.

3. SPOON enough of the meat mixture into the prepared baking dish to cover the bottom. Arrange about 1¾ tortillas on top, cutting or tearing to fit properly. Top with one-third of the sour cream, ¾ cup of the cheese, half of the remaining meat mixture, and half of the corn. Repeat layers with 1¾ tortillas, one-third of the sour cream, ¾ cup of the cheese, the remaining meat mixture, and the corn. Repeat the layers with 1¾ tortillas, the remaining sour cream, and the remaining ¾ cup cheese. Cover with aluminum foil.

4. BAKE for 40 minutes, or until bubbling. Remove and let rest for 10 minutes before serving.

PER SERVING 298 calories, 10 g fat, 5 g saturated fat, 20 g protein, 35 g carbohydrates, 2 g fiber, 441 mg calcium, 831 mg sodium

Pasta Fagioli

6 SERVINGS

39 MINUTES

1. **HEAT** a large saucepan over medium-high heat. Add the bacon and cook for 5 to 6 minutes, or until just starting to brown. Add the onion, garlic, celery, and carrots, and cook for 2 to 3 minutes, or until just starting to soften.

2. **POUR** in the broth, tomatoes, pasta, and beans. Cover and bring to a boil. Uncover and cook for 12 to 15 minutes, or until the rotini is tender. Remove from the heat and stir in the parsley, basil, and pepper.

2 slices center-cut (30% less fat) bacon, chopped

1 onion, chopped (about 1 cup)

4 garlic cloves, minced

3 celery ribs, chopped (about ¾ cup)

2 carrots, chopped (about ½ cup)

4 cups fat-free, reduced-sodium chicken broth

1 can (14.5 ounces) no-salt-added diced tomatoes

6 ounces whole wheat blend rotini (such as Ronzoni Healthy Harvest)

1 can (15 ounces) dark-red kidney beans, rinsed and drained

¼ cup chopped fresh parsley

¼ cup chopped fresh basil

⅛ teaspoon ground black pepper

PER SERVING 202 calories, 3 g fat, 1 g saturated fat, 10 g protein, 33 g carbohydrates, 8 g fiber, 74 mg calcium, 503 mg sodium

Vegetable and Barley Ragout

1 tablespoon olive oil

½ onion, chopped (about ½ cup)

8 ounces baby portobello or cremini mushrooms, halved

1 sweet potato, cut into 1" chunks

1½ teaspoons minced fresh rosemary

½ teaspoon dried thyme

½ teaspoon salt

¼ cup dry red wine (optional)

1 cup vegetable broth or water

½ cup quick-cooking barley

8 ounces broccoli florets, cut into marble-size pieces

¼ teaspoon ground black pepper

4 SERVINGS

45 MINUTES

1. **HEAT** the oil in a large pot over medium-high heat. Add the onion, mushrooms, sweet potato, rosemary, thyme, and salt. Stir to mix. Cover and cook, stirring occasionally, for 5 minutes, or until the mushrooms shrink and are glazed. Add the wine, if using. Cook for 4 minutes, or until the liquid evaporates.

2. **ADD** the broth or water and barley. Cover and reduce the heat to medium-low. Simmer for 10 minutes, or until the barley is tender.

3. **PLACE** broccoli in a medium skillet with enough water to come ½" up the pan sides. Cover and cook over high heat for 2 to 3 minutes, or until the broccoli is crisp-tender. Drain and stir into the stew. Add the pepper. Cover and let stand for 5 minutes for the flavors to blend.

PER SERVING 209 calories, 5 g fat, 1 g saturated fat, 7 g protein, 34 g carbohydrates, 8 g fiber, 64 mg calcium, 440 mg sodium

Creamy Mac and Three Cheeses

9
SERVINGS

1
HOUR

1. **PREHEAT** the oven to 350°F. Coat a 13" × 9" (3-quart) baking dish with cooking spray.

2. **COOK** the macaroni according to package directions. Drain and rinse. Return to the pot and set aside.

3. **POUR** the oil into a medium saucepan over medium heat. When the oil is hot, whisk in the flour. Cook, whisking, for 1 minute, or until the flour is dissolved. Whisk in the milk. Simmer, whisking occasionally, for 5 minutes, or until thickened. Add the American and Cheddar. Cook, whisking, until the cheese melts and the sauce is smooth. Add the hot sauce, if using. Pour the mixture over the macaroni. Stir to mix. Pour into the prepared dish. Combine the bread crumbs and Parmesan in a small bowl. Sprinkle on top of the mixture. Cover the dish with a lid or foil.

4. **BAKE** for 15 minutes. Remove the cover or foil. Bake for 15 minutes, or until bubbly and golden.

1 pound whole wheat elbow macaroni

$\frac{1}{4}$ cup canola oil

$\frac{1}{4}$ cup flour

1 cup fat-free milk

1 cup (4 ounces) shredded or chopped reduced-fat American cheese

1 cup (4 ounces) shredded or chopped reduced-fat Cheddar cheese

$\frac{1}{4}$ teaspoon hot sauce (optional)

$\frac{1}{4}$ cup panko bread crumbs

2 tablespoons ($\frac{1}{2}$ ounce) grated Parmesan cheese

PER SERVING 325 calories, 11 g fat, 3 g saturated fat, 16 g protein, 45 g carbohydrates, 4 g fiber, 347 mg calcium, 272 mg sodium

Creamy Peanut Noodles

12 ounces whole wheat spaghetti

½ cup creamy natural peanut butter

½ cup fat-free evaporated milk

3 tablespoons reduced-sodium soy sauce

1 teaspoon toasted sesame oil

1 small cucumber, thinly sliced (about 1 cup)

1 large carrot, shredded (about 1 cup)

18 sugar snap peas

6 SERVINGS

23 MINUTES

1. COOK the pasta according to package directions, omitting salt.

2. COMBINE the peanut butter, milk, soy sauce, and oil in a large bowl. Using an immersion mixer, blend until smooth. (Mixture may also be processed in a blender.)

3. DRAIN the pasta. Rinse under cool running water to stop the cooking. Add to the peanut butter mixture. Toss until evenly coated.

4. DIVIDE into 6 bowls. Top with the cucumber, carrot, and sugar snap peas.

PER SERVING 379 calories, 12 g fat, 2 g saturated fat, 16 g protein, 54 g carbohydrates, 10 g fiber, 95 mg calcium, 429 mg sodium

Cuban Black Beans

4 SERVINGS

30 MINUTES

1. **COMBINE** the oil, onion, pepper, garlic, bay leaves, cumin, oregano, and salt in a large pot. Cook over medium heat, stirring occasionally, for 4 minutes, or until softened. Stir in the beans. Cook for 1 minute to coat with the seasonings. Add the broth. Reduce the heat to medium-low. Cover and cook, stirring occasionally, for 15 minutes for the flavors to blend.

2. **COMBINE** the water and rice in a small saucepan. Cover and set over medium-high heat for 3 minutes, or until the water boils. Reduce the heat so the mixture simmers. Cook for 10 to 12 minutes, or until the water is absorbed.

3. **REMOVE** and discard the bay leaves from the beans. Stir in the hot-pepper sauce. If desired, smash some of the beans with the side of a large spoon. Fluff the rice with a fork. Serve the beans over the rice.

- 2 tablespoons olive oil
- 1 onion, chopped (about 1 cup)
- 1 green bell pepper, chopped (about 1 cup)
- 2 large garlic cloves, minced
- 2 bay leaves
- 1½ teaspoons ground cumin
- 1 teaspoon dried oregano
- ¼ teaspoon salt
- 1½ cans (15–19 ounces each) black beans, rinsed and drained (about 3 cups)
- 1 cup fat-free, reduced-sodium chicken or vegetable broth
- 1 cup water
- ½ cup instant brown rice, such as Uncle Ben's
- ½ teaspoon hot-pepper sauce

PER SERVING 411 calories, 10 g fat, 1 g saturated fat, 17 g protein, 64 g carbohydrates, 14 g fiber, 61 mg calcium, 180 mg sodium

Chunky Vegetable Shepherd's Pie

3 pounds sweet potatoes, peeled and cut into large chunks

1 tablespoon olive oil

1 large onion, coarsely chopped

3 carrots, sliced

1 large celery rib, sliced

8 ounces cremini mushrooms, halved

2 large garlic cloves, minced

1 teaspoon seasoning blend (such as Mrs. Dash Original Blend)

1 can (15–19 ounces) cannellini beans, rinsed and drained

1 box (9 ounces) frozen Italian green beans

1 can (14 ounces) vegetable broth

3 tablespoons whole wheat pastry flour

½ cup cold water

4 plum tomatoes, cut into ¾" pieces

8 SERVINGS

1 HOUR

40 MINUTES

1. PLACE the potatoes in a soup pot or Dutch oven and cover with cold water. Bring to a boil. Cover the pot, reduce the heat, and simmer for 15 to 20 minutes, or until tender. Drain in a colander and set aside.

2. PREHEAT the oven to 375°F.

3. HEAT the oil over medium heat in the same pot. Add the onion, carrots, and celery. Cook, stirring occasionally, for 5 minutes, or until the onion softens. Stir in the mushrooms, garlic, and seasoning blend. Cook, stirring frequently, for 5 minutes, or until the mushrooms soften. Add the cannellini beans, green beans, and broth. Bring to a boil. Whisk ½ cup cold water and flour in a small bowl until smooth, then stir into the vegetables. Reduce the heat and simmer for 3 minutes. Stir in the tomatoes. Pour into a 13" × 9" baking dish.

4. MASH the sweet potatoes in the same pot. Spoon around the edge of the baking dish. Bake for 35 minutes, or until bubbly in the center. Let stand for 5 minutes before serving.

PER SERVING 270 calories, 3 g fat, 0 g saturated fat, 8 g protein, 54 g carbohydrates, 10 g fiber, 114 mg calcium, 180 mg sodium

Fettuccine Alfredo Pizza

8 SERVINGS

39 MINUTES

1. **PREHEAT** the oven to 450°F. Coat a large round pizza pan with cooking spray. Sprinkle with the cornmeal.

2. **BRING** a medium saucepan of water to a boil. Add the fettuccine and stir. Cook according to package directions until al dente. Drain and rinse with cold running water. Set aside.

3. **PLACE** a medium saucepan coated with cooking spray over medium heat. Add the onion and garlic. Cook, stirring often, for 3 minutes, or until soft.

4. **WHISK** milk and flour in a small bowl until well blended. Add to the pan with the onion. Cook, whisking often, for 4 minutes, or until thickened. Remove from the heat. Add the basil, salt, and nutmeg. Add the fettuccine. Toss to coat.

5. **TURN** the dough out onto a lightly floured work surface. Roll into a 12" circle. Place on the prepared pan. Spread evenly with the fettuccine mixture, leaving a ¼" border. Sprinkle with the mozzarella and Parmesan.

6. **BAKE** for 10 to 12 minutes, or until the crust is golden brown.

- 1 tablespoon cornmeal
- 4 ounces fettuccine
- 1 small onion, chopped
- 2 garlic cloves, finely chopped
- 1 cup 1% milk
- 1 tablespoon unbleached or all-purpose flour
- 3 tablespoons chopped fresh basil
- ¼ teaspoon salt
- ¼ teaspoon ground nutmeg
- 1 tube (10 ounces) refrigerated pizza dough
- ¾ cup (3 ounces) shredded low-fat mozzarella cheese
- ½ cup (2 ounces) grated Parmesan cheese

PER SERVING 243 calories, 5 g fat, 3 g saturated fat, 12 g protein, 37 g carbohydrates, 2 g fiber, 280 mg calcium, 419 mg sodium

Skinny Pasta Primavera

2/3 cup reduced-fat ricotta cheese

1 cup vegetable broth

1 tablespoon olive oil

1 small onion, finely chopped

4 ounces white button mushrooms, sliced

1/2 pound plum tomatoes, chopped

2 large garlic cloves, minced

1/4 teaspoon salt

1/4 teaspoon ground black pepper

1/2 pound multigrain spaghetti

3 cups small broccoli florets

1 carrot, cut into matchsticks

1/4 pound asparagus, cut into 1" pieces

3/4 cup frozen, shelled green soybeans (edamame), thawed

1/2 cup fresh basil, thinly sliced

1/3 cup (1 1/2 ounces) grated Parmesan cheese

4 SERVINGS

40 MINUTES

1. **COMBINE** ricotta and broth in a food processor. Process until smooth. Set aside. Bring a large pot of water to a boil.

2. **HEAT** the oil in a large nonstick skillet over medium-high heat. Add the onion and mushrooms. Cook, stirring frequently, for 3 minutes, or until the mushrooms begin to brown. Reduce the heat to medium. Stir in the tomatoes, garlic, salt, and pepper. Cook for 2 minutes, or until the tomatoes begin to soften. Reduce the heat to very low and cover to keep warm.

3. **COOK** the pasta according to package directions. Two minutes before the pasta is finished cooking, add the broccoli, carrot, asparagus, and soybeans. Drain.

4. **RETURN** the hot pasta and vegetables to the pot. Add the basil, reserved mushroom mixture, and reserved ricotta. Toss to combine. Serve sprinkled with the Parmesan.

PER SERVING 401 calories, 9 g fat, 3 g saturated fat, 21 g protein, 62 g carbohydrates, 12 g fiber, 246 mg calcium, 423 mg sodium

Chickpea Skillet Supper

4 SERVINGS

1 HOUR

6 MINUTES

1. **PLACE** a 10" nonstick skillet coated with cooking spray over medium-high heat until hot. Add the oil, onions, carrots, broccoli, cauliflower, and garlic. Cook, stirring, for 3 minutes, or until the broccoli is bright-green. Add the chickpeas, beans, apple juice, curry powder, and celery seeds. Bring to a boil. Cover and cook for 35 minutes, or until thick.

2. **COOK** the rice according to package directions. Add to the skillet. Top with the cheese.

1 teaspoon olive oil

2 onions, chopped

2 carrots, sliced

1 cup broccoli florets

1 cup cauliflower florets

3 large garlic cloves, minced

1½ cans (15–19 ounces) chickpeas, rinsed and drained (about 3 cups)

1 cup rinsed and drained canned navy beans

¾ cup apple juice

¾ teaspoon curry powder

½ teaspoon celery seeds

1 cup long-grain white rice

⅓ cup (1½ ounces) grated Parmesan cheese

PER SERVING 561 calories, 7 g fat, 2 g saturated fat, 23 g protein, 102 g carbohydrates, 19 g fiber, 232 mg calcium, 178 mg sodium

Italian Vegetable Stir-Fry over Polenta

Polenta

- 4 cups water
- ¼ teaspoon salt
- 1 cup yellow cornmeal
- ½ cup (2 ounces) grated Parmesan cheese

Stir-Fry

- 1 tablespoon olive oil
- 1 red onion, thinly sliced
- 1 red bell pepper, thinly sliced
- 1 small fennel bulb, trimmed, quartered, cored, and thinly sliced
- 1 large zucchini, halved lengthwise and thinly sliced
- 1 can (15–19 ounces) chickpeas, rinsed and drained
- 1 large garlic clove, minced
- ¼ teaspoon red-pepper flakes
- ¼ teaspoon salt
- 2 large tomatoes, coarsely chopped
- ¼ cup chopped fresh basil

6 SERVINGS

55 MINUTES

1. TO MAKE THE POLENTA: Bring the water and salt to a boil in a large saucepan. Slowly whisk in the cornmeal. Reduce the heat to low. Cover and simmer, stirring frequently, for 30 to 35 minutes, or until the polenta thickens. Stir in the cheese. Cover and keep warm.

2. TO MAKE THE STIR-FRY: Heat the oil in a large nonstick skillet over medium-high heat. Add the onion, bell pepper, and fennel. Cook, stirring frequently, for 2 to 3 minutes, or until the vegetables begin to soften. Add the zucchini, chickpeas, garlic, red-pepper flakes, and salt. Cook, stirring constantly, for 2 to 3 minutes, or until the vegetables are crisp-tender. Add the tomatoes. Cook, stirring frequently, for 1 minute, or until the tomatoes soften. Stir in the basil. Serve over the polenta.

PER SERVING 224 calories, 7 g fat, 2 g saturated fat, 9 g protein, 34 g carbohydrates, 7 g fiber, 135 mg calcium, 312 mg sodium

Stuffed Spaghetti Squash

4 SERVINGS

1 HOUR

15 MINUTES

1. PLACE the squash halves cut side down on a microwave-safe plate. Microwave on high power for 10 to 12 minutes, or until the squash is easily pierced with a fork. Cool until easy to handle. Spoon out and discard the seeds. Separate the flesh into strands with a fork and place in a large bowl. Reserve the squash shells.

2. PREHEAT the oven to 350°F.

3. HEAT the oil in a large nonstick skillet over medium heat. Add the pepper, peas, scallions, garlic, oregano, and mint. Cook, stirring frequently, for 5 minutes, or until the vegetables are tender. Stir in the tomato juice and bring to a boil. Stir in the couscous. Cover, remove from the heat, and let stand for 5 minutes, or until soft. Fluff with a fork.

4. ADD the couscous mixture and cheese to the bowl with the squash. Toss to mix well. Divide among the reserved squash shells. Cover each shell with foil, place in a 13" × 9" nonstick baking dish, and bake for 15 to 20 minutes, or until heated through.

2 small spaghetti squash, halved lengthwise

1 tablespoon olive oil

1 large red bell pepper, chopped

1 cup frozen peas

8 scallions, chopped

2 garlic cloves, minced

1 teaspoon dried oregano

1 teaspoon dried mint

1½ cups tomato juice

1 cup couscous

1 cup (4 ounces) crumbled feta cheese

PER SERVING 272 calories, 7 g fat, 3 g saturated fat, 10 g protein, 44 g carbohydrates, 7 g fiber, 168 mg calcium, 417 mg sodium

Chapter

9

DESSERTS

Ginger–Sweet Potato Cheesecake

| 16 SERVINGS |
| 4 HOURS |
| 25 MINUTES |

1. **PREHEAT** the oven to 350°F. Coat a 9" spring-form pan with cooking spray.

2. **COMBINE** the potatoes in a large saucepan over high heat with enough cold water to cover by 2". Bring to a boil. Cook for 12 to 15 minutes, or until the potatoes are tender. Drain and mash. Cool. Meanwhile, bring 1 cup of water to a boil in a small saucepan over high heat. Remove from the heat, add the apricots, and let stand for 10 minutes before draining.

3. **COMBINE** the cookies and cereal in the bowl of a food processor and process until finely ground. Transfer to a bowl and add the margarine. Mix well. Firmly press mixture into the bottom and 1" up the sides of the prepared pan. Bake for 10 minutes, or until crisped, then cool on a wire rack. Reduce the oven temperature to 325°F.

4. **PLACE** the cooled mashed sweet potatoes and the cheeses in the bowl of an electric mixer. Beat on high speed for 1 to 2 minutes, or until smooth. Add the yogurt, egg whites, sugar, flour, pumpkin pie spice, vanilla extract, and salt and beat well. Sprinkle the apricots over the bottom of the prepared crust. Pour the potato mixture over the apricots. Bake for 42 to 45 minutes, or until the cheesecake is almost set. Turn the oven off and let the cheesecake stand for 1 hour. Remove from the oven and allow to cool to room temperature. Cover with plastic wrap and chill for at least 3 hours before serving. Scatter the ginger on top.

2 sweet potatoes, peeled and cut into 1" pieces

1 cup dried apricots, chopped

15 gingersnap cookies

3/4 cup high-fiber cereal, such as Fiber One

2 tablespoons trans-free spreadable/tub margarine, melted

8 ounces fat-free cream cheese, softened

8 ounces Neufchâtel cheese, softened

1 cup fat-free plain yogurt

3 egg whites

2/3 cup packed light brown sugar

1 tablespoon whole wheat flour

2 teaspoons pumpkin pie spice

2 teaspoons vanilla extract

1/8 teaspoon salt

3 tablespoons slivered crystallized ginger

PER SERVING 160 calories, 5 g fat, 3 g saturated fat, 6 g protein, 24 g carbohydrates, 2 g fiber, 88 mg calcium, 240 mg sodium

Banana Snack Cake

1 cup whole wheat pastry flour

½ teaspoon baking soda

½ teaspoon baking powder

Dash of salt

1 egg, separated

2 egg whites

½ cup granulated sugar

¼ cup canola oil

½ cup mashed ripe banana

¼ cup low-fat buttermilk

2 teaspoons confectioners' sugar

2 teaspoons unsweetened cocoa powder

9 SERVINGS

55 MINUTES

1. PREHEAT the oven to 350°F. Coat an 8" × 8" baking pan with cooking spray. Dust with flour. Set aside.

2. COMBINE the flour, baking soda, baking powder, and salt on a sheet of waxed paper or in a bowl. Whisk to combine. Set aside.

3. PLACE the 3 egg whites in the bowl of an electric mixer. Beat on high speed for 2 minutes, or until foamy. Continue beating, while adding 2 tablespoons of the granulated sugar, for 1 minute, or until the whites hold their peaks. Set aside.

4. COMBINE the oil and remaining granulated sugar in a clean mixing bowl using a spoon or spatula. Beat until smooth. One at a time, beat in the egg yolk, banana, and buttermilk, mixing well. Gradually add the reserved dry ingredients. Stir a large spoonful of the reserved egg whites into the batter. Fold in the remaining whites. Pour the batter into the prepared pan. Spread the top evenly.

5. BAKE for 30 to 35 minutes, or until golden and the cake starts to come away from sides of the pan. Allow to cool in the pan on a rack 5 minutes. Turn onto the rack to cool completely.

6. COMBINE the confectioners' sugar and cocoa in a small bowl. Place in a small sieve and sift over the cake.

PER SERVING 164 calories, 7 g fat, 1 g saturated fat, 3 g protein, 23 g carbohydrates, 2 g fiber, 33 mg calcium, 136 mg sodium

Iced Lemon Cupcakes

12 SERVINGS (1 CUPCAKE PER SERVING)

30 MINUTES

1. PREHEAT the oven to 350°F. Line a 12-cup muffin pan with paper liners. Lightly coat the inside of the liners with cooking spray.

2. COMBINE the flours, baking powder, baking soda, and salt in a mixing bowl. Stir to blend. Set aside.

3. BEAT ⅓ cup margarine in the bowl of an electric mixer for 1 minute, or until smooth. Add ½ cup of the sugar and the lemon zest. Beat for 30 seconds, or until smooth. Add the eggs, one at a time, beating after each addition. Add the yogurt and lemon extract. Mix on low speed to blend. Gradually add the reserved dry ingredients, mixing on low speed to blend. Dollop the batter into the prepared cups.

4. BAKE for 15 minutes, or until the cupcakes are lightly browned and spring back when pressed. Remove to a rack to cool completely.

5. COMBINE the remaining ½ cup sugar, 2 teaspoons margarine, and 2 teaspoons lemon juice in a small bowl. Whisk until smooth. Add up to 1 teaspoon more lemon juice if needed to make a spreadable consistency. Spread over the cupcakes.

¾ cup all-purpose flour

⅓ cup fat-free soy flour

¾ teaspoon baking powder

½ teaspoon baking soda

Pinch of salt

⅓ cup + 2 teaspoons trans-free spreadable/tub margarine, at room temperature

1 cup confectioners' sugar

1½ teaspoons freshly grated lemon zest

2 eggs

½ cup fat-free plain yogurt

½ teaspoon lemon extract

3 teaspoons freshly squeezed lemon juice

PER SERVING 130 calories, 5 g fat, 2 g saturated fat, 4 g protein, 18 g carbohydrates, 1 g fiber, 40 mg calcium, 150 mg sodium

Blueberry Cheese Blintzes

- ²/₃ cup fat-free milk
- ¹/₃ cup whole wheat pastry flour
- ¹/₄ cup liquid egg substitute
- ¹/₂ teaspoon baking powder
- 1¹/₂ cups low-fat sour cream
- 2 tablespoons honey
- 1 tablespoon freshly grated orange zest
- ¹/₄ teaspoon ground cinnamon
- 1 teaspoon canola oil
- 2 cups fresh or frozen and thawed blueberries
- 1 cup applesauce

8 SERVINGS

25 MINUTES

1. **COMBINE** the milk, flour, egg substitute, and baking powder in a blender. Blend until smooth, scraping down the sides of the container as needed.

2. **PLACE** a small nonstick skillet coated with cooking spray over medium-high heat. Ladle in about 3 tablespoons of the batter and swirl it around to coat the bottom of the pan.

3. **COOK** the blintz for 1 minute, or until the top is dry and the bottom is lightly browned. Flip onto a rack or tea towel by turning the pan upside down. Continue making blintzes with the remaining batter. You should have 8.

4. **MIX** 1 cup of the sour cream, the honey, orange zest, and cinnamon in a small bowl.

5. **SPOON** 1 rounded tablespoon of the filling onto the middle of each blintz. Fold the bottom of the blintz over the filling, then fold in the sides. Finish by rolling the whole thing into a little pouch.

6. **PLACE** a large nonstick skillet coated with cooking spray over medium heat until hot. Add the oil and cook the blintzes for a few minutes on each side to lightly brown.

7. **SERVE** topped with the blueberries, applesauce, and the remaining ¹/₂ cup sour cream.

PER SERVING 145 calories, 7 g fat, 4 g saturated fat, 4 g protein, 19 g carbohydrates, 2 g fiber, 101 mg calcium, 73 mg sodium

Strawberry Meringue Tart

8
SERVINGS

55
MINUTES

1. PREHEAT the oven to 300°F. Line a baking sheet with parchment paper or foil and coat lightly with cooking spray.

2. MIX the cornstarch, almonds, and ¼ cup of the sugar in a small bowl.

3. PLACE the egg whites, cream of tartar, and salt in a large bowl. Beat until soft peaks form, using an electric mixer on medium speed. Slowly add the remaining ½ cup sugar and beat until stiff, glossy peaks form, with the mixer at medium-high speed. Beat in the vanilla extract. Gently fold in the almond mixture.

4. SPREAD enough of the egg white mixture on the baking sheet to form an 8" or 9" circle about ¾" thick, using a large spoon. Drop spoonfuls of the remaining whites around the edge to form a border about 1" high. (Or use a pastry bag fitted with a large rosette tip to pipe a fancier border.)

5. BAKE on the bottom rack of the oven for 30 minutes, or until light tan and crisp. Cool on a rack for 5 minutes. Carefully peel off the paper or foil.

6. PLACE the shell on a serving plate. Fill with the strawberries.

7. PLACE the preserves and water in a small saucepan. Melt over low heat. Lightly glaze the strawberries with melted preserves, using a pastry brush. Serve the tart at room temperature.

¼ cup cornstarch
¼ cup finely ground blanched almonds
¾ cup sugar
3 large egg whites, at room temperature
⅛ teaspoon cream of tartar
Pinch of salt
1 teaspoon vanilla extract
1½ pints fresh strawberries, hulled and halved
2 tablespoons seedless raspberry all-fruit preserves
2 teaspoons water

PER SERVING 151 calories, 3 g fat, 0 g saturated fat, 3 g protein, 30 g carbohydrates, 2 g fiber, 20 mg calcium, 41 mg sodium

Chocolate Pudding Cake

2/3 cup unsweetened cocoa powder

2 ounces semisweet chocolate, chopped, or semisweet chocolate chips

2 tablespoons unsalted butter

2 tablespoons canola oil

3/4 cup granulated sugar

1/3 cup packed light brown sugar

1/2 cup all-purpose flour

1/4 cup whole wheat pastry flour or whole wheat flour

2 teaspoons baking powder

1/3 cup fat-free milk

1 tablespoon vanilla extract

1/4 teaspoon salt

1 egg yolk

1 1/2 cups brewed coffee, cooled

9 SERVINGS

1 HOUR

15 MINUTES

1. **PREHEAT** the oven to 400°F. Coat an 8" × 8" baking dish with cooking spray.

2. **COMBINE** 1/3 cup of the cocoa, the semisweet chocolate, butter, and oil in a microwaveable bowl. Cook on high power, stirring often, for 1 to 3 minutes, or until smooth. Set aside.

3. **COMBINE** 1/4 cup of the granulated sugar, the brown sugar, and the remaining 1/3 cup cocoa in a small bowl until well mixed with no lumps. Set aside.

4. **COMBINE** the flours and baking powder in a medium bowl. Set aside.

5. **COMBINE** the milk, vanilla extract, salt, and remaining 1/2 cup granulated sugar in a large bowl. Whisk until smooth. Whisk in the egg yolk and then the reserved melted chocolate mixture until well combined. Stir in the reserved flour mixture until well mixed. Pour the batter into the prepared baking dish. Sprinkle the reserved brown sugar mixture evenly over the batter. Pour the coffee gently over the brown sugar mixture.

6. **BAKE** for about 40 minutes, or until bubbly and the cake just starts to pull away from the edge of dish. Remove to a rack to cool for 20 to 30 minutes. Serve warm.

PER SERVING 227 calories, 9 g fat, 3 g saturated fat, 3 g protein, 36 g carbohydrates, 2 g fiber, 85 mg calcium, 182 mg sodium

Raspberry Brownies

15
SERVINGS
(1 BROWNIE
PER
SERVING)

40
MINUTES

1. **PREHEAT** the oven to 325°F. Coat a 13" × 9" baking pan with cooking spray.

2. **HEAT** the fruit spread in a small saucepan over low heat, stirring constantly, for 1 to 2 minutes, or until thin enough to pour. Set aside.

3. **COMBINE** the brownie mix, yogurt, vanilla extract, and the amount of water called for on the mix box in a large bowl. Stir by hand until well combined. Pour into the prepared pan. Drop teaspoonfuls of the fruit spread on top of the batter. Swirl the spread through the batter with a butter knife, making a marbleized effect.

4. **BAKE** for 25 to 30 minutes, or until a toothpick inserted 2" from the edge of the pan comes out clean or almost clean. Remove and allow to cool. Cut into 15 brownies.

$\frac{1}{3}$ cup all-fruit seedless raspberry spread

1 box (18–21 ounces) brownie mix

$\frac{1}{2}$ cup fat-free plain or vanilla yogurt

Water

1 teaspoon vanilla extract

PER SERVING 195 calories, 6 g fat, 1 g saturated fat, 2 g protein, 35 g carbohydrates, 1 g fiber, 18 mg calcium, 128 mg sodium

Peanut Butter Sandies

1¾ cups whole wheat pastry flour

½ cup confectioners' sugar

2 tablespoons cornstarch

1½ teaspoons baking powder

½ teaspoon baking soda

¼ teaspoon salt

½ cup packed light brown sugar

⅓ cup reduced-fat chunky peanut butter

¼ cup canola oil

1 egg

2 tablespoons corn syrup

2 teaspoons vanilla extract

¼ cup granulated sugar

40
SERVINGS

33
MINUTES

1. PREHEAT the oven to 375°F. Coat 2 baking sheets with cooking spray.

2. COMBINE the flour, confectioners' sugar, cornstarch, baking powder, baking soda, and salt in a medium bowl. Mix well.

3. COMBINE the brown sugar, peanut butter, and oil in a large bowl. Beat on medium speed until well-blended using an electric mixer. Add the egg, corn syrup, and vanilla extract. Beat until well-combined. Stir in the flour mixture (dough will be crumbly).

4. FORM the mixture into 1" balls. Roll each ball in the granulated sugar and place on the prepared baking sheets, leaving 2" between balls. Flatten with the bottom of a glass.

5. BAKE 1 sheet at a time for 7 to 8 minutes, or until lightly browned. Remove from the oven and let stand on the baking sheet for 1 minute. Transfer to a rack to cool.

PER SERVING 70 calories, 3 g fat, 0 g saturated fat, 1 g protein, 11 g carbohydrates, 1 g fiber, 14 mg calcium, 60 mg sodium

Peanut Butter Cup Sundaes

2 SERVINGS

5 MINUTES

1. **COMBINE** the peanut butter and chocolate chips in a small microwaveable bowl. Cook on medium-high power for 20 to 30 seconds. Stir. Cook for 20 to 30 seconds longer, or until creamy.

2. **PUT** ½ cup of the ice cream or frozen yogurt in each serving dish. Divide the peanut butter mixture evenly and pour over ice cream. Sprinkle peanuts on top.

1½ tablespoons creamy peanut butter

1 tablespoon semisweet mini chocolate chips

1 cup slow-churned vanilla ice cream or low-fat frozen yogurt

1½ teaspoons chopped unsalted peanuts

PER SERVING 220 calories, 13 g fat, 5 g saturated fat, 7 g protein, 22 g carbohydrates, 1 g fiber, 69 mg calcium, 119 mg sodium

Spiced Coffee Custards

2 cups unsweetened light soy milk

½ cup brewed coffee

¼ cup coffee liqueur (such as Kahlua)

1 tablespoon instant coffee powder

1 teaspoon ground cinnamon

½ teaspoon ground allspice

2 eggs

2 egg whites

¼ cup sugar

⅛ teaspoon salt

Chocolate-covered espresso beans (optional)

6 SERVINGS

5 HOURS

5 MINUTES

1. PREHEAT the oven to 350°F. Set six 6- or 8-ounce ovenproof custard cups into a 13" × 9" baking dish. Place 2 to 3 cups of water in a teakettle or saucepan. Set over high heat and bring to a boil.

2. COMBINE the soy milk, coffee, liqueur, instant coffee powder, cinnamon, and allspice in a medium saucepan. Set over medium heat and cook for 4 minutes, or just until bubbles form around the edge of the pan. Remove from the heat. Whisk together the eggs, egg whites, sugar, and salt in a large bowl until well blended. Gradually stir in the milk mixture until blended. Ladle into the custard cups, dividing evenly. Add boiling water to the baking dish to come halfway up the sides of the custard cups.

3. BAKE for 40 to 45 minutes, or until a knife inserted into the center of a custard comes out clean. Carefully remove the cups from the water and cool on a rack. Cover with plastic wrap and refrigerate for 4 hours (or overnight), or until chilled. Garnish with espresso beans, if using.

PER SERVING 166 calories, 2 g fat, 1 g saturated fat, 5 g protein, 22 g carbohydrates, 1 g fiber, 117 mg calcium, 123 mg sodium

Cherry Rice Pudding

7 SERVINGS

30 MINUTES

1. **COMBINE** the water and rice in a small saucepan. Cover and set over medium-high heat for 3 minutes, or until the water boils. Reduce the heat so the mixture simmers. Cook for 10 to 12 minutes, or until the water is absorbed.

2. **PLACE** the cherries in a small bowl and cover with hot water. Set aside.

3. **COMBINE** the sugar, flour, and salt in a 3-quart saucepan. Whisk to mix well. Gradually whisk in the milk or half-and-half until smooth. Cook over medium heat, stirring often, for 12 to 15 minutes, or until simmering and slightly thickened.

4. **ADD** the rice to the pan. Cook over low heat, stirring frequently, for 5 to 8 minutes, or until thick and creamy. Remove from the heat. Add the vanilla extract and cinnamon. Stir. Drain the reserved cherries and stir into the rice mixture. Allow to cool slightly. Serve warm or cover and refrigerate for several hours to serve cold.

- $^3/_4$ cup water
- $^3/_4$ cup instant brown rice, such as Uncle Ben's
- $^1/_2$ cup dried cherries, chopped
- $^1/_2$ cup sugar
- 3 tablespoons flour
- $^1/_4$ teaspoon salt
- 3 cups 1% milk or fat-free half-and-half
- 1 teaspoon vanilla extract
- $^1/_2$ teaspoon ground cinnamon

PER SERVING 220 calories, 2 g fat, 1 g saturated fat, 7 g protein, 45 g carbohydrates, 3 g fiber, 141 mg calcium, 135 mg sodium

Pear Crisp with Creamy Orange Sauce

Fruit

- 1 tablespoon confectioners' sugar
- 2 teaspoons cornstarch
- 4 cups (about 2 pounds) peeled and sliced Anjou or Bartlett pears
- 2 teaspoons vanilla extract

Topping

- 1/2 cup old-fashioned oats
- 2 tablespoons slivered almonds
- 1/4 teaspoon ground nutmeg
- 2 tablespoons cold trans-free spreadable/tub margarine

Sauce

- 1 cup fat-free plain yogurt
- 1 tablespoon maple syrup
- 1/4 teaspoon orange extract

9 SERVINGS

1 HOUR 20 MINUTES

1. **PREHEAT** the oven to 350°F. Coat an 8" × 8" baking dish with cooking spray. Set aside.

2. **TO PREPARE THE FRUIT:** Combine the confectioners' sugar and cornstarch in a bowl. Stir until well blended. Add the pears and vanilla. Toss to coat evenly. Transfer to the reserved dish and set aside.

3. **TO PREPARE THE TOPPING:** Wipe the bowl dry with a paper towel. Add the oats, almonds, and nutmeg. Toss with a fork to mix. Break the spread into small chunks, using the fork. Add to the mixture. Use the fork to blend the margarine with the oats mixture. Sprinkle over the reserved fruit. Bake for 55 minutes, or until bubbly.

4. **TO PREPARE THE SAUCE:** Combine the yogurt, syrup, and extract in a small bowl. Stir to mix. Serve the crisp warm or at room temperature, topped with the sauce.

PER SERVING 128 calories, 3 g fat, 1 g saturated fat, 2 g protein, 24 g carbohydrates, 4 g fiber, 48 mg calcium, 37 mg sodium

Anytime Blueberry–
Raspberry Shortcakes

6
SERVINGS

25
MINUTES

1. PREHEAT the oven to 400° F. Line a 6-cup muffin pan with paper liners.

2. COMBINE the baking mix, milk, egg substitute, margarine, and 2 tablespoons of the sugar in a mixing bowl. Stir until a batter forms but don't over mix. Fill the prepared muffin cups two-thirds full.

3. BAKE for 15 minutes, or until puffed and golden. Remove the muffins from the pan immediately and place on a rack to cool slightly.

4. COMBINE the blueberries, raspberries, lemon zest, and the remaining 4 tablespoons sugar in a medium saucepan. Bring to a boil over high heat. Reduce the heat so the mixture simmers. Cook, stirring occasionally, for 10 minutes, or until the juices thicken slightly.

5. SPLIT the cakes in half to serve. Place the bottoms on plates. Spoon ½ cup of the berry sauce on top. Cover with the remaining cake halves. Spoon on the remaining berry sauce.

1 cup baking mix, such as Bisquick

¼ cup fat-free milk

2 tablespoons liquid egg substitute

1 tablespoon trans-free spreadable/tub margarine

6 tablespoons sugar, divided

1 bag (12 ounces) frozen blueberries, thawed

1 bag (12 ounces) frozen raspberries, thawed

Freshly grated zest of 1 lemon

PER SERVING 191 calories, 6 g fat, 1 g saturated fat, 3 g protein, 35 g carbohydrates, 5 g fiber, 53 mg calcium, 282 mg sodium

Peach Crunch

½ cup fat-free plain yogurt

3 teaspoons apple pie spice

½ cup whole grain nugget cereal, such as Grape-Nuts

2 teaspoons honey

1 teaspoon unsalted butter

1 package (16 ounces) frozen unsweetened peach slices, thawed, or 3½ cups peeled, pitted, and sliced peaches

4 SERVINGS

17 MINUTES

1. MIX the yogurt and 1½ teaspoons of the apple pie spice in a small bowl.

2. MIX the cereal, honey, and the remaining 1½ teaspoons apple pie spice in another small bowl.

3. COAT a small nonstick skillet with cooking spray. Add the butter and place over medium heat until melted. Add the cereal mixture. Cook and stir for 2 minutes, or until the butter is absorbed.

4. SPOON the peaches into 4 dessert bowls. Top with the yogurt mixture and sprinkle with the cereal mixture.

PER SERVING 137 calories, 1 g fat, 1 g saturated fat, 4 g protein, 29 g carbohydrates, 2 g fiber, 52 mg calcium, 113 mg sodium

Oatmeal-Date Bars

18 SERVINGS (1 BAR PER SERVING)

1 HOUR

5 MINUTES

1. PREHEAT the oven to 375°F. Line a 10½" × 7" baking dish with foil and coat with cooking spray.

2. TO MAKE THE FILLING: Combine the applesauce, dates, and pumpkin pie spice in a small nonstick saucepan. Bring to a bare simmer and cook, stirring and mashing occasionally with a heatproof spatula, for 10 minutes, or until thickened. Stir the vanilla extract into the filling until blended. Set the filling aside to cool while preparing the crust.

3. TO MAKE THE CRUST: Whisk together the flour, oats, baking powder, baking soda, and salt in a medium bowl. Place the mixture on a sheet of waxed paper. Beat the sugar, butter, and sour cream in the same bowl with an electric mixer on high speed for 1 minute, or until smooth. Stir in the oat mixture with a wooden spoon until combined.

4. PLACE a sheet of plastic wrap on a small baking sheet. Remove 1 cup of the dough and crumble it onto the plastic wrap. Cover loosely with plastic and freeze while assembling the bars. Drop the remaining dough by spoonfuls into the prepared baking dish. Cover with a sheet of plastic wrap coated with cooking spray and press the dough into an even layer. Remove the wrap.

5. DROP the filling by spoonfuls over the dough and spread in an even layer. Crumble the chilled dough evenly over the filling.

6. BAKE for 25 minutes, or until golden brown. Cool completely in a pan on a rack. Remove from the pan and gently remove the foil. Divide into 18 squares, cutting in thirds lengthwise and sixths crosswise. Store airtight for up to 1 week, or freeze for up to 2 months.

Filling

- 1 cup cinnamon applesauce, sweetened with apple juice concentrate
- 1 cup chopped dates
- ½ teaspoon pumpkin pie spice
- 1 teaspoon vanilla extract

Crust

- 1 cup whole wheat pastry flour
- 1 cup old-fashioned oats
- ½ teaspoon baking powder
- ½ teaspoon baking soda
- ½ teaspoon salt
- ⅔ cup packed light brown sugar
- 3 tablespoons unsalted butter, at room temperature
- 3 tablespoons reduced-fat sour cream

PER SERVING 121 calories, 3 g fat, 1 g saturated fat, 2 g protein, 24 g carbohydrates, 2 g fiber, 29 mg calcium, 118 mg sodium

EAT THE WOW WAY

PART
three

10

28 DAYS
OF WOW
MENUS

IMAGINE AN ENTIRE DAY when you dine like a queen while sticking to your weight-loss goals!

The 4-week menu plan in this chapter shows you how to put the WOW principles (outlined in the first three chapters) into action without spending a lot of time planning, shopping, and cooking. No more fretting or calculating about what and how much to eat.

Don't think of these menus as a strict regimen. If you want to eat the meals for Day 10 on Day 20, that's fine. You can tweak these meals a bit to account for your tastes, as long as the calories are equal. If you want a peach instead of a nectarine or cauliflower instead of broccoli, go for it.

Tossed salads appear frequently. Select your preferred salad-type veggies—baby spinach, red leaf romaine, tomato, cucumber, red onion, carrots, or radishes—and toss with reduced-fat salad dressing.

For meals that don't include beverages, use the opportunity to drink green tea or water. Remember, you're striving for three cups of green tea and five 8-ounce glasses of water daily.

Day 1

BREAKFAST
1 serving California-Style Eggs Benedict (page 49)

20 medium strawberries

1 cup fat-free milk

LUNCH
1 Mediterranean Pocket (page 91)

1 cup grapes

1 cup fat-free milk

SNACK
1 serving Honey-Nut Walking Stix (page 45)

Green tea

DINNER
1 Grilled Pork Chop (page 124)

1 serving Buttermilk-Smashed Red Potatoes with Scallions (page 111)

1 serving Roasted Beet Salad (page 98)

1 cup fat-free milk

SNACK
1 serving Creamy Citrus Dip for Fruit (page 36)

1 medium apple

5 medium strawberries

PER SERVING 1,775 calories; 37 g fat; 10 g saturated fat; 96 g protein; 284 g carbohydrates; 32 g fiber; 1,553 mg calcium; 2,579 mg sodium

Day 2

BREAKFAST
1 serving Lemon-Blueberry Clafouti (page 64)

¾ cup fat-free vanilla yogurt

LUNCH
1 serving Honey-Grilled Chicken Salad (page 103) on a bed of 1 cup romaine

6 whole wheat crackers

1 cup fat-free milk

SNACK
1 small banana

2 tablespoons semisweet chocolate chips

DINNER
1 serving Creamy Peanut Noodles (page 156)

1 cup tossed salad

1 tablespoon reduced-fat salad dressing

1 cup fat-free milk

SNACK
1 serving Chocolate Pudding Cake (page 170)

PER SERVING 1,761 calories; 51 g fat; 14 g saturated fat; 79 g protein; 264 g carbohydrates; 23 g fiber; 1,446 mg calcium; 2,111 mg sodium

Day 3

BREAKFAST

1 serving Salmon Artichoke Hash (page 57)

¾ cup 100% fruit juice of your choice

LUNCH

Egg Salad Sandwich: 2 slices 100% whole wheat/grain bread;
1 hard-cooked egg, chopped; and 2 teaspoons reduced-fat mayonnaise

1 serving leftover Roasted Beet Salad (page 98)

1 cup fat-free milk

SNACK

1 ounce baked tortilla chips

3 tablespoons salsa

3 tablespoons mashed avocado

DINNER

1 serving Chicken Parmesan (page 132)

½ cup cooked whole wheat penne

¼ cup low-sodium spaghetti sauce

½ cup cooked green beans

¼ teaspoon trans-free spreadable/tub margarine

½ cup fat-free milk

SNACK

1 serving Honey-Nut Walking Stix (page 45)

PER SERVING 1,838 calories; 54 g fat; 11 g saturated fat; 102 g protein; 248 g carbohydrates; 30 g fiber; 1,038 mg calcium; 1,996 mg sodium

Day 4

BREAKFAST

1 serving Whole Grain French Toast with Nutmeg-Scented Fruit (page 61)

Green tea

LUNCH

1 cup low-sodium vegetable soup

4 whole wheat crackers

1 cup fat-free vanilla yogurt

$\frac{1}{2}$ cup blueberries

SNACK

1 medium apple

1 tablespoon peanut butter

DINNER

1 serving Mexican Lasagna (page 152)

$1\frac{1}{2}$ cups tossed salad

$1\frac{1}{2}$ tablespoons reduced-fat salad dressing

1 cup fat-free milk

SNACK

1 Peanut Butter Cup Sundae (page 173)

PER SERVING 1,731 calories; 46 g fat; 14 g saturated fat; 76 g protein; 272 g carbohydrates; 29 g fiber; 1,522 mg calcium; 2,470 mg sodium

Day 5

BREAKFAST

1 serving Banana-Ginger Smoothie (page 69)

2 slices 100% whole wheat/grain toast

1 teaspoon trans-free spreadable/tub margarine

1 teaspoon honey

LUNCH

1 serving Southwest Cobb Salad (page 105)

1 medium (2$\frac{1}{2}$") whole wheat roll

1 medium apple

1 cup fat-free milk

SNACK

2 fun-size candy bars, like 3 Musketeers

10 no-salt-added peanuts

DINNER

1 Flounder and Broccoli Roll-Up (page 138)

1 medium (2$\frac{1}{2}$") whole wheat roll

1 cup tossed salad

1 tablespoon reduced-fat salad dressing

1 cup fat-free milk

SNACK

1 serving leftover Chocolate Pudding Cake (page 170)

PER SERVING 1,766 calories; 43 g fat; 12 g saturated fat; 101 g protein; 262 g carbohydrates; 34 g fiber; 1,597 mg calcium; 2,361 mg sodium

Day 6

BREAKFAST
1 egg, prepared as you like in a nonstick skillet

2 slices whole wheat/grain toast

1 teaspoon trans-free spreadable/tub margarine

½ large grapefruit

1 cup fat-free milk

LUNCH
1 serving leftover Mexican Lasagna (page 152)

1 medium orange

1 cup fat-free milk

SNACK
10 unsalted walnut halves

3 tablespoons dried, sweetened cranberries (such as Craisins)

DINNER
1 serving Seared Salmon with Mango Salsa (page 148)

1 serving Creamy Macaroni Salad (page 104)

1 serving Snow Peas with Basil (page 113)

½ cup fat-free milk

SNACK
1 Banana Chocolate Chip Macadamia Muffin (page 46)

PER SERVING 1,800 calories; 63 g fat; 14 g saturated fat; 96 g protein; 221 g carbohydrates; 21 g fiber; 1,523 mg calcium; 2,131 mg sodium

BREAKFAST
1 serving Date-Walnut Pudding (page 67)

1 small banana

½ cup 100% fruit juice of your choice

LUNCH
Turkey Apple Panini (page 93)

³⁄₄ apple leftover from panini

½ cup baby carrots

1 tablespoon reduced-fat ranch dip/dressing

½ cup fat-free milk

SNACK
2 sticks reduced-fat string cheese

5 whole wheat crackers

DINNER
1 serving South of France Baked Cod (page 146)

³⁄₄ cup cooked brown rice

1 cup tossed salad

1 tablespoon reduced-fat salad dressing

1 cup fat-free milk

SNACK
1 serving Mustard-Glazed Snack Mix (page 44)

½ cup fat-free milk

PER SERVING 1,817 calories; 41 g fat; 8 g saturated fat; 92 g protein; 286 g carbohydrates; 42 g fiber; 1,491 mg calcium; 1,936 mg sodium

Day 8

BREAKFAST
1 serving Sunrise Casserole (page 51)

1 slice whole wheat/grain toast

1/2 teaspoon trans-free spreadable/tub margarine

1/2 cup 100% orange juice

LUNCH
1 Tomato Avocado Open-Faced Sandwich (page 83)

3/4 ounce baked tortilla chips

1/2 cup fat-free vanilla yogurt

1/2 cup sliced strawberries

SNACK
1 leftover Banana Chocolate Chip Macadamia Muffin (page 46)

DINNER
1 serving Hoisin Pork Stir-Fry (page 126)

1 cup cooked brown rice

1 cup fat-free milk

SNACK
1 serving Crudités with Spicy Peanut Dipping Sauce (page 38)

PER SERVING	1,755 calories; 49 g fat; 9 g saturated fat; 91 g protein; 243 g carbohydrates; 27 g fiber; 1,125 mg calcium; 2,406 mg sodium

Day 9

BREAKFAST

1 Orange Bran Muffin (page 68)

½ cup fat-free vanilla yogurt

1 medium peach

LUNCH

Grilled Swiss Cheese Sandwich: 2 slices whole wheat/grain bread, 1 teaspoon trans-free spreadable/tub margarine, and 1 ounce reduced fat/sodium Swiss cheese

¾ cup reduced-sodium tomato soup

1 small banana

Green tea

SNACK

1 serving Avocado-Peach Salsa with Multigrain Chips (page 36)

DINNER

1 serving Chicken Chili with Black Beans (page 76)

7 saltines

1½ cups tossed salad

1½ tablespoons reduced-fat salad dressing

½ cup grapes

1 cup fat-free milk

SNACK

1 Oatmeal-Date Bar (page 179)

1 cup fat-free milk

PER SERVING 1,783 calories; 44 g fat; 10 g saturated fat; 81 g protein; 283 g carbohydrates; 36 g fiber; 1,474 mg calcium; 2,169 mg sodium

Day 10

BREAKFAST
1 serving Breakfast Bread Pudding (page 58)

1 medium nectarine

1 cup fat-free milk

LUNCH
1 Tex-Mex Turkey, Mango, and Pineapple Wrap (page 92)

$\frac{1}{2}$ cucumber, sliced

1 tablespoon reduced-fat ranch dip/dressing

$\frac{1}{2}$ cup juice-packed mandarin oranges

1 cup fat-free milk

3 dark chocolate Hershey's Kisses

SNACK
1 serving Mustard-Glazed Snack Mix (page 44)

$\frac{1}{2}$ cup fat-free milk

DINNER
1 serving Shrimp-and-Crab Cakes (page 151)

1 medium (2$\frac{1}{2}$"–3") baked potato

1 teaspoon trans-free spreadable/tub margarine

1 tablespoon reduced-fat sour cream

1 serving Cajun-Blackened Zucchini (page 115)

1 cup fat-free milk

SNACK
$\frac{1}{2}$ cup fat-free vanilla yogurt

$\frac{1}{2}$ cup sliced strawberries

2 tablespoons slivered almonds

PER SERVING 1,785 calories; 41 g fat; 10 g saturated fat; 116 g protein; 257 g carbohydrates; 27 g fiber; 2,130 mg calcium; 1,973 mg sodium

Day 11

BREAKFAST

1 Ricotta and Fig Breakfast Sandwich (page 58)

1 cup fat-free milk

LUNCH

1 serving leftover Chicken Chili with Black Beans (page 76)

7 saltines

1 medium peach

1 cup fat-free milk

SNACK

1 leftover Orange Bran Muffin (page 68)

DINNER

1 Portobello Swiss Cheese Burger with Caramelized Onions (page 84)

1 serving Sesame Spinach (page 114)

1 cup tossed salad

1 tablespoon reduced-fat salad dressing

1 medium banana

1 cup fat-free milk

SNACK

1 serving leftover Avocado-Peach Salsa with Multigrain Chips (page 36)

PER SERVING 1,712 calories; 38 g fat; 6 g saturated fat; 86 g protein; 278 g carbohydrates; 45 g fiber; 1,628 mg calcium; 2,331 mg sodium

Day 12

BREAKFAST
1 serving Cheese and Pepper Frittata (page 50)

1 slice whole wheat/grain toast

$\frac{1}{2}$ teaspoon trans-free spreadable/tub margarine

1 medium plum

$\frac{3}{4}$ cup fat-free milk

LUNCH
1 California Club Sandwich (page 88)

$\frac{1}{2}$ ounce lightly salted potato chips

$\frac{1}{2}$ medium red bell pepper, sliced

2 teaspoons reduced-fat ranch dip/dressing

1 medium nectarine

1 cup fat-free milk

SNACK
1 Oatmeal-Date Bar (page 179)

1 cup fat-free milk

DINNER
1 serving Rosemary Roast Chicken (page 134)

1 serving Cheesy Broccoli Salad (page 99)

$\frac{3}{4}$ cup boiled red potatoes

1 teaspoon trans-free spreadable/tub margarine

1 medium ($2\frac{1}{2}$") whole wheat roll

Green tea

SNACK
2 servings Zesty Dill Spread on Whole Grain Crackers (page 37)

1 cup baby carrots

PER SERVING	1,699 calories; 51 g fat; 15 g saturated fat; 102 g protein; 219 g carbohydrates; 30 g fiber; 1,632 mg calcium; 2,515 mg sodium

Day 13

BREAKFAST

2 slices cinnamon-swirl toast

1 tablespoon peanut butter

1/2 medium banana

3/4 cup fat-free milk

LUNCH

Big salad: 2 cups Bibb lettuce, 1 medium tomato, 1/2 sliced cucumber, 1/4 cup shredded carrots and topped with 2 ounces leftover sliced Rosemary Roast Chicken (page 134)

3 tablespoons balsamic vinaigrette

1 medium (2 1/2") whole wheat roll

1 medium orange

1 cup fat-free milk

SNACK

3/4 ounce unsalted pistachio nuts

2 tablespoons dried cherries

DINNER

Seafood and Brown Rice Paella (page 142)

1 cup cooked carrots

1 1/2 cups tossed salad

1 1/2 tablespoons reduced-fat salad dressing

1 cup fat-free milk

SNACK

1 serving Mustard-Glazed Snack Mix (page 44)

1/2 cup fat-free milk

PER SERVING 1,767 calories; 59 g fat; 9 g saturated fat; 91 g protein; 236 g carbohydrates; 38 g fiber; 1,505 mg calcium; 2,345 mg sodium

Day 14

BREAKFAST

1 serving Multigrain Cereal (page 66)

1 cup fat-free milk

³/₄ cup grapes

¹/₂ cup 100% fruit juice of your choice

LUNCH

Turkey Sandwich: 2 slices whole wheat/grain bread, 1¹/₂ ounces reduced-sodium deli turkey, and 2 teaspoons reduced-fat mayonnaise

1 serving leftover Cheesy Broccoli Salad (page 99)

1 medium apple

³/₄ cup fat-free milk

SNACK

2 Peanut Butter Sandies (page 172)

DINNER

1 serving Beef Stew (page 119) served over ²/₃ cup cooked brown rice

1 cup tossed salad

1 tablespoon reduced-fat salad dressing

1 cup fat-free milk

SNACK

Fruit Bruschetta: 2 graham crackers (2¹/₂" x 2¹/₂") topped with 1¹/₂ teaspoons mascarpone cheese, 2 chopped grapes, 2 chopped walnuts, 2 chopped strawberries, and ¹/₂ teaspoon honey

¹/₂ cup fat-free milk

PER SERVING 1,794 calories; 39 g fat; 11 g saturated fat; 96 g protein; 277 g carbohydrates; 30 g fiber; 1,816 mg calcium; 2,045 mg sodium

Day 15

BREAKFAST

1 serving Cornmeal Flapjacks with Berries (page 63)

1 teaspoon trans-free spreadable/tub margarine

2 tablespoons maple syrup

$\frac{1}{2}$ cup fat-free milk

LUNCH

1 Almond, Tarragon, and Chicken Salad Sandwich (page 89)

$\frac{3}{4}$ cup fat-free vanilla yogurt

$\frac{3}{4}$ cup cherries

SNACK

15 medium strawberries

1 fat-free chocolate pudding cup

1 graham cracker ($2\frac{1}{2}$" x $2\frac{1}{2}$")

DINNER

2 slices Fettuccine Alfredo Pizza (page 159)

8 spears steamed asparagus

$\frac{1}{2}$ teaspoon trans-free spreadable/tub margarine

1 cup tossed salad

1 tablespoon reduced-fat salad dressing

Iced green tea

SNACK

2 Peanut Butter Sandies (page 172)

$\frac{1}{2}$ cup fat-free milk, heated in the microwave on high power for 45 to 60 seconds, or until hot, mixed with $\frac{1}{2}$ teaspoon vanilla extract

PER SERVING 1,803 calories; 36 g fat; 9 g saturated fat; 85 g protein; 296 g carbohydrates; 27 g fiber; 1,267 mg calcium; 2,589 mg sodium

Day 16

BREAKFAST
1 serving Garlic and Tomato Frittata (page 56)

1 cup diced melon

1 cup fat-free milk

LUNCH
1 serving leftover Beef Stew (page 119)

1 medium banana

1 cup fat-free milk

SNACK
1/2 cup fat-free vanilla yogurt

10 grapes

12 unsalted pistachio nuts

DINNER
1 serving Honey-Mustard Pork Tenderloin (page 125)

1 serving Green and White Bean Salad (page 107)

1 cup tossed salad

1 tablespoon reduced-fat salad dressing

1 medium (2½") whole wheat roll

SNACK
1 Anytime Blueberry-Raspberry Shortcake (page 177)

PER SERVING 1,716 calories; 36 g fat; 9 g saturated fat; 113 g protein; 250 g carbohydrates; 33 g fiber; 1,603 mg calcium; 2,306 mg sodium

Day 17

BREAKFAST

1 serving Cocoa-Espresso Waffles (page 62)

$^1/_2$ **cup sliced strawberries**

1 tablespoon confectioners' sugar

LUNCH

1 serving Fruited Spinach Salad with Ham and Toasted Walnuts (page 97)

1 medium (2$^1/_2$") whole wheat roll

1 container (6 ounces) low-fat fruit-flavored yogurt

SNACK

$^1/_2$ **whole grain or multigrain bagel (3$^1/_2$" wide) topped with a mixture of 1 tablespoon reduced-fat cream cheese, 1 teaspoon honey, and 1$^1/_2$ teaspoons chopped walnuts**

4 medium strawberries

$^1/_2$ **cup fat-free milk**

DINNER

1 serving Turkey Meatballs and Linguine (page 128)

1 cup tossed salad

1 tablespoon reduced-fat salad dressing

1 cup fat-free milk

SNACK

$^1/_2$ **cup 1% cottage cheese**

$^1/_2$ **cup crushed pineapple packed in juice, drained**

PER SERVING	1,723 calories; 35 g fat; 8 g saturated fat; 91 g protein; 278 g carbohydrates; 37 g fiber; 1,272 mg calcium; 2,248 mg sodium

Day 18

BREAKFAST

1 serving Breakfast Strata (page 54)

1 cup 100% orange juice

LUNCH

Roast Beef Sandwich: 2 slices whole wheat/grain bread, 2 ounces low-sodium, deli-style roast beef, and 2 teaspoons spicy brown mustard

5 celery sticks (4" long)

1 tablespoon reduced-fat ranch dip/dressing

1 medium pear

1 cup fat-free milk

SNACK

1 cup baby carrots

¼ cup hummus

DINNER

1 serving Tortellini Corn Chowder (page 74)

5 whole wheat crackers

½ cup steamed broccoli

½ teaspoon trans-free spreadable/tub margarine

1½ cups tossed salad

1½ tablespoons reduced-fat salad dressing

1 large apple

Iced green tea

SNACK

leftover Anytime Blueberry-Raspberry Shortcake (page 177)

PER SERVING	1,708 calories; 44 g fat; 10 g saturated fat; 80 g protein; 266 g carbohydrates; 43 g fiber; 1,366 mg calcium; 2,437 mg sodium

Day 19

BREAKFAST

1 Apricot-Currant Scone (page 67)

³/₄ cup fat-free vanilla yogurt

¹/₂ cup juice-packed mandarin oranges

Green tea

LUNCH

1 serving French Roasted Vegetable Sandwich (page 85)

1 cup fat-free vanilla yogurt

¹/₂ cup raspberries

SNACK

1 serving Grilled Cumin Pita with White Bean Dip (page 39)

¹/₂ medium red bell pepper, sliced

DINNER

1 serving Chunky Vegetable Shepherd's Pie (page 158)

1 medium (2") whole wheat roll

1¹/₂ cups tossed salad

1¹/₂ tablespoons reduced-fat salad dressing

1 cup fat-free milk

SNACK

2 Peanut Butter Sandies (page 172)

¹/₂ cup fat-free milk

PER SERVING	1,734 calories; 28 g fat: 4 g saturated fat; 68 g protein; 310 g carbohydrates; 36 g fiber; 1,683 mg calcium; 1,826 mg sodium

Day 20

BREAKFAST

1 serving German Apple Pancake (page 65)

1 medium pear

1 cup fat-free milk

LUNCH

Tuna Melt: 2 ounces drained water-packed tuna mixed with
1½ teaspoons reduced-fat mayonnaise spread on ½ multigrain English
muffin, topped with 1 slice tomato and 1½ teaspoons reduced-fat
shredded Cheddar cheese, broiled until cheese melts

1 serving leftover Green and White Bean Salad (page 107)

1 medium peach

1 cup fat-free milk

SNACK

1 serving Buffalo-Style Chicken Bites (page 42)

½ cup fat-free milk

DINNER

1 serving Beef and Black Bean Picadillo over Brown Rice (page 122)

1 cup tossed salad

1 tablespoon reduced-fat salad dressing

SNACK

2 servings Curried Snack Mix with Golden Raisins (page 43)

PER SERVING 1,766 calories; 38 g fat; 9 g saturated fat; 104 g protein; 261 g carbohydrates; 41 g fiber; 1,311 mg calcium; 2,301 mg sodium

Day 21

BREAKFAST
1 serving Ham and Vegetable Omelet Wrap (page 53)

1 medium banana

1 cup fat-free milk

LUNCH
1 serving leftover Chunky Vegetable Shepherd's Pie (page 158)

³⁄₄ cup juice-packed peach slices

1 cup fat-free milk

SNACK
1 Fruit 'n' Nut Muffin (page 47)

Green tea

DINNER
1 serving Mediterranean Flounder (page 140)

1 serving Onion, Caper, and Orange Salad (page 101)

1 medium (2¹⁄₂") whole wheat roll

1 cup fat-free milk

SNACK
1 leftover Apricot-Currant Scone (page 67)

2 teaspoons apricot fruit spread

Green tea

PER SERVING 1,750 calories; 32 g fat; 8 g saturated fat; 88 g protein; 286 g carbohydrates; 30 g fiber; 1,432 mg calcium; 1,950 mg sodium

Day 22

BREAKFAST
Huevos Rancheros Wrap (page 55)

$\frac{1}{2}$ cup diced papaya

1 cup fat-free milk

LUNCH
1 serving Baked Potato Chowder (page 73)

4 whole wheat crackers

1 small apple

Green tea

SNACK
$\frac{1}{2}$ cup edamame

1 ounce reduced-fat Cheddar cheese

DINNER
2 Veracruz Shrimp Tacos (page 87)

Spanish Rice: $\frac{1}{4}$ medium red bell pepper, diced, sautéed in 1 teaspoon olive oil and mixed with $\frac{1}{2}$ cup cooked brown rice, $\frac{1}{2}$ cup corn kernels, and $\frac{1}{4}$ teaspoon cumin

1 cup fat-free milk

SNACK
1 serving Banana Snack Cake (page 166)

$\frac{1}{2}$ cup fat-free milk

PER SERVING 1,818 calories; 50 g fat; 15 g saturated fat; 99 g protein; 261 g carbohydrates; 29 g fiber; 1,817 mg calcium; 2,273 mg sodium

BREAKFAST
2 Banana Pancakes with Maple-Walnut Syrup (page 59)

³/₄ cup fat-free milk

LUNCH
1 Roast Beef and Charred Vegetable Sandwich (page 94)

1 ounce baked tortilla chips

1¹/₂ cups diced melon

1 cup fat-free milk

SNACK
³/₄ cup fat-free vanilla yogurt

¹/₂ cup blueberries

DINNER
1 serving Stir-Fried Orange Chicken and Broccoli (page 131)

³/₄ cup cooked brown rice mixed with 2 tablespoons slivered almonds

Iced green tea

SNACK
1 Fruit 'n' Nut Muffin (page 47)

PER SERVING 1,760 calories; 38 g fat; 6 g saturated fat; 91 g protein; 282 g carbohydrates; 22 g fiber; 1,519 mg calcium; 1,880 mg sodium

Day 24

BREAKFAST
1 serving Apple Pie Oatmeal (page 66)

Green tea

LUNCH
1 Chicken Salad Roll-Up (page 90)

1 cup baby carrots

1 tablespoon reduced-fat ranch dip/dressing

³/₄ cup pineapple chunks, fresh or packed in juice

1 cup fat-free milk

SNACK
³/₄ ounce reduced-fat Cheddar cheese

4 whole wheat crackers

1 small apple

DINNER
1 serving Old-Fashioned Meat Loaf (page 121)

1 serving Mashed Sweet Potatoes and Carrots (page 112)

1 cup tossed salad

1 tablespoon reduced-fat salad dressing

1 cup fat-free milk

SNACK
1 slice whole wheat/grain toast

1 tablespoon peanut butter

¹/₂ cup fat-free milk

PER SERVING 1,726 calories; 39 g fat; 11 g saturated fat; 97 g protein; 258 g carbohydrates; 32 g fiber; 1,604 mg calcium; 2,477 mg sodium

Day 25

BREAKFAST
1 serving Spinach, Mushroom, and Mozzarella Omelet (page 52)

1 medium grapefruit

2 teaspoons sugar

1 cup fat-free milk

LUNCH
Cuban-Style Sandwich (page 95)

³/₄ cup grapes

³/₄ cup fat-free milk

SNACK
1 medium red bell pepper, sliced

¹/₃ cup hummus

DINNER
1 serving Grilled Grouper with Chili-Lime Sauce (page 144)

1 serving Roasted Green Beans with Candied Walnuts (page 109)

1 medium (2¹/₂") whole wheat roll

1 cup tossed salad

1 tablespoon reduced-fat salad dressing

³/₄ cup fat-free milk

SNACK
1 serving Banana Snack Cake (page 166)

¹/₂ cup fat-free milk

PER SERVING 1,774 calories; 58 g fat; 12 g saturated fat; 122 g protein; 206 g carbohydrates; 33 g fiber; 1,612 mg calcium; 2,082 mg sodium

Day 26

BREAKFAST
Parfait Presto (page 69)

1 whole grain English muffin

1 tablespoon peanut butter

LUNCH
Leftover Old-Fashioned Meat Loaf (page 121) **Sandwich:** 1 slice meat loaf, 2 slices whole wheat/grain toast, and 1 teaspoon reduced-fat mayonnaise

1 medium orange

green tea

SNACK
2 servings Curried Snack Mix with Golden Raisins (page 43)

DINNER
1 serving Creamy Mac and Three Cheeses (page 155)

1 serving Sweet-and-Sour Broccoli (page 113)

8 medium strawberries drizzled with 2 tablespoons chocolate syrup

Green tea

SNACK
1 serving Pesto Dip (page 37)

2 whole grain Wasa Crispbreads

PER SERVING 1,795 calories; 47 g fat; 11 g saturated fat; 83 g protein; 282 g carbohydrates; 43 g fiber; 1,060 mg calcium; 2,261 mg sodium

Day 27

BREAKFAST

1¼ cups **Cheerios**

1 small **banana**

½ cup sliced **strawberries**

¾ cup fat-free **milk**

½ cup 100% **orange juice**

LUNCH

1 serving **Sicilian Tuna on Whole Grain Bread** (page 86)

1 cup fat-free **vanilla yogurt**

½ cup **raspberries**

SNACK

1 serving **Pesto Dip** (page 37)

2 whole grain **Wasa Crispbreads**

DINNER

1 serving **Italian Vegetable Stir-Fry over Polenta** (page 162)

2 cups **tossed salad**

2 tablespoons reduced-fat **salad dressing**

¾ cup **fruit cocktail, packed in juice**

Iced green tea

SNACK

½ multigrain **English muffin**

2 teaspoons **peanut butter**

1 small **banana**

PER SERVING 1,745 calories; 34 g fat; 6 g saturated fat; 77 g protein; 311 g carbohydrates; 46 g fiber; 1,632 mg calcium; 2,087 mg sodium

Day 28

BREAKFAST
1 serving Orange French-Toasted English Muffins (page 60)

1 cup fat-free milk

LUNCH
1 serving leftover Creamy Mac and Three Cheeses (page 155)

1 serving leftover Sweet-and-Sour Broccoli (page 113)

3 apricots

Green tea

SNACK
3 (2½" x 2½") graham crackers

1 medium nectarine

¾ cup fat-free milk

DINNER
1 serving Chicken Tortilla Soup (page 75)

1 ounce baked tortilla chips

1 cup tossed salad

1 tablespoon reduced-fat salad dressing

1 cup fat-free milk

SNACK
1 Spiced Coffee Custard (page 174)

8 medium strawberries

PER SERVING 1,779 calories; 43 g fat; 9 g saturated fat; 86 g protein; 269 g carbohydrates; 32 g fiber; 1,916 mg calcium; 2,254 mg sodium

BUILD YOUR OWN WOW MENUS

JUST AS PHYSICAL SUPPLENESS is a big plus in your WOW program, flexibility in the kitchen can help equip you for success in cutting excess calories. For those of you who want more wiggle room in your daily meal choices, Build Your Own WOW Menus is the answer. As with 28 Days of WOW Menus, all of the tiresome calculations and planning are done. All you have to do is mix and match your preferred meals and snacks to create the daily eating plan that's just right for you!

The same options apply: If you're not crazy about a certain fruit or veggie, pick another. When no specific beverage is listed, reach for refreshing water or sodium-free sparkling water spiked with a lemon, lime, or orange wedge. Or choose hot or cold green tea.

For your tossed salads, remember the rainbow and choose your ingredients accordingly—dark-green lettuce, crimson tomatoes, garnet shredded red cabbage and red onions, orange carrots, and other raw vegetables to enjoy with reduced-fat dressing.

Mix & Match Menus

BREAKFASTS

MEAL 1

Orange Bran Muffin (page 68)

1 cup fat-free milk, heated in the microwave on high power for 45 to 60 seconds, or until hot, mixed with 1 teaspoon vanilla extract

20 medium strawberries

PER SERVING: 366 calories, 9 g fat, 1 g saturated fat, 15 g protein, 65 g carbohydrates, 10 g fiber, 437 mg calcium, 414 mg sodium

MEAL 2

³/₄ cup low-fat, low-sodium cottage cheese

³/₄ cup peach slices, packed in juice

1 multigrain English muffin

1 teaspoon trans-free spreadable/tub margarine

PER SERVING: 375 calories, 7 g fat, 2 g saturated fat, 27 g protein, 57 g carbohydrates, 10 g fiber, 183 mg calcium, 253 mg sodium

MEAL 3

1¹/₂ cups whole grain cereal, such as Total

¹/₄ cup blueberries

2 tablespoons chopped walnuts

1 cup fat-free milk

PER SERVING: 400 calories, 11 g fat, 1 g saturated fat, 15 g protein, 66 g carbohydrates, 7 g fiber, 2,322 mg calcium, 483 mg sodium

MEAL 4

1 egg scrambled in a nonstick pan with 2 tablespoons shredded reduced-fat Cheddar cheese

2 slices whole wheat/grain toast

1 teaspoon trans-free spreadable/tub margarine

³/₄ cup 100% orange juice

PER SERVING: 366 calories, 14 g fat, 4 g saturated fat, 19 g protein, 43 g carbohydrates, 4 g fiber, 305 mg calcium, 482 mg sodium

MEAL 5

Breakfast Bread Pudding (page 58)

1 cup fat-free milk

1 medium orange

PER SERVING: 370 calories, 2 g fat, 1 g saturated fat, 20 g protein, 69 g carbohydrates, 5 g fiber, 596 mg calcium, 312 mg sodium

MEAL 6

2 heat-and-eat whole grain waffles topped with ¹/₂ cup fat-free vanilla yogurt, ³/₄ cup sliced strawberries, and 2 tablespoons confectioners' sugar

PER SERVING: 390 calories, 7 g fat, 1 g saturated fat, 12 g protein, 74 g carbohydrates, 5 g fiber, 338 mg calcium, 505 mg sodium

MEAL 7

2 slices whole wheat/grain toast

4 teaspoons apple butter

1 cup fat-free milk, heated in the microwave on high power for 45 to 60 seconds, or until hot, mixed with 1 teaspoon vanilla extract

1 medium pear

PER SERVING: 379 calories, 3 g fat, 1 g saturated fat, 17 g protein, 75 g carbohydrates, 11 g fiber, 390 mg calcium, 400 mg sodium

MEAL 8

1 packet (28 grams) instant oatmeal, prepared according to package directions with ²/₃ cup fat-free milk, 2 tablespoons raisins, and 1 tablespoon maple syrup, topped with ¹/₃ cup fat-free milk and 2 tablespoons chopped pecans

PER SERVING: 392 calories, 13 g fat, 1 g saturated fat, 14 g protein, 61 g carbohydrates, 5 g fiber, 439 mg calcium, 187 mg sodium

MEAL 9

2 slices whole wheat/grain toast

2 teaspoons Nutella

1 cup fat-free milk

1 small banana

PER SERVING: 389 calories, 6 g fat, 2 g saturated fat, 18 g protein, 68 g carbohydrates, 8 g fiber, 376 mg calcium, 395 mg sodium

MEAL 10

1 (3" diameter) whole wheat bagel

2 tablespoons reduced-fat cream cheese

¹/₂ cup sliced strawberries

1 cup fat-free milk

PER SERVING: 365 calories, 7 g fat, 4 g saturated fat, 20 g protein, 58 g carbohydrates, 8 g fiber, 424 mg calcium, 515 mg sodium

MEAL 11

Banana-Ginger Smoothie (page 69)

1 multigrain English muffin

1 tablespoon peanut butter or cashew butter

PER SERVING: 351 calories, 11 g fat, 2 g saturated fat, 15 g protein, 61 g carbohydrates, 11 g fiber, 236 mg calcium, 301 mg sodium

MEAL 12

WOW Breakfast Sandwich: multigrain English muffin, toasted, spread with 1 teaspoon reduced-fat mayonnaise mixed with a dash of hot pepper sauce and filled with 1 egg cooked in a nonstick pan and 1 ounce reduced-fat American cheese

1 medium peach

1 cup fat-free milk

PER SERVING: 387 calories, 11 g fat, 3 g saturated fat, 27 g protein, 54 g carbohydrates, 10 g fiber, 572 mg calcium, 638 mg sodium

Mix & Match Menus

MEAL 13

1 packet (28 grams) instant oatmeal prepared according to package directions with $2/3$ cup fat-free milk and $1/4$ teaspoon cinnamon, topped with $1/3$ cup fat-free milk and 2 tablespoons chopped walnuts

1 medium banana

PER SERVING: 386 calories, 12 g fat, 1 g saturated fat, 16 g protein, 61 g carbohydrates, 7 g fiber, 433 mg calcium, 184 mg sodium

MEAL 14

1$1/4$ cups whole grain cereal, such as Total

2 tablespoons raisins

2 tablespoons slivered almonds

1 cup fat-free milk

PER SERVING: 382 calories, 8 g fat, 1 g saturated fat, 15 g protein, 68 g carbohydrates, 7 g fiber, 2,017 mg calcium, 421 mg sodium

LUNCHES

MEAL 1

Veggie burger on half of a whole wheat hamburger bun topped with 1 slice ($3/4$ ounce) reduced-fat Cheddar cheese, 1 slice tomato, and 1 lettuce leaf

1 cup baby carrots with 2 tablespoons fat-free, plain yogurt mixed with salt-free seasoning, such as Mrs. Dash

1 medium apple

$1/2$ cup fat-free milk

PER SERVING: 452 calories, 10 g fat, 4 g saturated fat, 26 g protein, 69 g carbohydrates, 13 g fiber, 455 mg calcium, 799 mg sodium

MEAL 2

Dilly tuna salad: 3 ounces water-packed tuna, drained, mixed with $1^1/2$ tablespoons reduced-fat mayonnaise, $1/4$ cup grated carrot, and $1/2$ teaspoon dried dill

7 whole wheat crackers

1 cup fat-free milk

1 medium nectarine

PER SERVING: 467 calories, 15 g fat, 3 g saturated fat, 33 g protein, 51 g carbohydrates, 6 g fiber, 360 mg calcium, 807 mg sodium

MEAL 3

Pork and Corn Salad with Tomato-Basil Dressing (page 106)

1 medium (2$\frac{1}{2}$") whole wheat roll

1 medium apple

1 cup fat-free milk

PER SERVING: 495 calories, 10 g fat, 2 g saturated fat, 31 g protein, 77 g carbohydrates, 12 g fiber, 410 mg calcium, 506 mg sodium

MEAL 4

Pan-Seared Salmon Salad (page 108)

1 (4" diameter) whole wheat pita

$\frac{3}{4}$ cup fat-free milk

1 cup raspberries

1 fat-free chocolate pudding cup

PER SERVING: 490 calories, 11 g fat, 2 g saturated fat, 28 g protein, 73 g carbohydrates, 14 g fiber, 417 mg calcium, 602 mg sodium

MEAL 5

Superfast Herbed White Bean Soup (page 72)

7 whole wheat crackers

1 medium orange

1 cup fat-free milk

PER SERVING: 468 calories, 11 g fat, 2 g saturated fat, 22 g protein, 73 g carbohydrates, 14 g fiber, 439 mg calcium, 386 mg sodium

MEAL 6

Hearty Country Vegetable Soup (page 80)

7 whole wheat crackers

1 medium banana

1 cup fat-free milk

2 dark chocolate Hershey's Kisses

PER SERVING: 489 calories, 10 g fat, 3 g saturated fat, 18 g protein, 86 g carbohydrates, 10 g fiber, 412 mg calcium, 423 mg sodium

MEAL 7

Sandwich of Honey-Grilled Chicken Salad (page 103) on 2 slices whole wheat/grain toast

$\frac{1}{2}$ cup fat-free milk

PER SERVING: 492 calories, 15 g fat, 2 g saturated fat, 37 g protein, 54 g carbohydrates, 6 g fiber, 259 mg calcium, 526 mg sodium

MEAL 8

Turkey and Swiss cheese sandwich:
1 ounce reduced-sodium, deli-style turkey and 1 ounce reduced-sodium, low-fat Swiss cheese on 2 slices whole wheat/grain bread spread with 2 teaspoons reduced-fat Thousand Island dressing

$\frac{1}{2}$ medium red bell pepper, sliced, with 2 tablespoons fat-free, plain yogurt mixed with 1 teaspoon salt-free seasoning, such as Mrs. Dash

1 medium plum

1 cup fat-free milk

PER SERVING: 442 calories, 10 g fat, 5 g saturated fat, 33 g protein, 56 g carbohydrates, 7 g fiber, 667 mg calcium, 679 mg sodium

Mix & Match Menus

MEAL 9

Salmon salad: 2 cups tossed salad (greens, tomato, cucumber, carrots, etc.) topped with 2 ounces drained water-packed salmon and 2 tablespoons balsamic vinaigrette

2 whole grain Wasa Crispbreads

1 cup grapes

1 cup fat-free milk

PER SERVING: 499 calories, 12 g fat, 2 g saturated fat, 28 g protein, 77 g carbohydrates, 11 g fiber, 561 mg calcium, 765 mg sodium

MEAL 10

Grilled cheese and tomato sandwich: 1 ounce reduced-fat American cheese, and 1 slice tomato on 2 slices whole wheat/grain bread spread with 1/2 teaspoon trans-free spreadable/tub margarine

1/2 cup steamed broccoli with salt-free seasoning

1 medium peach

1 ounce whole wheat pretzels

1 cup fat-free milk

PER SERVING: 480 calories, 7 g fat, 2 g saturated fat, 29 g protein, 80 g carbohydrates, 11 g fiber, 625 mg calcium, 733 mg sodium

MEAL 11

Creamy Broccoli Soup with Parmesan Crisps (page 71)

1 cup pineapple chunks packed in juice, mixed with 1 carton (6 ounces) low-fat banana yogurt and 1 tablespoon shredded coconut

PER SERVING: 466 calories, 10 g fat, 5 g saturated fat, 19 g protein, 82 g carbohydrates, 8 g fiber, 560 mg calcium, 478 mg sodium

MEAL 12

Pepper Steak Soup (page 79)

2 ounces Italian bread

1 cup fat-free milk

10 medium strawberries

PER SERVING: 498 calories, 10 g fat, 3 g saturated fat, 37 g protein, 64 g carbohydrates, 7 g fiber, 421 mg calcium, 771 mg sodium

MEAL 13

Bruschetta pizza: 1 multigrain English muffin topped with 1/2 tomato, chopped; 1 tablespoon finely chopped red onion; 1 1/2 teaspoons minced fresh basil; 1 teaspoon olive oil; and 2 tablespoons shredded reduced-fat mozzarella, baked in a 375°F oven for 8 to 12 minutes

1 medium apple

1 cup fat-free milk

5 vanilla wafer cookies

PER SERVING: 450 calories, 12 g fat, 3 g saturated fat, 20 g protein, 79 g carbohydrates, 14 g fiber, 619 mg calcium, 437 mg sodium

MEAL 14

Tossed salad with egg: 1 cup baby spinach; 1 cup other green (red leaf romaine, radicchio, or shredded red cabbage); 1 slice tomato chopped; and $\frac{1}{4}$ cup chopped red onion topped with 1 large hard-cooked egg, sliced or chopped, and 2 tablespoons reduced-fat Catalina or French dressing

5 whole wheat crackers

1 cup fat-free milk

1 medium pear

PER SERVING: 485 calories, 15 g fat, 2 g saturated fat, 21 g protein, 71 g carbohydrates, 12 g fiber, 415 mg calcium, 633 mg sodium

DINNERS

MEAL 1

4-ounce boneless, skinless chicken breast sprinkled with sodium-free seasoning mix and grilled

1 large baked sweet potato

$\frac{3}{4}$ cup steamed cauliflower topped with 1 teaspoon melted trans-free spreadable/tub margarine mixed with $\frac{1}{2}$ teaspoon whole grain bread crumbs

1 medium ($2\frac{1}{2}$") whole wheat roll

1 cup fat-free milk

PER SERVING: 527 calories, 8 g fat, 2 g saturated fat, 43 g protein, 73 g carbohydrates, 11 g fiber, 440 mg calcium, 472 mg sodium

MEAL 2

Old-Fashioned Meat Loaf (page 121)

Apple and Sweet Potato Hash Browns (page 110)

1 cup frozen baby peas, cooked

1 cup fat-free milk

PER SERVING: 542 calories, 12 g fat, 4 g saturated fat, 40 g protein, 65 g carbohydrates, 10 g fiber, 426 mg calcium, 682 mg sodium

MEAL 3

Braised Pork Cutlets with Cider Sauce
  (page 123)

Roasted Vegetable Medley (page 115)

1 cup tossed salad

1 tablespoon reduced-fat dressing

1 cup fat-free milk

PER SERVING: 541 calories, 21 g fat, 6 g saturated fat, 32 g protein, 58 g carbohydrates, 7 g fiber, 410 mg calcium, 551 mg sodium

MEAL 4

Southwestern Chicken Sauté (page 136)

³/₄ cup cooked brown rice

³/₄ cup diced mango

1 cup fat-free milk

PER SERVING: 561 calories, 6 g fat, 1 g saturated fat, 43 g protein, 86 g carbohydrates, 10 g fiber, 391 mg calcium, 497 mg sodium

MEAL 5

Home-Style Turkey Pot Pie (page 129)

1 cup tossed salad

1 tablespoon reduced-fat salad dressing

1 medium orange

1 cup fat-free milk

PER SERVING: 560 calories, 15 g fat, 5 g saturated fat, 35 g protein, 75 g carbohydrates, 10 g fiber, 454 mg calcium, 726 mg sodium

MEAL 6

4 ounces salmon, grilled, topped with 1 teaspoon trans-free spreadable/tub margarine and seasoned with fresh or dried dill

1 medium baked potato with 1 tablespoon reduced-fat sour cream and 1 teaspoon chives

1 cup steamed broccoli

1 cup fat-free milk

PER SERVING: 550 calories, 19 g fat, 5 g saturated fat, 40 g protein, 58 g carbohydrates, 9 g fiber, 437 mg calcium, 266 mg sodium

MEAL 7

Pasta Fagioli (page 153)

7 whole wheat crackers

¹/₂ cup fat-free milk

10 strawberries drizzled with 1¹/₂ tablespoons chocolate syrup

PER SERVING: 519 calories, 8 g fat, 2 g saturated fat, 21 g protein, 92 g carbohydrates, 16 g fiber, 275 mg calcium, 768 mg sodium

MEAL 8

Beef Cottage Pie (page 120)

1 cup tossed salad

1 tablespoon reduced-fat salad dressing

1 cup fat-free milk

PER SERVING: 542 calories, 10 g fat, 3 g saturated fat, 45 g protein, 71 g carbohydrates, 7 g fiber, 515 mg calcium, 629 mg sodium

MEAL 9

Herb and Crumb–Topped Tilapia
(page 139)

1 cup cooked carrots with 1 teaspoon trans-free spreadable/tub margarine

$\frac{1}{2}$ cup cooked wild rice

1 medium banana

1 cup milk

PER SERVING: 545 calories, 12 g fat, 2 g saturated fat, 42 g protein, 73 g carbohydrates, 11 g fiber, 362 mg calcium, 318 mg sodium

MEAL 10

3 ounces (93–95% lean) ground beef burger, cooked, on a whole wheat bun

Creamy Macaroni Salad (page 104)

Cauliflower, Green Bean, and Tomato Gratin (page 116)

green tea

PER SERVING: 524 calories, 14 g fat, 5 g saturated fat, 39 g protein, 59 g carbohydrates, 8 g fiber, 185 mg calcium, 684 mg sodium

MEAL 11

Grilled Pork Chop (page 124)

Potato Salad with Warm Bacon Dressing (page 102)

1 cup grilled zucchini

1 medium (2$\frac{1}{2}$") whole wheat roll

1 cup fat-free milk

PER SERVING: 573 calories, 11 g fat, 3 g saturated fat, 39 g protein, 85 g carbohydrates, 11 g fiber, 446 mg calcium, 650 mg sodium

MEAL 12

Cuban Black Beans (page 157)

$\frac{1}{2}$ cup corn kernels

$\frac{1}{2}$ cup diced papaya

$\frac{1}{2}$ cup fat-free milk

PER SERVING: 546 calories, 11 g fat, 2 g saturated fat, 24 g protein, 91 g carbohydrates, 18 g fiber, 232 mg calcium, 245 mg sodium

MEAL 13

1 cup cooked whole grain spaghetti

$\frac{3}{4}$ cup reduced-sodium spaghetti sauce

1 medium (2$\frac{1}{2}$") whole wheat roll

1 cup tossed salad

1 tablespoon reduced-fat salad dressing

$\frac{3}{4}$ cup fat-free milk

PER SERVING: 557 calories, 10 g fat, 2 g saturated fat, 22 g protein, 99 g carbohydrates, 17 g fiber, 376 mg calcium, 441 mg sodium

MEAL 14

Salmon and Onions Baked in Foil
(page 149)

Braised Burgundy Cabbage (page 117)

1 medium (2$\frac{1}{2}$") whole wheat roll

1 cup fat-free milk

PER SERVING: 567 calories, 22 g fat, 5 g saturated fat, 40 g protein, 53 g carbohydrates, 8 g fiber, 471 mg calcium, 649 mg sodium

Mix & Match Menus

SNACKS

MEAL 1

1 cup baby carrots

1½ tablespoons peanut butter

PER SERVING: 194 calories, 12 g fat, 3 g saturated fat, 7 g protein, 17 g carbohydrates, 4 g fiber, 37 mg calcium, 170 mg sodium

MEAL 2

¾ cup fat-free milk mixed with 1 tablespoon chocolate syrup

3 graham crackers (2½" x 2½")

PER SERVING: 201 calories, 2 g fat, 0 g saturated fat, 8 g protein, 37 g carbohydrates, 1 g fiber, 235 mg calcium, 217 mg sodium

MEAL 3

1 medium apple

1 tablespoon peanut butter or cashew butter

PER SERVING: 189 calories, 8 g fat, 2 g saturated fat, 4 g protein, 28 g carbohydrates, 5 g fiber, 18 mg calcium, 75 mg sodium

MEAL 4

Banana Chocolate Chip Macadamia Muffin (page 46)

Green tea

PER SERVING: 225 calories, 9 g fat, 2 g saturated fat, 4 g protein, 33 g carbohydrates, 2 g fiber, 38 mg calcium, 225 mg sodium

MEAL 5

¾ cup fat-free vanilla yogurt

½ cup sliced strawberries

PER SERVING: 194 calories, 1 g fat, 0 g saturated fat, 10 g protein, 39 g carbohydrates, 2 g fiber, 340 mg calcium, 127 mg sodium

MEAL 6

20 unsalted almonds

2 tablespoons raisins

PER SERVING: 192 calories, 12 g fat, 1 g saturated fat, 6 g protein, 20 g carbohydrates, 4 g fiber, 72 mg calcium, 2 mg sodium

MEAL 7

1 stick reduced-fat string cheese

7 whole wheat crackers

PER SERVING: 204 calories, 11 g fat, 4 g saturated fat, 10 g protein, 20 g carbohydrates, 3 g fiber, 214 mg calcium, 425 mg sodium

MEAL 8

2 servings Curried Snack Mix with Golden Raisins (page 43)

PER SERVING: 179 calories, 4 g fat, 0 g saturated fat, 4 g protein, 33 g carbohydrates, 4 g fiber, 51 mg calcium, 290 mg sodium

MEAL 9

2 cups plain popcorn mixed with 2 tablespoons raisins and 2 teaspoons melted peanut butter

PER SERVING: 179 calories, 6 g fat, 1 g saturated fat, 5 g protein, 29 g carbohydrates, 4 g fiber, 14 mg calcium, 52 mg sodium

MEAL 10

Avocado-Peach Salsa with Multigrain Chips (page 36)

PER SERVING: 178 calories, 10 g fat, 1 g saturated fat, 2 g protein, 20 g carbohydrates, 3 g fiber, 22 mg calcium, 249 mg sodium

MEAL 11

2 Peanut Butter Sandies (page 172)

³/₄ cup fat-free milk

PER SERVING: 205 calories, 5 g fat, 1 g saturated fat, 9 g protein, 32 g carbohydrates, 1 g fiber, 239 mg calcium, 168 mg sodium

MEAL 12

1 medium red bell pepper, cut into strips

¹/₃ cup hummus

PER SERVING: 170 calories, 8 g fat, 0 g saturated fat, 4 g protein, 21 g carbohydrates, 5 g fiber, 8 mg calcium, 431 mg sodium

MEAL 13

Iced Lemon Cupcake (page 167)

³/₄ cup fat-free milk

PER SERVING: 196 calories, 5 g fat, 2 g saturated fat, 10 g protein, 27 g carbohydrates, 1 g fiber, 269 mg calcium, 225 mg sodium

MEAL 14

Banana Snack Cake (page 166)

¹/₂ cup fat-free milk

PER SERVING: 217 calories, 7 g fat, 1 g saturated fat, 7 g protein, 31 g carbohydrates, 2 g fiber, 179 mg calcium, 187 mg sodium

Appendix

THE WALK OFF WEIGHT PLAN

THE KEY TO BURNING WEIGHT three times as fast isn't just walking—it's the special blend of interval walks and strength routines that change each week to help you avoid the plateau effect and keep on losing. Intervals train your body to be a fat-burning machine, so you blast more fat even when you're doing noninterval workouts. While all types of cardio exercise improve your body's fat-burning ability, interval training can get those results in less time with less exercise. When we invited real women to try the program, the most successful losers were those who combined the program below with the WOW diet, which is the basis for all the recipes in this book. On average, the women who combined diet and exercise lost almost 4 pounds more over 8 weeks than women who did exercise alone. Now, with both the cookbook and the weight-loss plan in hand, you have the potential to achieve your best body—and health—for years to come. For more exercises, photos, and tips on perfecting your walking technique, see *Walk Off Weight* by Michele Stanten (www.walkoffweightbook.com).

WARM-UP

STARTING SLOWLY IS KEY to improving your performance and results and reducing your risk of injury. All of the walking routines in the WOW program lead off with a 3- to 5-minute warm-up in which you'll be strolling at an easy pace. This gradual start will raise your heart rate, send blood to your working muscles, ramp up your respiration, increase your body temperature, and boost your calorie burn.

NOTE: If you do the strength workouts separately or before a walk, make sure you include a warm-up. See the individual routines for warm-up suggestions.

COOL-DOWN

FINISH ALL OF YOUR WALKS by gradually slowing your pace to an easy intensity for 2 to 5 minutes. During exercise, blood accumulates in your working muscles. Easing out of your workout, instead of stopping abruptly, prevents the blood from pooling in your legs, which can cause dizziness or nausea. It also helps remove lactate that can build up in muscles, so you'll feel less fatigued. By taking some time to cool down, you'll feel better and be more likely to look forward to your next workout because you're finishing your current one on a high note.

STRETCH

THE BEST TIME TO STRETCH to increase flexibility is after your cool-down, when your muscles and joints are at their warmest. This will help to counter the decrease in range of motion that occurs as you get older and makes everyday tasks, such as reaching for things on high shelves and bending over to put on your socks, more difficult. The following exercises stretch all of your walking muscles without the hassle of getting down on the ground, so you can easily make them a habit by automatically adding them to the end of your walks, after your cool-down, when your muscles and joints are still warm and pliable. Think of stretching as the finishing touch to a perfect workout. Hold each stretch for 10 seconds, pause for a second, then repeat two more times for a total of 30 seconds.

LUNGE & REACH (Stretches calves, hips, and sides of torso)
Stand with your right foot 2 to 3 feet in front of your left, toes pointing straight ahead. Bend your right knee, keeping your left leg straight and your heel on the ground, stretching your calf and hip. Reach your left arm overhead and toward the right to feel a stretch along your left side. Hold, then switch sides.

SIT BACK (Stretches back and hamstrings)
You can segue from the preceeding stretch directly into this one. Stay in the same position, with your left leg in front, but move your right foot forward a few inches. Straighten your left leg, raising your toes off the ground. Place your hands on your right thigh and bend your right knee and hips. Press your left heel into the ground, stick out your butt, and sit back until you feel a stretch in the back of your left leg. Hold, then switch sides.

BENT-LEG BALANCE (Stretches quads and hips)

Balance on your left leg (hold on to something sturdy for support, such as a tree or the back of a bench, if you need to). Bend your right knee, grasp the top of your foot, and pull your heel upward toward your butt. Keep your right knee pointing toward the ground, and press your right foot against your right hand to feel a stretch in the front of your thigh. Hold, then switch sides.

FIGURE 4 (Stretches hips and glutes)

Hold on to something sturdy for balance and rest your left ankle on your right thigh. Place your right hand on your hip and slowly sit back until you feel a stretch in your left hip and glute area. Hold, then switch sides.

Intensity Levels

ACTIVITY	INTENSITY LEVEL	PACE	HOW IT FEELS	SPEED ESTIMATES**
Inactive	1–2	Barely moving	Easy; you could do it for a very long period of time	<2.0 MPH
Easy*	3–5	Leisurely stroll	Light effort, rhythmic breathing; you can sing	2.0–3.5 MPH
Moderate	5–6	Purposeful	Some effort, breathing somewhat hard; you can talk in full sentences	3.0–4.0 MPH
Brisk	6–7	In a bit of a hurry	Hard effort, slightly breathless; you can only talk in brief phrases	3.5–4.5 MPH
Fast	7–8	Late for an appointment	Very hard effort, breathless; yes/no responses are all you can manage	4.0–5.0 MPH
Very Fast	8–9	Trying to catch a bus as it's pulling away	Maximum effort; no breath for any talking	4.5–5.5 MPH
Sprint	10	Racing for your life	All-out effort; you can't maintain it for more than a minute	5.5+ MPH

* Use this for warm-up and cool-down.

** These are only rough estimates, with the midpoint based on someone who is moderately fit. If you're just starting out, you'll probably hit each intensity level at a slower pace, closer to the lower end of the speed range or even below. If you've been walking regularly and you're very fit, you may have to walk faster, aiming toward the higher end of the range, to achieve the recommended effort levels. Pay attention to your body and do what feels right to you.

How Exercise Should Feel

Anytime you're doing something that's out of your comfort zone—which is the intention of exercise in order for your body to change—it's going to be uncomfortable. That's normal, but some symptoms aren't normal and shouldn't be ignored. Here are guidelines for how exercise should feel, what's abnormal, and what to do if you experience any abnormal symptoms.

NORMAL	ABNORMAL	WHAT TO DO
Heart pumping rhythmically harder and faster	Chest pain, pressure, or tightness; skipped heartbeats or palpitations	Stop immediately and call 911.
Breathing faster and harder	Difficult or uncomfortable breathing that doesn't improve when you decrease your intensity or stop exercising	Stop immediately and call your doctor.
Muscle soreness or burning	Sharp, shooting pain or pain in a joint	Stop and rest and ice the area. If pain persists, call your doctor.
General fatigue	Light-headedness or dizziness	Stop immediately.

How to Use the Resistance Band

You'll need a resistance band for some of the following moves. Position the band as described, and check that it's secure before you begin the exercise. If you're instructed to make a loop from the band, be aware that the larger the loop, the easier the resistance will be; the smaller the loop, the harder it will be. For a floor-level anchor, slide the band under a heavy piece of furniture or tie it around a railing. For a waist-level anchor, tie it to a doorknob. If you need to tie the band in a loop around your lower legs for an exercise, you can wrap it around your legs twice for maximum resistance. For upper-body exercises, increase resistance by shortening the band; fold it lengthwise, move your hands closer together, or wrap the band around your hands. You can also increase the resistance by moving farther away from the anchor point.

Just remember, don't sacrifice good form for increased challenge. Stretching and releasing the band's resistance with control is key to maximizing toning and avoiding injury. Don't let the band snap back once you've reached the top of the move; pause, then slowly release, resisting against the band's pull as you do.

PHASE 1

WEEK	DAY 1	DAY 2	DAY 3	DAY 4	DAY 5	DAY 6	DAY 7
1	**Basic Interval Walk I** 30 min **Lower-Body Strength Workout** 15 min **45 MIN TOTAL**	**Toning Walk I** (upper body) **20 MIN TOTAL**	**Basic Interval Walk I** 30 min **Core Strength Workout** 15 min **45 MIN TOTAL**	**Toning Walk I** (upper body) **20 MIN TOTAL**	**Basic Interval Walk I** 30 min **Lower-Body Strength Workout** 15 min **45 MIN TOTAL**	**Long Walk I** 45 min **Core Strength Workout** 15 min **60 MIN TOTAL**	Rest
2	**Basic Interval Walk I** 30 min **Lower-Body Strength Workout** 15 min **45 MIN TOTAL**	**Toning Walk I** (upper body) **20 MIN TOTAL**	**Basic Interval Walk I** 30 min **Core Strength Workout** 15 min **45 MIN TOTAL**	**Toning Walk I** (upper body) **20 MIN TOTAL**	**Basic Interval Walk I** 30 min **Lower-Body Strength Workout** 15 min **45 MIN TOTAL**	**Long Walk II** 60 min **Core Strength Workout** 15 min **75 MIN TOTAL**	Rest
3	**Basic Interval Walk II** 45 min **Lower-Body Strength Workout** 15 min **60 MIN TOTAL**	**Toning Walk II** (upper body) **25 MIN TOTAL**	**Basic Interval Walk II** 45 min **Core Strength Workout** 15 min **60 MIN TOTAL**	**Toning Walk II** (upper body) **25 MIN TOTAL**	**Basic Interval Walk II** 45 min **Lower-Body Strength Workout** 15 min **60 MIN TOTAL**	**Long Walk III** 75 min **Core Strength Workout** 15 min **90 MIN TOTAL**	Rest
4	**Basic Interval Walk II** 45 min **Lower-Body Strength Workout** 15 min **60 MIN TOTAL**	**Toning Walk II** (upper body) **25 MIN TOTAL**	**Basic Interval Walk II** 45 min **Core Strength Workout** 15 min **60 MIN TOTAL**	**Toning Walk II** (upper body) **25 MIN TOTAL**	**Basic Interval Walk II** 45 min **Lower-Body Strength Workout** 15 min **60 MIN TOTAL**	**Long Walk IV** 90 min **Core Strength Workout** 15 min **105 MIN TOTAL**	Rest

Lower-Body Strength Workout

These moves target all of your major walking muscles from the butt down. A recent study found that simply doing one move to strengthen your quads (the fronts of your thighs) could increase your walking speed by 15 percent. That's equivalent to increasing your pace from 3.5 MPH to 4 MPH! Imagine what you could do if you shape up all of your lower-body muscles. These exercises also challenge your balance, giving your core muscles an extra workout, and improve your posture for a stronger, pain-free stride.

During phase 1 of the WOW program, you'll be doing this routine twice a week, taking a 30- to 60-second break between moves. Each week, you'll be increasing the number of repetitions of each exercise. Here's what you should try to aim for, repeating on each side when appropriate.

Week 1: 6–8 reps
Week 2: 8–10 reps
Week 3: 10–12 reps
Week 4: 12–15 reps

If you're doing this workout separate from your walks, start out by taking about 5 minutes to warm up by walking at an easy pace.

Lightly hold on to something sturdy, such as the back of a chair or the wall, to help you maintain your balance if you find that you're wobbly when doing any of these moves; you'll get more muscle building and firming out of the exercises and reduce your risk of injury if you're steady. Over time, even within just a few weeks, your balance will improve, and you can eventually try the moves without holding on.

CROSS LEG SWING (Targets inner thighs)
Attach the resistance band near the floor around a sturdy furniture leg or railing or under a heavy piece of furniture so that it forms a loop. Stand so that the band is on your left. Put the band around your left foot near your ankle. Step away from the anchor point until the band is taut when your left leg is extended out to the side, toes pointed. Flex your left foot, contract your inner thigh, and swing your leg across the front of your body toward your right leg. Hold, then slowly return to start without letting your left foot touch the floor between reps.

ONE-LEG SQUAT (Targets quads, glutes, and hamstrings)
Balance on your right leg with the toes of your left foot lightly touching the floor and your arms at your sides. Bend your hips and right knee and sit back as if you were lowering halfway into a chair. Let your arms swing forward to about chest height. Keep your right knee behind your toes. Press into your right foot and stand back up.

REAR KICK (Targets glutes and hamstrings)
Attach the resistance band near the floor around a sturdy furniture leg or a railing or under a heavy piece of furniture so that it forms a loop. Stand facing the anchor point, and put the

band around your right foot near your ankle. Step backward if needed so the band is taut. Balancing on your left leg with your left knee slightly bent, press your right leg back with your foot flexed, and squeeze your butt. Hold and slowly lower without touching your foot to the floor between reps.

REVERSE LUNGE (Targets quads, glutes, and calves)

Stand with your feet together and your arms at your sides. Step 2 to 3 feet behind you with your right foot, toes pointing forward, and bend your knees so that the right one is almost to the floor (your right heel will come off the floor). Simultaneously, swing your arms forward to about chest height. Keep your left knee directly over your left ankle; if it's coming forward, shift your hips back or take a bigger step back. Press into your front foot and stand back up, bringing your feet together. Repeat, stepping back with the left leg. Continue alternating legs until you complete the recommended number of reps with each leg.

MOVING SQUAT (Targets quads, glutes, and outer thighs)

Stand with your feet together and your arms at your sides. Step your right foot out to the side 2 to 3 feet, bend your hips and knees, and sit back as if you're lowering into a chair. Simultaneously, swing your arms forward to about chest height. Keep your knees over your feet, not out past your toes or rolling in toward each other. Your upper body will lean forward about 45 degrees. Stand back up, bringing your left foot toward your right. Step to the right again. Continue moving to the right until you run out of space or you've completed all of the reps. Then repeat to the left. You may need to alternate going side to side, depending on how much space you have.

Toning Exercises

For on-the-go firming, you'll do these upper-body moves with a resistance band while you walk. Don't worry, with a little practice you can do it—all of our test panelists did. It's also a great way to improve your coordination. Do this routine twice a week. Instead of counting reps like you do for the lower-body and core strength routines, you'll be doing each exercise for a specific time interval (45 seconds during Weeks 1 and 2, and 60 seconds during Weeks 3 and 4). Using controlled movements, you'll complete as many reps as possible in that time (usually 20 to 30), then you'll drape the resistance band around your neck and walk briskly for 1 minute before doing the next exercise.

PULL-DOWN (Targets upper and mid back and biceps)

With arms extended overhead, hold the center of a resistance band with your hands about shoulder-width apart, palms forward, and elbows bent slightly. Keeping your left hand stationary, pull your right arm down and out to the side, without bending your elbow, until your hand is at about shoulder level. Hold for a second, then slowly return to the start position.

FRONT PRESS (Targets chest and triceps)

Loop a resistance band around your upper back and under your arms. Grasp an end of the band in each hand. Position your hands near your chest, palms forward and elbows bent out. Extend your arms straight in front of you at chest level. Hold for a second, then slowly return to the start position.

ROW (Targets mid back and biceps)

With your arms extended in front of you at chest level, hold the center of a resistance band with both hands. Keeping your left arm stationary as an anchor, bend your right elbow and pull your arm back, keeping it close to your body, until your hand is near your hip and your elbow is pointing behind you. Hold for a second, then slowly return to the start position.

OVERHEAD PRESS (Targets shoulders and triceps)

Loop a resistance band around your upper back and under your arms. Grasp an end of the band in each hand, with your elbows bent and pointing down and out to the sides. Your hands should be near your shoulders, palms forward. Press your hands straight up overhead. Hold for a second, then slowly return to the start position.

FRONT PULL (Targets shoulders)

With your arms extended out in front of you, hold a resistance band at chest height with your hands about shoulder-width apart. Keeping your arms straight, pull your hands apart, squeezing your shoulder blades together and bringing your hands almost directly out to the sides. Hold for a second, then slowly return to the start position.

ARM PULL (Targets triceps)

Drape a resistance band around your neck and grasp each side with your arms bent and your hands by your shoulders. Press your hands down and straighten your arms. Hold for a second, then slowly return to the start position, keeping your upper arms stationary throughout.

Core Exercises

Walking may seem like a lower-body-only exercise, but the action of walking really starts within your core with the psoas muscles, which lie deep in your pelvis and attach your spine to your thighs, and the abdominals. In fact, research shows that strengthening your ab and back muscles—exactly what these exercises target—helps you walk faster. Strong core muscles also keep your pelvis in a neutral position, which is important for good walking posture. Do this routine twice a week, taking a 30- to 60-second break between moves. Each week, you'll be increasing the number of repetitions of each exercise. Here's what you should aim for (unless otherwise noted), repeating on each side when appropriate.

Week 1: 6–8 reps
Week 2: 8–10 reps
Week 3: 10–12 reps
Week 4: 12–15 reps

If you're doing this workout separate from your walks, make sure that you warm up first by walking at an easy pace for about 5 minutes. Then do these upper-body moves to prepare your torso muscles for their workout: Roll your shoulders forward and back; twist your torso to the left and right, reaching the opposite arm across your chest; and reach each arm overhead, stretching to the opposite side.

PLANK (Targets abs, back, glutes, shoulders, chest, and triceps)

Lie facedown with your forearms on the floor, hands clasped, elbows under your shoulders, and toes tucked. Contract your abs and raise your belly, hips, and legs off the floor, keeping your body in line from head to heels. Don't bend at the waist. Hold for 15 seconds the first week, then increase by 15 seconds each week. Do just one time.

TABLETOP BALANCE (Targets back, abs, glutes, hamstrings, and shoulders)

Get down on all fours, hands under your shoulders and knees under your hips. Keeping your abs tight, raise your right arm and left leg simultaneously until they are in line with your spine, squeezing your glutes as you do. Hold for a second, then lower. Repeat with the opposite arm and leg.

SIDE PLANK (Targets back and side abs)

Lie on your right side with your legs stacked and the bottom one bent behind you. Prop yourself up on your right elbow with your right palm flat on the floor and your left hand on your left hip. Contract your abs and raise your right hip and leg off the floor. Slowly lower your right hip toward the floor without touching, then lift back up.

ROLL DOWN (Targets abs and back)

Sit on the floor with your knees bent, feet flat on the floor, and arms extended in front of you. Pull your abs in, round your back, and inhale as you roll down about halfway toward the floor. Exhale and slowly roll back up, sitting tall.

BICYCLE (Targets front and side abs and quads)

Lie on your back, pulling your knees in toward your chest so that both your hips and knees are bent 90 degrees. Place your hands behind your head. Exhale as you curl your head and shoulders off the floor and twist your torso to the right. At the same time, pull your right knee in toward your chest and extend your left leg so that it's at about a 45-degree angle to the floor. Crunch, bringing your left shoulder toward your right knee. Inhale as you slowly lower. Repeat, twisting to the left. Continue alternating sides for 10 to 20 total reps.

Weeks 1 and 2

BASIC INTERVAL WALK 1

TIME	ACTIVITY	INTENSITY
0:00–5:00	Warm-Up (5 min)	3→5
5:00–6:00	Moderate (1 min)	5–6
6:00–6:30	Fast (30 sec)	7–8
6:30–24:30	Alternate Moderate (1 min) and Fast (30 sec) for 18 minutes.	
24:30–25:30	Moderate (1 min)	5–6
25:30–30:00	Cool-Down (4.5 min)	5→3

TONING WALK 1

TIME	ACTIVITY	INTENSITY
0:00–4:00	Warm-Up (4 min)	3→5
4:00–4:45	Pull-Down, right arm (45 sec; 20 reps)	5–6
4:45–5:45	Brisk Walk (1 min)	6–7
5:45–6:30	Pull-Down, left arm (45 sec; 20 reps)	5–6
6:30–7:30	Brisk Walk (1 min)	6–7
7:30–8:15	Front Press (45 sec; 20 reps)	5–6
8:15–9:15	Brisk Walk (1 min)	6–7
9:15–10:00	Row, right arm (45 sec; 20 reps)	5–6
10:00–11:00	Brisk Walk (1 min)	6–7
11:00–11:45	Row, left arm (45 sec; 20 reps)	5–6
11:45–12:45	Brisk Walk (1 min)	6–7
12:45–13:30	Overhead Press (45 sec; 20 reps)	5–6
13:30–14:30	Brisk Walk (1 min)	6–7
14:30–15:15	Front Pull (45 sec; 20 reps)	5–6
15:15–16:15	Brisk Walk (1 min)	6–7
16:15–17:00	Arm Pull (45 sec; 20 reps)	5–6
17:00–18:00	Brisk Walk (1 min)	6–7
18:00–20:00	Cool-Down (2 min)	5→3

LONG WALK 1

TIME	ACTIVITY	INTENSITY
0:00–5:00	Warm-Up (5 min)	3→5
5:00–40:00	Easy to Moderate (35 min)	4–6
40:00–45:00	Cool-Down (5 min)	5→3

LONG WALK 2		
TIME	ACTIVITY	INTENSITY
0:00–5:00	Warm-Up (5 min)	3→5
5:00–55:00	Easy to Moderate (50 min)	4–6
55:00–60:00	Cool-Down (5 min)	5→3

Weeks 3 and 4

BASIC INTERVAL WALK 2		
TIME	ACTIVITY	INTENSITY
0:00–5:00	Warm-Up (5 min)	3→5
5:00–6:00	Moderate (1 min)	5–6
6:00–6:30	Fast (30 sec)	7–8
6:30–39:30	Alternate Moderate (1 min) and Fast (30 sec) for 33 minutes.	
39:30–40:30	Moderate (1 min)	5–6
40:30–45:00	Cool-Down (4.5 min)	5→3

TONING WALK 2		
TIME	ACTIVITY	INTENSITY
0:00–5:00	Warm-Up (5 min)	3→5
5:00–6:00	Pull-Down, right arm (1 min; 30 reps)	5–6
6:00–7:00	Brisk Walk (1 min)	6–7
7:00–8:00	Pull-Down, left arm (1 min; 30 reps)	5–6
8:00–9:00	Brisk Walk (1 min)	6–7
9:00–10:00	Front Press (1 min; 30 reps)	5–6
10:00–11:00	Brisk Walk (1 min)	6–7
11:00–12:00	Row, right arm (1 min; 30 reps)	5–6
12:00–13:00	Brisk Walk (1 min)	6–7
13:00–14:00	Row, left arm (1 min; 30 reps)	5–6
14:00–15:00	Brisk Walk (1 min)	6–7
15:00–16:00	Overhead Press (1 min; 30 reps)	5–6
16:00–17:00	Brisk Walk (1 min)	6–7
17:00–18:00	Front Pull (1 min; 30 reps)	5–6
18:00–19:00	Brisk Walk (1 min)	6–7
19:00–20:00	Arm Pull (1 min; 30 reps)	5–6
20:00–21:00	Brisk Walk (1 min)	6–7
21:00–25:00	Cool-Down (4 min)	5→3

LONG WALK 3		
TIME	ACTIVITY	INTENSITY
0:00–5:00	Warm-Up (5 min)	3→5
5:00–70:00	Easy to Moderate (65 min)	4–6
70:00–75:00	Cool-Down (5 min)	5→3

LONG WALK 4		
TIME	ACTIVITY	INTENSITY
0:00–5:00	Warm-Up (5 min)	3→5
5:00–85:00	Easy to Moderate (80 min)	4–6
85:00–90:00	Cool-Down (5 min)	5→3

PHASE 2

AT-A-GLANCE Higher-intensity, shorter-duration training

WEEK	DAY 1	DAY 2	DAY 3	DAY 4	DAY 5	DAY 6	DAY 7
5	Supercharged Interval Walk I	Recovery Walk 20 min Total-Body Strength Workout 20 min	Supercharged Interval Walk I	Recovery Walk 20 min Total-Body Strength Workout 20 min	Supercharged Interval Walk I	Speed Walk	Rest
	20 MIN TOTAL	**40 MIN TOTAL**	**20 MIN TOTAL**	**40 MIN TOTAL**	**20 MIN TOTAL**	**30 MIN TOTAL**	
6	Supercharged Interval Walk I	Recovery Walk 20 min Total-Body Strength Workout 20 min	Supercharged Interval Walk I	Recovery Walk 20 min Total-Body Strength Workout 20 min	Supercharged Interval Walk I	Speed Walk	Rest
	20 MIN TOTAL	**40 MIN TOTAL**	**20 MIN TOTAL**	**40 MIN TOTAL**	**20 MIN TOTAL**	**30 MIN TOTAL**	
7	Supercharged Interval Walk II	Recovery Walk 25 min Total-Body Strength Workout 20 min	Supercharged Interval Walk II	Recovery Walk 25 min Total-Body Strength Workout 20 min	Supercharged Interval Walk II	Speed Walk	Rest
	30 MIN TOTAL	**45 MIN TOTAL**	**30 MIN TOTAL**	**45 MIN TOTAL**	**30 MIN TOTAL**	**30 MIN TOTAL**	
8	Supercharged Interval Walk II	Recovery Walk 25 min Total-Body Strength Workout 20 min	Supercharged Interval Walk II	Recovery Walk 25 min Total-Body Strength Workout 20 min	Supercharged Interval Walk II	Speed Walk	Rest
	30 MIN TOTAL	**45 MIN TOTAL**	**30 MIN TOTAL**	**45 MIN TOTAL**	**30 MIN TOTAL**	**30 MIN TOTAL**	

Total-Body Strength Workout

These moves work your upper and lower body at the same time. Do this routine two or three times a week, taking a 30- to 60-second break between moves. Each week, you'll be increasing the number of repetitions. Here's what you should aim for, repeating on each side when appropriate.

Week 5: 8–10 reps
Week 6: 10–12 reps
Week 7: 15–17 reps
Week 8: 18–20 reps

If you find that you're wobbly when doing any of these moves, lightly hold on to something sturdy, such as the back of a chair or the wall, to help maintain your balance, at least to start out.

If you're doing this workout separate from your walks, warm up first by walking at an easy pace for about 5 minutes. Then do these moves to prepare your torso muscles for their workout: Roll your shoulders forward and back; twist your torso to the left and right, reaching the opposite arm across your chest; and reach each arm overhead, stretching to the opposite side.

BALANCING DEADLIFT WITH ARM RAISE
(Targets glutes, legs, abs, and shoulders)
Stand with one end of a resistance band under your right foot and hold the other end in your right hand. With your left hand, lightly hold on to a chair for balance. Slowly hinge forward from your hips, lowering your torso toward the floor as your left leg rises behind you as far as comfortable, or until your body and leg are parallel to the floor. Choke up on the band as you lower. Squeeze your glutes and stand back up, raising your left knee in front of you. Release a little of the band, then raise your right arm out to the side up to shoulder height. Hold, then slowly lower and repeat.

BRIDGE WITH PRESS (Targets chest, arms, abs, back, glutes, and legs)
Sit on the floor and loop a resistance band around your upper back so that it's under your armpits. Lie on your back with your knees bent and your feet about a foot from your butt. Grasp each end of the band with your hands near your chest, palms facing forward, and your elbows pointing out. Contract your abs and glutes and lift your butt off the floor so that your body forms a straight line from your shoulders to your knees. At the same time, straighten your arms, pressing your hands toward the ceiling. Hold for a second before lowering your arms, then your body.

ROTATING LUNGE (Targets legs, glutes, and obliques)
Anchor the center of a resistance band at about waist level by tying it to a door handle or putting a knot in the band and pinching it in a door (check that it's secure before you begin). Stand facing the band, holding the ends with both hands so the band is taut. Your feet should be together, your arms out in front at about waist height, and your elbows bent. Step your left

foot behind you 2 to 3 feet, with your toes pointing forward. Bend your knees and lower until your right knee is bent 90 degrees, keeping your knee over your ankle. At the same time, rotate your torso to the right. Hold, then press into your right foot to stand back up and rotate back to center.

ROW WITH LEG SWING (Targets upper back, hips, and glutes)
Anchor a resistance band at about waist level. Stand facing the band, holding an end in each hand, with your feet together and your arms extended in front of you. Bend your elbows and pull your arms back, squeezing your shoulder blades together and keeping your arms close to your body, until your hands are near your hips and your elbows are pointing behind you. At the same time, raise your left knee in front of you to hip height. Extend your arms back out in front of you and swing your left leg behind you, flexing your foot and squeezing your glutes as you do. Continue without lowering your left foot to the floor.

CRUNCH AND EXTEND (Targets abs and arms)
Anchor the center of a resistance band near the floor and lie so that it's behind your head. Grasp each end with your hands and bend your arms so that your elbows point up and your hands are on either side of your head. Contract your abs and curl your head and shoulders off the floor, keeping your arms stationary. Hold the crunch position and extend your arms. Hold, then slowly bend your arms and lower your head.

ELEVATED SQUAT WITH CURL (Targets legs, butt, and arms)
Stand with a resistance band under the balls of your feet, with your feet about shoulder-width apart, your toes pointing forward, and your arms at your sides. Holding one end of the band in each hand, bend your hips and knees, sitting back as if you were lowering into a chair. Choke up on the band for resistance, then stand up. Release some of the band to bend your elbows and raise your hands toward your shoulders. Finally, lift your heels off the floor so that you're balancing on your toes. Lower your heels, then your arms.

Weeks 5 and 6

SUPERCHARGED INTERVAL WALK 1		
TIME	**ACTIVITY**	**INTENSITY**
0:00–5:00	Warm-Up (5 min)	3→5
5:00–6:00	Moderate (1 min)	5–6
6:00–6:15	Very Fast (15 sec)	8–9
6:15–6:45	Easy to Moderate (30 sec)	4–6
6:45–7:00	Very Fast (15 sec)	8–9
7:00–16:00	Alternate Easy to Moderate (30 sec) and Very Fast (15 sec) for 9 minutes.	
16:00–16:30	Easy to Moderate (30 sec)	4–6
16:30–20:00	Cool-Down (4.5 min)	5→3

RECOVERY WALK		
TIME	ACTIVITY	INTENSITY
0:00–3:00	Warm-Up (3 min)	3→5
3:00–18:00	Moderate Walk (15 min)	5–6
18:00–20:00	Cool-Down (2 min)	5→3

SPEED WALK	
ACTIVITY	INTENSITY
Warm-Up (5 min)	3→5
Brisk to Very Fast Walk (times will vary)*	6–8
Cool-Down (5 min)	5→3

*During this walk, you want to walk 1 mile as fast as you can.

Weeks 7 and 8

SUPERCHARGED INTERVAL WALK 2		
TIME	ACTIVITY	INTENSITY
0:00–5:00	Warm-Up (5 min)	3→5
5:00–6:00	Moderate (1 min)	5–6
6:00–6:15	Very Fast (15 sec)	8–9
6:15–6:45	Easy to Moderate (30 sec)	4–6
6:45–7:00	Very Fast (15 sec)	8–9
7:00–25:00	Alternate Easy to Moderate (30 sec) and Very Fast (15 sec) for 18 minutes.	
25:00–25:30	Easy to Moderate (30 sec)	4–6
25:30–30:00	Cool-Down (4.5 min)	5→3

RECOVERY WALK		
TIME	ACTIVITY	INTENSITY
0:00–3:00	Warm-Up (3 min)	3→5
3:00–23:00	Moderate Walk (20 min)	5–6
23:00–25:00	Cool-Down (2 min)	5→3

SPEED WALK	
ACTIVITY	INTENSITY
Warm-Up (5 min)	3→5
Brisk to Very Fast Walk (times will vary)*	6–8
Cool-Down (5 min)	5→3

*During this walk, you want to walk 1 mile as fast as you can.

Endnotes

CHAPTER 1

[1] www.mayoclinic.com/health/exercise/ SM00109

[2] www.usda.gov/factbook/chapter2.pdf

[3] www.cdc.gov/nchs/data/hestat/overweight/ overweight_adult.htm

[4] www.americanheart.org/presenter. jhtml?identifier=3069203

[5] www.americanheart.org/presenter. jhtml?identifier=2152

[6] diabetes.niddk.nih.gov/dm/pubs/overview/ #scope

[7] J. M. Pascual, et al., "Body weight variation and control of cardiovascular risk factors in essential hypertension," *Blood Press* 2009; 18(5): 247-54.

CHAPTER 2

[1] L. A. Tucker and K. S. Thomas, "Increasing total fiber intake reduces risk of weight and fat gains in women," *Journal of Nutrition*, 139, no. 3 (2009): 576–81.

[2] K. H. Poddar, et al., "Low-fat dairy intake and body weight and composition changes in college students," *Journal of the American Dietetic Association* 109 (2009): 1433–38.

[3] www.brighamandwomens.org/ healtheweightforwomen/special_topics/ DodgingWeightGainWithVitaminD. aspx?subID=submenu10

[4] www.americanheart.org/presenter. jhtml?identifier=3045795

[5] www.hsph.harvard.edu/nutritionsource/ questions/omega-3/index.html

[6] D. Parra, et al., "A diet rich in long chain omega-3 fatty acids modulates satiety in overweight and obese volunteers during weight loss," *Appetite* 51, no. 3 (2008): 676–80.

[7] http://www.cdc.gov/DHDSP/library/sodium. htm

[8] http://www.iom.edu/Global/ News%20Announcements/~/media/ 442A08B899F44DF9AAD083D86164C75B .ashx

[9] http://www.cdc.gov/DHDSP/library/pdfs/ Sodium_Fact_Sheet.pdf

[10] M. A. Veldhorst, et al., "Effects of high and normal soy protein breakfasts on satiety and subsequent energy intake, including amino acid and 'satiety' hormone responses," *European Journal of Nutrition* 48, no. 2 (2009): 92–100.

[11] J. D. Stookey, et al., "Drinking water is associated with weight loss in overweight dieting women independent of diet and activity," *Obesity* 16 (2008): 2481–88.

[12] K. C. Maki, et al., "Green tea catechin consumption enhances exercise-induced abdominal fat loss in overweight and obese adults," *Journal of Nutrition* 139 (2009): 264–70.

[13] R. J. Green, et al., "Common tea formulations modulate in vitro digestive recovery of green tea catechins," *Molecular Nutrition & Food Research* 59, no. 9 (2007): 1152–62.

[14] https://admin.beef.org/deImagesBN/ 18-226-29Cuts-NutBang-08-2.jpg

CHAPTER 3

[1] J. E. Flood and B. J. Rolls, "Soup preloads in a variety of forms reduce meal energy intake," *Appetite*, 49 no. 3 (2007): 626–34.

[2] J. M. de Castro, "The time of day of food intake influences overall intake in humans," *Journal of Nutrition*, 134 no. 1 (2004): 104–11.

[3] L. Djoussé, J.A. Driver, and J.M. Gaziano, "Relation between modifiable lifestyle factors and lifetime risk of heart failure," *Journal of the American Medical Association*, no. 4 (2009); 302: 394–400.

Conversion Chart

These equivalents have been slightly rounded to make measuring easier.

VOLUME

U.S.	IMPERIAL	METRIC
1/4 tsp	–	1 ml
1/2 tsp	–	2 ml
1 tsp	–	5 ml
1 Tbsp	–	15 ml
2 Tbsp (1 oz)	1 fl oz	30 ml
1/4 cup (2 oz)	2 fl oz	60 ml
1/3 cup (3 oz)	3 fl oz	80 ml
1/2 cup (4 oz)	4 fl oz	120 ml
2/3 cup (5 oz)	5 fl oz	160 ml
3/4 cup (6 oz)	6 fl oz	180 ml
1 cup (8 oz)	8 fl oz	240 ml

WEIGHT

U.S.	METRIC
1 oz	30 g
2 oz	60 g
4 oz (1/4 lb)	115 g
5 oz (1/3 lb)	145 g
6 oz	170 g
7 oz	200 g
8 oz (1/2 lb)	230 g
10 oz	285 g
12 oz (3/4 lb)	340 g
14 oz	400 g
16 oz (1 lb)	455 g
2.2 lb	1 kg

LENGTH

U.S.	METRIC
1/4"	0.6 cm
1/2"	1.25 cm
1"	2.5 cm
2"	5 cm
4"	11 cm
6"	15 cm
8"	20 cm
10"	25 cm
12" (1')	30 cm

PAN SIZES

U.S.	METRIC
8" cake pan	20 × 4 cm sandwich or cake tin
9" cake pan	23 × 3.5 cm sandwich or cake tin
11" × 7" baking pan	28 × 18 cm baking tin
13" × 9" baking pan	32.5 × 23 cm baking tin
15" × 10" baking pan	38 × 25.5 cm baking tin (Swiss roll tin)
1 1/2 qt baking dish	1.5 liter baking dish
2 qt baking dish	2 liter baking dish
2 qt rectangular baking dish	30 × 19 cm baking dish
9" pie plate	22 × 4 or 23 × 4 cm pie plate
7" or 8" springform pan	18 or 20 cm springform or loose-bottom cake tin
9" × 5" loaf pan	23 × 13 cm or 2 lb narrow loaf tin or pâté tin

TEMPERATURES

FAHRENHEIT	CENTIGRADE	GAS
140°	60°	–
160°	70°	–
180°	80°	–
225°	105°	1/4
250°	120°	1/2
275°	135°	1
300°	150°	2
325°	160°	3
350°	180°	4
375°	190°	5
400°	200°	6
425°	220°	7
450°	230°	8
475°	245°	9
500°	260°	–

Index

Underscored page references indicate boxed text. An asterisk (*) indicates recipe photos are shown in the color inserts.

WALK INTO YOUR BEST SHAPE EVER!

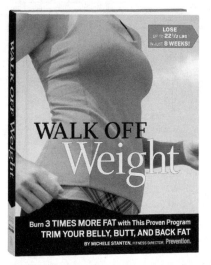

LOSE UP TO 22½ LBS IN JUST 8 WEEKS!

WALK OFF Weight

Burn 3 TIMES MORE FAT with This Proven Program
TRIM YOUR BELLY, BUTT, AND BACK FAT
BY MICHELE STANTEN, FITNESS DIRECTOR, *Prevention.*

Walk Off Weight

Slim down and firm up for life with this revolutionary walking program from *Prevention* magazine. In just 8 weeks, learn innovative interval walking and workout techniques that will help you blast fat and tone all your trouble spots three times as fast as conventional walking. We'll help you every step of the way with:

- Step-by-step illustrations of each routine
- A flexible, delicious, go-anywhere diet plan designed to help optimize your weight loss
- Tips on proper walking and exercise form to boost metabolism, reduce the risk of injury, and maximize fat burning

LOSE UP TO 22½ LBS IN JUST 8 WEEKS!

ALSO AVAILABLE:

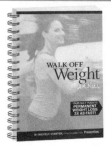

Also available for download onto your MP3 player!

Walk Off Weight Journal

With weekly exercise overviews and technique focus tips, this customizable 16-week journal is the essential tool to keep you committed to walking into the best shape of your life!

Lace up your sneakers— and start writing!

Walk Off Weight Strength Workout

Including 4 new metabolism-revving workouts with body-firming strength moves, this energizing DVD will help you stay motivated and keep the weight off for good.

Take your program to the next level.

Walk Off Weight MP3 Player and Podcasts

Clip on this portable music player featuring audio workouts that talk you through each interval and toning walk so you never need to memorize the steps or check your watch.

Get your own personal coach!

Walk Off Weight Quick & Easy Cookbook

Packed with 150 fast, full-flavored dishes designed to maximize your workouts, this easy-to-use cookbook is perfect for your on-the-go lifestyle. Mix and match your favorites to customize your meal plan and lose weight faster.

Fuel your walks with our tasty, body-slimming recipes.

Visit www.walkoffweightbook.com to order today!